HOLISTIC LEARNING AND SPIRITUALITY IN EDUCATION

Holistic Learning and Spirituality in Education

Breaking New Ground

Edited by
JOHN P. MILLER
SELIA KARSTEN
DIANA DENTON
DEBORAH ORR
AND
ISABELLA COLALILLO KATES

STATE UNIVERSITY OF NEW YORK PRESS

State University of New York Press, Albany

For information, contact State University of New York Press, Albany, NY
www.sunypress.edu

Production by Marilyn P. Semerad
Marketing by Michael Campochiaro

Library of Congress Cataloging in Publication Data

Holistic learning and spirituality in education : breaking new ground / edited by
  John P. Miller ... [et al.].
    p. cm.
  Includes bibliographical references and index.
  ISBN 0-7914-6351-6 — ISBN 0-7914-6352-4 (pbk. : alk. paper)
    1. Holistic education—Congresses. 2. Learning—Congresses. 3. Spiritual life—
Congresses. I. Miller, John P., 1943–

  LC990.H65 2005
  370.112—dc22   2004043457

ISBN- 13: 978-0-7914-6351-2 (hardcover : alk. Paper)
ISBN- 13: 978-0-7914-6352-9 (pbk. : alk. Paper)

                    10 9 8 7 6 5 4 3 2 1

Contents

PART 2
Practices: Integrating Self, Soul, and Spirit in the Classroom

PART 3
Inspiring Wholeness:
The Poetics of Holistic Education

Acknowledgments

This book is the result of several conferences on Holistic Education held at the Ontario Institute for Studies in Education at the University of Toronto (OISE/UT). The first conference was held in 1997 and since then three more have taken place and another one is planned for 2005. We are indebted to all the participants who made the conferences possible.

The editors would like to thank all of those at OISE/UT who supported the conferences. This includes the Department of Curriculum, Teaching and Learning and faculty and students involved in holistic education within the department. Special thanks to Gayle Grisdale who has been conference coordinator for three conferences and to the many individuals who served on the planning committees.

We very much appreciate the work that Kristen Moss and Maria Fryman have done in preparing the manuscript. Kristen transferred all of the individual chapters into a coherent manuscript while Maria worked on the manuscript so that it conformed to the publication guidelines provided by SUNY Press. We are also grateful to Anne Dhir for completing the indexing for this book.

Our appreciation is also extended to those at SUNY Press for their work on this book. First we thank Lisa Chesnel who guided the book through the editorial review process. With regards to production we appreciate the work of Marilyn P. Semerad, our production editor at SUNY, as well as the copyeditor for the manuscript, Margaret Copeley. We thank them for the care they have taken in preparing the manuscript for publication. Finally, our thanks to Priscilla Ross who provided the initial encouragement and interest in this book from SUNY Press.

We are grateful to *Encounter* for giving us permission to publish Anna Lemkow's chapter previously published in that journal as "Reflections on our Common, Life-long Educational Journey," Vol. 11, No. 2, Summer 1998, pp. 4–9, and *Orbit* for giving us permission to publish "Nourishing Adolescents' Spirituality in Secular Schools" by Rachael Kessler, Vol. 30, No. 2, 1999, pp. 30–33.

Cover photo by Selia Karsten.

                                                              The Editors

Introduction

Holistic Learning

JOHN P. MILLER

The vision of human wholeness is an ancient one. It can be found in the cultures of indigenous peoples as well as in the ancient cultures of Greece, India, and China. It is a different story today. Our culture and education systems have become obsessed with acquisition and achievement. In schools the move to high-stakes testing has narrowed the focus of teaching and learning to "standards" that are easily measurable. Our present culture is not interested in educating the whole person but rather in what James Hillman (1999) has called the "objective observer":

> Mr. Objective Observer. This characterless abstraction runs corporations, constructs the International Style of architecture, writes the language of official reports. He enforces the methods of scientific research, prefers systems to people, numbers to images. He defines the educational programs and the standards for testing them. He has also succeeded in separating the practices of law, science, medicine and commerce from the character of the practitioner. . . . The same characterless abstraction made possible the gulag and the KZ lager. The one death that has caused so much death in the past century is the death of character. (pp. 238–239)

As Hillman points out, education has been an integral part of this process.

In contrast, there are people who have a different vision of education: a holistic view. They still hold to the ancient perspective of educating the whole person and not just training students to compete in a global economy. Some of

1

these people have been participating in conferences held on holistic education in Toronto over the past six years and this book contains some of the work done at those gatherings.

HOLISTIC EDUCATION

What is holistic education? First, holistic education attempts to nurture the development of the whole person. This includes the intellectual, emotional, physical, social, aesthetic, and spiritual. Perhaps the defining aspect of holistic education is the spiritual. Progressive education and humanistic education dealt with the first five factors but generally ignored the spiritual dimension. Recently we have seen a rapidly expanding interest in this last dimension with the publication of several books (Glazer, 1999; Kessler, 2000; Lantieri, 2001; J. Miller 2000; J. Miller and Nakagawa, 2002). Addressing spirituality in the curriculum can mean reawakening students to a sense of awe and wonder. This can involve deepening a sense of connection to the cosmos.

Ron Miller (2000) believes that there are levels of wholeness that are important to holistic education. Besides the whole person there needs to be wholeness in the *community*. People need to be able to relate to one another openly and directly and to foster a sense of care. Communities need to operate on democratic principles and support pluralism. There also should be holism in *society* that allows for more local control and citizen participation. Holistic educators are concerned that the ideology of the marketplace dominates society and they call for more humane approaches to our social structures. Another level of wholeness is the *planet*. Holistic educators generally look at the planet in terms of ecological interdependence. Finally, there is the wholeness of the *cosmos*. This again involves the spiritual dimension that I referred to earlier.

Elsewhere I have described three basic principles of holistic education: *connectedness*, *inclusion*, and *balance* (Miller, 2001). Connectedness refers to moving away from a fragmented approach to curriculum toward an approach that attempts to facilitate connections at every level of learning. Some of these connections include integrating analytic and intuitive thinking, linking body and mind, integrating subjects, connecting to the community, providing links to the earth, and connecting to soul and spirit. Inclusion refers to including all types of students and providing a broad range of learning approaches to reach these students. Finally, balance is based on the concepts of the Tao and yin/yang which suggest that at every level of the universe there are complementary forces and energies (e.g., the rational and the intuitive) that need to be recognized and nurtured. In terms of education this means recognizing these complementary energies in the classroom. Generally our education has been dominated by yang energies such as a focus on rationality and individual com-

petition, and has ignored yin energies such as fostering intuition and cooperative approaches to learning.

Ramon Gallegos Nava (2001), a holistic educator from Mexico, has made
several distinctions between mechanistic approaches to teaching and holistic
education. These are shown in the table below:

It is important to recognize that holistic education cannot be reduced to a
set of techniques or ideologies. Ultimately holistic education rests in the hearts
and minds of the teachers and students. Education has tended to focus on the
head to the exclusion of the rest of our being. Holistic education attempts to
provide learnings that are much more broadly conceived.

THEORY, PRACTICES, AND POETICS

Educators sharing in the vision of wholeness have gathered every other year in
Toronto since 1997 for a conference on holistic learning. These conferences
have included educators from Australia, Canada, Japan, Korea, the United
Kingdom, and the United States. They have been hosted and sponsored by the
Holistic and Aesthetic Education Graduate Focus at the Ontario Institute for
Studies in Education at the University of Toronto (hereafter referred to as
OISE/UT). This collection of readings includes papers submitted by keynote
speakers and workshop presenters at these conferences.

Theory

The editors of this volume have placed the chapters into three different categories: theory, practices, and the poetic. The first chapters include those that
focus on theories and perspectives related to holistic learning. Thomas Moore,
author of several books on the soul, begins the book with a paper on "Educating for the Soul." According to Moore, education for the soul can begin with
teaching people "how to live poetically and aesthetically, how to step into eternity." Anna F. Lemkow was one of the keynote speakers at our first conference
in 1997 and here outlines the main features of a holistic perspective. Another
theoretical piece comes from Douglas Sloan, who writes about the "Modern
Assault on Being Human" and then discusses ways to nurture body, soul, and
spirit in our children.

Riane Eisler, who has written several books on the theme of partnership,
discusses specifically how we can approach partnership education in our schools
and classrooms. Edmund O'Sullivan discusses the concept of "strange attractors,"
which are those systems, or people, that hold the creative edge to change.

Professor Bok Young Kim from Korea writes about Teilhard de Chardin.
South Korea has become one of the centers of activity for holistic education in

TABLE 1.1
Comparison of Educational Paradigms

Mechanistic Education	Holistic Education
Guiding metaphor: the 19th-century machine	Guiding metaphor: 21st-century network organizations
Interdisciplinarity	Transdisciplinarity
Fragmentation of knowledge	Integration of knowledge
Systemic	Holistic
Empirical-analytical	Empirical-analytical-holistic
Development of thought	Development of intelligence
Scientistic-dogmatic	Secular-spiritual
Reductionist	Integral
Focused on teaching	Focused on learning
Static, predetermined curriculum	Open, dynamic curriculum
Curriculum focused on disciplines	Curriculum focused on human knowledge
Superficial changes in behavior	Profound changes in awareness
Academic disciplines	Inquiry based
Mechanistic psychology	Perennial psychology
Explores the external quantitative dimension of the universe	Explores the external/internal and quantitative/qualitative dimensions of the universe
We can know the planet without knowing ourselves	Only by knowing ourselves can we know the planet
There exists only one intelligence: logical-mathematical	There are at least seven equally valid intelligences
Based on bureaucratic organizations	Based on communities of learning
Based on the mechanistic science of Descartes-Newton-Bacon	Based on the cutting-edge science of Bohm-Prigogine-Pribram
Paradigm of simplification	Paradigm of complexity
Predatory conscience	Ecological conscience

SOURCE: Gallegos Nava 2001, pp. 35–36. (Reprinted with permission.)

Asia and Professor Kim is one of leaders of the holistic education movement there. Working from her background in philosophy, Deborah Orr discusses the work of Wittgenstein and Buddhist philosopher Nagarjuna to develop the notion of a holistic embodied spirituality found in such feminist works as Audre Lorde's *Uses of the Erotic*.

Rachael Kessler also contributes a chapter on soulful education. Kessler has worked for many years with adolescents and from this work has identified seven gateways to soul that are based on essential yearnings of young people. Finally, Young Mann Park and Min Young Song have written about Won Hyo, a Korean Buddhist scholar who lived in the 7th century. Park and Song are also very active in the holistic education movement in Korea.

Practices

Several chapters in this book focus on practices. Some of these are classroom practices while other chapters focus on practices and learning strategies that the authors used in their workshop at the conference at OISE/UT.

Gary Babiuk has contributed a chapter on the work he did as principal of a school in a small community in Alberta. He describes how the school staff helped create a holistic learning community. Care was a primary value in the school.

Atsuhiko Yoshida has contributed a chapter about how Waldorf schooling is being introduced in Japan. Professor Yoshida is one of the leaders of the holistic education movement in Japan and has written and translated several books on the topic. Marni Binder has written about the work she does in her school. Specifically, she describes a project on storytelling at Lord Dufferin Public School in Toronto.

Rina Cohen has written about a holistic approach to teaching in mathematics. In particular she describes the work of a grade 7 teacher who has students keep math journals. David Forbes has written about a project he initiated with twelve members of a high school football team. He introduced these young men to meditation practice.

Some of the contributors have described their work with adults. Susan A. Schiller has contributed a chapter describing a holistic process that she uses in her workshops and teaching. This process includes writing a poem, meditating, and contemplating place.

Leslie Owen Wilson writes about how we can create rites of passage for children in our schools. She describes programs that are already being used in some schools.

John P. Miller

Poetics

In the final section of this collection, the chapters have a poetic focus. Diana Denton has described a "pedagogy of compassion" that is based on a phenomenology of the heart, which she has used in her workshops. Isabella Colalillo Kates has written a chapter describing how she teaches creative writing in her classes and workshops. Isabella sees creativity as spiritual activity that involves the soul in holistic learning.

Christopher Reynolds states that conferences have been a gathering of orphans. He suggests that the voice of the orphan can be deeply healing and thus needs to be heard. Celeste Snowber has written about the eros of teaching as she focuses on the importance of embodied learning and knowing.

Finally, Ayako Nozawa describes the workshops that she has done on art and meditation, in which she presents drawing and painting as contemplative activities.

This book provides an alternative to the narrow vision of education that we are confronted with today. The vision presented here focuses on how human beings can reclaim meaning, purpose, and wholeness. It involves a remembering, or recalling of, the visions given to us by the shamans, ancients, sages, and saints over the centuries. Yet we must find a way to make the vision of wholeness a reality in today's world. This book can help us create that reality.

REFERENCES

Gallegos Nava, R. (2001). *Holistic education: Pedagogy of universal love*. Brandon, VT: Foundation for Educational Renewal.

Glazer, S. (1999). *The heart of learning: Spirituality in education*. New York: Jeremy P. Tarcher/Putnam.

Hillman, J. (1999). *The force of character and the lasting life*. New York: Random House.

Kessler, R. (2000). *The soul of education: Helping students find connection, compassion, and character at school*. Alexandria, VA: Association for Supervision and Curriculum Development.

Lantieri, L. (2001). *Schools with spirit: Nurturing the inner lives of children and teachers*. Boston: Beacon.

Miller, J. (2000). *Education and the soul: Toward a spiritual curriculum*. Albany: State University of New York Press.

Miller, J. (2001) *The holistic curriculum*. Toronto, ON: OISE Press.

Miller, J. and Nakagawa, Y. (2002). *Nurturing our wholeness: Perspectives on spirituality in education*. Brandon, VT: Foundation for Educational Renewal.

Miller, R. (2000). *Caring for a new life: Essays on holistic education*. Brandon, VT: Foundation for Educational Renewal.

PART 1

Theorizing a Pedagogy of Wholeness

Awakening Self, Soul, and Spirit

CHAPTER 1

Educating for the Soul

THOMAS MOORE

Everything a human being does, including learning and teaching, is filtered through many layers of the imagination. Our childhood and our parents are always with us, setting the stage. The worldview of the society in which we live is always pressing. Our fears and our hopes, our fantasies of the future, all those things we feel as needs—this entire mass of images, soaked in emotions, profoundly influences how we imagine learning to take place and how we go about teaching and learning. And this world of imagination is largely unconscious, doing its work in the background as we develop our strategies and forge our theories on the surface of experience.

A case could be made that the current focus on accountability and testing stems from anxiety, the fear that our students may not learn as much as they should or that they may be given the wrong facts and the wrong ideas. I see two problems here. First, whenever we try to be creative out of anxiety, we are doomed to failure. Anxiety always has a place, but as the basic emotion shaping the thrust of our activity, it is a destructive starting point. Second, no matter how much testing we do, we will still get it wrong. It's the nature of learning to be a mixture of insight and dimness, facts and mistakes. We know all too well that what one generation takes to be proven truth a later generation transcends and revises. It might be better to incorporate ignorance into the design of teaching and learning.

Before elaborating on that point, let me proclaim as clearly as possible that my concern is the soul. Our current focus on facts and science and skills highlights a certain dimension of human reality but overlooks others. An emphasis on mind has generated a neglect of soul. The matter of soul is taken up today by the fringe writers who are generally outside the culture of academia and professionalism, digging in the murky swamps of self-help and popular psychology. I think we need to bring soul more into the center, where we can study it seriously and allow it to have an impact on the culture at large.

But how do you educate the soul, and is that the proper way to formulate the issue? Do we cultivate the soul, or do we shape our ideas and practices so that soul is included? Let me phrase my concern as "educating for the soul"—teaching certain subjects and doing it in a way that brings the soul forward into our awareness and our list of priorities.

WHAT THE SOUL NEEDS AND WANTS

As a starting point, we might realize that the soul is essentially different, though by no means disconnected, from the mind and body. It has its own qualities, which give rise to its own requirements. Because it is so mysterious, it is difficult to list those qualities without many caveats, but generally I feel comfortable saying that the soul is eternal, unique, contemplative, poetic, erotic, aesthetic, and transcendent. To lay out an approach to educating for the soul all we would have to do is consider each of these elements and see how we might become more sophisticated in our knowledge and practice of them.

Before going through the list, let me point out that eros is the dynamic of the soul. It works by desire—by want, need, and longing. It's easy to quickly pass by this important realization, but it is crucial. As my colleagues in archetypal psychology used to say, "What does the soul want?" That is the first question. Not, what will improve it or make it excellent or help it to function, but what does it want? As a therapist, I saw over and over how people were brought to a recognition of their soul through desperate feelings of need, lack, and confusion. As a musician and artist, I know, too, that people can become keenly aware of soul in the process of their art and their longing for beauty and insight.

If we understand eros in its classical and mythological origins, we might appreciate that desire and need are aspects of the erotic dynamic of the soul, and if we are going to educate for the soul, then we have to give full attention to these strongly felt emotions and realizations. Eros, then is not just a quality of soul but the very energy that sustains it and causes it to increase.

POETIC VISION AND KNOWLEDGE

We live in a quite literal-minded, fact-loving society, and so it is difficult to appreciate the soul's language and dialects. It is at home in poetic imagery and language, and that is not surprising given the soul's tendency toward mystery and multiple levels of meaning. A dream is a perfect example of soul speech. It usually connects strongly with the dreamer's daily life, it is full of obscure imagery, and it hints at far broader, collective, and eternal issues. It demands a poetic sensitivity if we are to take any insight from it. But these are directions of soul in everything it touches.

Soul-centered education would emphasize the many dimensions of poetic existence: poetry as such, literature and art, a poetic reading of science and nature (advocated and described by soul specialist Ralph Waldo Emerson), and a generally imagistic approach to all human interactions. We glimpse soul through insight rather than through direct analysis. We see it in reflection—implied, distorted, obscured, camouflaged. Soul is like poetry as described by the American poet Wallace Stevens—"like a pheasant disappearing behind a bush."

So let us try to resist the temptation to define soul, to establish a once-and-for-all theory of it, to make a school of soul experts, to program its study on models not inherently appropriate to it. Our best model is the poet, who may or may not speak explicitly about it. Our approach could be mythological, lyric, narrative, epic, comic, ironic, absurdist. We could be cautious in the genre of our speech about it, knowing that certain styles that are beautifully elegant for the mind and for fact are entirely inappropriate for the soul.

ETERNITY IN A MOMENT

If the poetics of soul is a stumbling block for educators in the modern setting, the notion of eternity is even more difficult. We live in a secularist society. The word *secular* refers to our age, our time and place. We focus our attention more on what is happening now and on a futurism that is equally literal. We imagine a future that has more and better of what we already know, and for the most part that future is a material one. I have yet to hear a futurist talk about how children will be fed, nurtured, brought up, and taught in profoundly fulfilling ways in the future.

Eternity is not the same as afterlife. Eternity is now, if it is anything. Marsilio Ficino, who single-handedly did much to promote education for soul in the 15th century and had an influence far beyond that, said that soul exists in both eternity and time. The eternal is that which is beyond time and yet fully present. A beautiful object may stop time for a moment, allowing a moment of refreshing withdrawal from the pressures of the temporal. A brief period of contemplation, whether it is formal sitting and meditation or informal absorption in a child playing or a few bars of music, may take us out of time, and the soul increases in this moment.

I use the word *moment* because the eternal is not limited or conditioned by time. A few seconds of reverie equal hours of hard work at the temporal level. Educators could keep in mind this principle as they develop a curriculum for the soul. It doesn't require grand new schemes of coursework and activities, but it may ask for attention to gardens, empty rooms, empty times, paintings, good sounds (a beautiful bell)—anything that might foster a mere moment of contemplation.

The soul has a spiritual dimension, and the eternal is certainly part of that spirituality. But it is never far removed from ordinary existence and from the material earth and the human body. The sound of the resonant bell doesn't just inspire the eternal; it is itself participation in the eternal, and its physicality is essential. The soul's spirituality is also as deep as it is high and as diverse as it is intense. I picture the soul as a sphere surrounded by its eternal dimensions, its spirituality as rich deep in its body as at its periphery.

EXQUISITELY UNIQUE

Talk of the soul is filled with paradox. Dreams teach us that eternal, archetypal, mythic themes lie at the base of our daily lives. We are always living a myth, being human and incarnating human potential. Soul writers favor mythology because it addresses these huge, cosmic themes.

But at the same time nothing is more unique and momentary than the soul. As Cicero said, it is the animus, the daimonic and driven aspect of soul, that gives us our identity. Modern psychology favors the idea of an ego, a kind of self-sufficient, self-constructing identity fully in our ken and control. But Cicero suggests something more in the line of the artist's ego, a sense of destiny and identity that rises up from passionate, uncontrolled, fate-filled dimensions of our entire existence. The ego is only a small portion of that volcanic power. Our idea of it reflects the shallowness of our very image of the human being, a mechanical ego lacking the profound vitality of a soul.

Cicero hints at the mystery and paradox by which the great archetypal ground of human being gives birth to a remarkable individual person. Like artists who must be in touch with the inspiring muse aspect of being for their supply of images and familiarity with the mysteries, any person thrives through such a funneling of powerful forces and possibilities that draw fatefully into a personality and a life story.

Therefore, in educating for the soul, the teacher will help the student meander in this paradoxical territory, a liminality, you might say, a capacity to stay on the border between the universal and the unique. We make a mistake when we reduce our psychological thinking to personal terms and dimensions. A person thrives from the great images as well as personal reflection. Our studies need not be made relevant to give them soul, and in fact confusing soul for personality psychologizes in the worst way our efforts at education. There is a vast difference between allowing soul into the classroom and making learning a personal experience. A person's uniqueness comes from the soul, not from a focus on personal particulars and a delimiting of learning to what is personally relevant. That is the problem, too, with learning for skill and financial success. These may be relevant to the ego, but they obscure the needs of the soul.

VITAL AND NECESSARY EROTICISM

The great story of Eros and Psyche, ancient in its roots and loved by many modern psychologies, tells us allegorically that the soul needs eros to work its way out of its primary narcissism, its concern for itself and its family—its literal and immediate roots. Orphic religion in Greece taught that Eros is a creative force, making worlds and keeping them alive. It is this terrifying profundity I have in mind when I say that educating for the soul is fundamentally erotic.

As teachers and learners we have to distinguish between what we think we need and what the soul desperately longs for. In therapy, I sit and watch as people struggle against the obvious and powerful desires that burn deep within them, but which seem to contradict what they consider best for themselves. Their healing would be the discovery of what the soul wants and the capacity to grant the soul its pleasure. Therapy is no more and no less than this, and neither is education.

As everyone knows from experience, eros is inevitably entangled with sexuality. In some ways they overlap and are essentially the same, provided you imagine sexuality as an experience of soul and mind as well as body. On the few occasions when I have addressed groups of educators on the theme of eros, I have met strong resistance, out of the fear, I believe, of sex.

Education is a highly sexual activity: intimate, physical, full of desire, involving a deeper tangle of souls than is usually admitted. It also involves the thrill of authority and power, on both sides. It might help to remind ourselves how these power issues can turn into sadomasochistic patterns, where the sexuality in the power struggle comes more into the foreground. Eugene Ionesco's play *The Lesson*, in which the teacher dominates and finally rapes his student, has always been instructive to me. In my studies of the Marquis de Sade, I also learned how sex and power, differences in age, and learning itself are all riddled with sexual colorings.

Whether or not we invite eros into education, it will be there. Better to cultivate it than to let it do its work outside any positive effort on our part to address it. I believe that the sexual demands in education can be satisfied through a more general attention to the erotics. Most Western education is highly saturnine in tone: we like order, hierarchies, grades, tests, a gloried past, control, deprivation, remoteness of various kinds, and weighty seriousness.

The saturnine has its pleasures, and we do indeed take pleasure giving and often taking tests and all the rest. The problem is really more one of monotheism, the exclusive attention to saturnine values, a focus that denies other legitimate pleasures. I often ask students to imagine a Venusian form of education. It might take place in lush gardens, where the body feels tended and pleasured. Desire would be in the foreground. Beauty everywhere. Of course, there would be venereal problems. Everything has its shadow. My point is to suggest a way to give eros some range.

COSMETICS IN THE SCHOOL

If I had another lifetime like this one, I'd want to study the sacred art of the world as a way of learning life's mysteries. In the gesture and details of art we glimpse truths about the nature of things. One of the most precious moments in my life took place when I was fifty and visiting Rome. I wandered the narrow streets by myself and visited the Museo Capitolino, in which I stood alone and quietly contemplated two sacred sculptures that have given my life meaning for many years: the *Capitoline Venus* and the *Eros* and *Psyche*. I wondered about Venus standing there naked with her hands in front of her breasts and some clothing and a vase beside her. She is often shown with a mirror, rising from water, wearing bracelets, and anklets, or, in the unsurpassable paintings of Lucas Cranach, with brilliant jewels.

Beauty, adornment, and cosmetics are all of great importance to the soul, even though they may seem secondary to an ego-centered life. Beauty arrests the attention so the soul can come into view. It does little for practical life but everything for that which makes human life meaningful and worth living. Shouldn't education be concerned with these issues, as well as understanding the physical world and getting along in it?

Writers often note that the word *cosmos* means adornment, and conversely we might say that cosmetics have a universal importance. Ficino said that sparkling sand and stone transmit the light they have absorbed from the brilliant stars. The cosmetic aspect of our experience similarly lets the mysterious light of the soul shine through, placing us at another liminal point between the eternal and the temporal.

Educators sometimes reject plans to bring beauty into the learning environment as being "merely" cosmetic. From the soul viewpoint, instructed in the mysteries of Venus, we would not make such a judgment but rather appreciate the importance of adornment in our schools, beauty in everything we do, and even the role of cosmetics for the body, an issue often discussed by school administrators who are usually fearful of the Venusian soul.

IN PRACTICE

I can see that these few, abbreviated reflections are really an outline for a book on educating for the soul. Each of these areas and many more need further development. The main point I want to make is that educating for the soul asks for an entirely new set of concerns and values. These may be compatible with other goals we ordinarily bring to education, but they are radically different and demand a fundamental shift in thinking. As I have tried to show, when you focus on the soul you necessarily turn some things upside down, as in the case of cosmetics.

At the beginning I referred briefly to education as a cultivation of a certain kind of ignorance and not just an assault on the uninformed mind. As many religions teach, not knowing is as important as knowing. This may mean simply not striving to know everything, not testing to the limit, recognizing that everyone will have unique and precious pockets of ignorance. The soul can't be forced into education or into a life; it appears when there is an opening, and ignorance can be such an opening, provided it is allowed its necessity.

Soul-oriented teachers need wisdom rather than information and a strong imagination. They have to be open to the deepest archetypal thrusts at work in human life and also focused on the absolutely unique individuals in front of them. They, the soul teachers, have to think and speak in images and pay attention to beauty, nuance, and ritual. All school actions address the soul as well as the temporal and practical concerns. This is where a rule or custom turns into ritual and a uniform or a classroom into an image.

wisdom + imagination

Soul teachers are never fully out of the realm of dream, for that is the natural environment of the soul. I don't mean they have to be dreamy, in the usual sense, but always aware of the image and narrative that saturates their work. This is by no means an impossible expectation. We are all born to live poetically. We are created to serve the soul. This kind of education is natural and relatively easy. We need only get out of the way and let it happen. It does take work and circumspection not to be entirely deluded by the normative myth of the society, but that, too, isn't impossible.

You educate for the soul by giving it the things in life it needs: love, beauty, spirit, pleasure. You teach a person how to focus on the soul, how to live poetically and aesthetically, how to step into eternity. In this kind of education, time and eternity always intersect; one doesn't dominate the other. You aim toward the fullness of life and its empty spaces, and you avoid the tendency to be overly busy and literally void. You create the conditions and allow the soul to manifest itself.

To accomplish this kind of learning, the teacher has to know what the soul is all about—not definitions and theories, but concrete understanding of how the soul exists in ordinary life. This vision will draw soul into every subject, every field, and every learning activity. This will result in education not of the soul or about the soul, but for the soul.

CHAPTER 2

Reflections on Our Common
Lifelong Learning Journey

ANNA F. LEMKOW

It has been said that words have mysterious powers, that a word can be a ladder or a bridge to a higher level of awareness. I believe this is true, and that *wholeness* is such a word. With respect to learning, wholeness invites us to contemplate it in its integrity—to contemplate it in the truest way we can. Wholeness suggests encompassing the different dimensions of human experience, because experience is perhaps our best teacher. It suggests as well contemplating the world—the arena of our experience. Wholeness suggests that one's life, experience, and learning are coextensive, and that learning is thus lifelong—perhaps, for all we know, many life times long. Learning, it may be said, is a prolonged journey in consciousness, in self-unfoldment. Wholeness suggests it is a holy and healing journey; even an obligatory journey since existence is not optional. Nor can we alter universal conditions, including the difficult universal human condition of having the power to choose but, together with everything else, being totally woven into the very fabric of existence, utterly dependent on our planet, on the cosmos, on the universe.

Speaking of the mysterious power of words, the two words *cosmos* and *universe* are nothing short of revelatory in what they say about our journey. *Universe,* from Latin, suggests a turning in a unitary direction—a dynamic unicity. The word *cosmos*, from Greek, means order; hence mind, intelligence. These two words combine to tell us that existence is one and indivisible, and that its dynamics are meaningful. By the same token, our own journey is an integral part of a common and meaningful journey.

In exploring learning, I believe we must start with ourselves, the learners, with what or who we believe ourselves to be. This determines what we believe we can know, how we understand our relationship to the world we live in, and the values we affirm. Here we immediately come up against a prevailing mind-set that is utterly incompatible with holistic learning, the idea that a human being is nothing but the totality of his or her biological, material self, that all human experience is nothing but biochemistry; for example, the beauty of a tree is nothing but the brain's dopamine and serotonin at work. If that were true, then we would be merely automatons, and all talk of learning and responsibility, let alone spiritual values, would be nonsense. But it is not true either scientifically, psychologically, or spiritually. If science introduced the reductionist self-image, science has now outdated it. For instance, it doesn't cohere with the emergent field theory. Frontier scientists, I'm told, including a number of respected medical doctors, believe that our nature, our mind, and our health are constantly influenced by and interacting with the energy fields in which we are embedded, especially the electromagnetic bioenergy field and a subtler energy field science calls the "holofield of the quantum vacuum," described as the fathomless energy sea in which all is embedded, with which we interact, which interconnects us and also nurtures us. It reminds one forcibly, does it not, of certain long-held spiritual intuitions, for instance, the Buddhist's boundless emptiness that is a plenum.

I heard a well-known astronomer the other day declare on TV, "I'm a committed reductionist. I believe that the universe is a whole consisting of the sum of its parts." He sounded almost defiant, as if he were defiantly rejecting an opposing view—the view in systems theory that a whole, an open or dynamic system, is more than the sum of its parts, and therefore *not* reducible to its parts. From a systems perspective, for instance, an atom is more than the sum of its subatomic particles; a cell is more than its component molecules; an animal more than a plant; a human being more than an animal. Systems science is a major development of recent decades whose effect is to reverse the reductionistic and mechanistic view of nature. Thanks to systems science, evolution itself is no longer viewed as mechanical but as a veritable whole-making process, a process that has generated and is ever generating a vast continuum of successively more inclusive, more capable, more autonomous wholes, or dynamic systems or "holons." A *holon*, the word coined some decades ago by Arthur Koestler, is an entity that is both a whole and a part, and in fact we know of no whole in nature that is not both a whole and a part of a greater whole. It becomes apparent from the systems view that the universe displays a grand cosmic design—that it organizes itself in the pattern of wholes within wholes, or, in systems parlance, systems within systems. By the same token, it is apparent that everything is dynamically interconnected—more than that, the entities comprising the universe interpenetrate. Without intending to, science here reveals a profound metaphysical truth—the radical unity of existence, something long intuited in mystical thought, as in St. Paul's dictum that we are all members of one another.

It is worth noting that each whole in the evolutionary continuum contains within itself a component of all succeeding levels. A human being thus embodies the components of all preceding levels, is not reducible to any of them, and is presumably going to transcend himself or herself into a still more inclusive entity. What apparently happens is that every entity differentiates itself, specializes, but then subordinates itself to the purposes of the next more inclusive holon—subordinates itself, transcends itself, as it were, for the sake of the greater whole in the making. As Arthur Koestler (1973) memorably put it, unity is achieved by a detour through diversity. Nature is surely a great teaching. In reality, the continuum of evolution is replete with meaning.

But to get back to the astronomer, I happened to mention the astronomer's remark to Jeffery Kane and he immediately quoted an extraordinarily apt poem by Walt Whitman entitled "When I Heard the Learn'd Astronomer." It makes the point I want to make here much more eloquently than I could.

> When I heard the learn'd astronomer,
> When the proofs, the figures, were ranged in columns before me
> When I was shown the charts and diagrams, to add, divide,
> and measure them,
> When I sitting heard the astronomer where he lectured with much
> applause in the lecture-room,
> How soon unaccountable I became tired and sick,
> Till rising and gliding out I wander'd off by myself,
> In the mystical moist night-air, and from time to time,
> Look'd up to perfect silence at the stars. (p. 221)

So much for reductionism!

Closely related to reductionism is rationalism. Rationalism, as we know, has prevailed in the West for several centuries. Rationalists extol reason and discount subjective experience as unreal. Thus, like reductionists, their idea of who we are and what we can know is inadequate. Rationalists tend not to perceive that marvelous and indispensable as our power of reason is, it is still a limited faculty. Reason *is* the mode for philosophical discourse. But while reason is the faculty we use for discussing truth, goodness, beauty, love, and compassion, reason alone cannot make them realities in our life. We don't love anyone because it's reasonable to do so. Reason alone can't conquer irrational feelings that are impervious to logic. Reason is not the source of inspiration for a great work of art. Nor is it the source of the experience of unity with others beyond all differences.

Before I comment on the transrational faculties we possess, I first must make mention of yet another ism—relativism. It, too, misapprehends who we are and what we can know. It is found mostly in political and cultural spheres, at least in our part of the world. Without wishing to discount relativist thought wholesale, I reject their disbelief in transcendent truths, their disbelief in our capacity to know transcendent truths. Not surprisingly, they find no basis for determining between right and wrong. Indeed, one of their mantras is that one should not be judgmental. For a relativist, the difference between right and wrong is simply a matter of where you happen to live. Morality is only relative to culture, not unlike manners and fashions. Relativists in effect and sometimes avowedly deny the existence of timeless truths or values that transcend different cultures and civilizations.

But the relativists' position is self-defeating: it asserts the nonexistence of universal truth while exempting its own would-be universal assertion. My impression is that relativism would deny the very thing we appreciate and enjoy most in the arts and cultures of different times and places—its universal aspects.

Presumably relativists would manage somehow to deny the undeniable universality of the world's myths of all times and places. Presumably, they would deny the undeniable universality of folklore. As one connoisseur of folk art put it, folk art is bewilderingly varied and astonishingly related; it shows that the whole world is hometown, that there are no foreigners. Could relativists deny that music and music making transcends time and place? Personally, I find moving the sight, frequent today, of an Oriental musician superbly performing Occidental works on a Western instrument. Perhaps today's greatest living cellist is Yo-Yo Ma.

I would like to remind relativists that human beings are all of one and the same species. We intermarry; a nuclear family's members may all differ in skin color; cultures are not only permeable but have rarely, if ever, developed in total isolation. (They were inevitably exposed to each other by virtue of the trade routes, the silk roads, the roads of faith.) And I'd also remind relativists that human thought is continuous throughout our species, that it travels through the air, as it were, that we send and receive each other's thoughts constantly. As Vaclev Havel (1994) put it, "It's as if something like an antenna were at our disposal, picking up signals from a transmitter that contains the experience of the entire human race" (p. 3).

If the arts and cultures of the worlds were indeed totally devoid of universal aspects, there could be no hope of common human understanding. There could be no hope for world peace. As it is, what we have in common far outweighs our differences.

Is it possible to discern the juncture we have collectively reached in our common journey in consciousness? I do not mean to imply that we are all at the same level. Obviously, individuals vary enormously in refinement of soul; they range in consciousness from the brute to the seer or sage. Yet I believe a predominant planetwide mentality is discernible, and it is that of separateness, divisiveness. It parallels the too-narrow self-identity—the truncated self-image I've been discussing. Huston Smith describes this mentality as "tunnel vision." Ken Wilber names this limited out-look "Flatland."

However named, this mind-set is one of ignorance of, disbelief in, or the dormancy of a human being's higher faculties. As we saw, it is common to the adherents of all the isms I discussed. The separative mind explains our present shallowness and cynicism. It goes a long way to explain the widespread prevalence of competitiveness, dishonesty, and corruption in government, politics, and business, not to speak of the horrible thing called "ethnic cleansing." In many places and quarters, competitiveness has now become so intensive it's downright pathological.

Many of us have grown very weary of all this. But more than that, the planetwide divisiveness over a range of old and new issues is very dangerous, given the degree of interdependence we have developed—materially, militarily, ecologically, and in every other way. It seems we've come to a fork in the road of our common learning journey. Many thinkers have long seen it coming and have pointed out that institutional change would not suffice to resolve the serious dilemma, that it demanded nothing short of a fundamental change in consciousness on the part of at least a critical number of us. The rise of the holistic education movement some decades ago is one of many responses aroused by the perception of the undesirable direction in human affairs.

Self-transformation can't occur without the exertion of our higher faculties—our intuitive, aesthetic, unitive, spiritual faculties. These components of ours include reason and the physical senses but transcend them. The reductionists, the rationalists, the relativists among us could not hope to transform their behavior and their values without reclaiming or awakening to their higher faculties. In reality, all of us will have to develop a stronger sense of our unity beyond all differences.

It's thought provoking that the human constitution parallels the pattern we saw in the evolutionary continuum. Thus, the reasoning mind includes but transcends the physical senses. The intuition includes but transcends the mind. Spirit includes but transcends the intuition. Spirit is not a personal faculty; it is impersonal and universal. Yet Spirit is the very source of our powers of knowing and of our illumination.

Self-observation shows that our different faculties work in tandem: one cannot think without feeling, and one cannot feel without thinking. To think without feeling is pathological. Experience also shows that to be divided within oneself is to feel uneasy, even to fall ill. Our deep need for wholeness is entirely self-evident.

This interactivity of a human being's powers of knowing implies a significant thing about knowledge: just as we are all of a piece, so is knowledge. In principle, knowledge is one and indivisible. In other words, science, philosophy, mystical religion, the arts, psychology, and so on are in principle mutually har-monious and complementary.

Take science and religion. They have been seriously at odds since the rise of modern science. But where the religion posited is mystical religion as distinct from dogmatic or fanatical types, and where the science posited is the newer, more organic, holistic, and integrative science, the essential harmony of religion and science begins to come into view. Albert Einstein defined their relationship most succinctly and memorably when he said that religion without science is lame, and science without religion is blind.

I've been suggesting the wholeness and dynamic oneness of everything, of the universe, of the evolution of the universe, of living nature, of ourselves, of our knowledge. On reflection, it is evident that wholeness pervades existence. And what is transpiring today in the sciences shows that most, if not all, scien-tific disciplines have encountered the problems of wholes and wholeness, that wholeness is emerging as a guiding principle in science. It has long been that in the spiritual domain. My book (1995/1990) on wholeness attempted inter alia to explore all this in a specific way. Wholeness, I think, points insistently beyond itself. It demands a consensual wisdom, a consensual philosophy that could illu-minate the meaning of wholeness. Just as critical thought calls for a critical theory to ground it, so holistic thought calls for a consensual wisdom, a consen-sual frame of reference.

As some are undoubtedly aware, humanity in fact possesses a consensual wisdom, a consensual philosophy, a perennial philosophy, called also theosophy, the tradition from which I myself come, ageless wisdom, integral philosophy, and *Atma Vidya*, among other names.

In the space available for this chapter it is not possible to do more than cite the most succinct yet satisfactory definition of the perennial philosophy found in Aldous Huxley's (1970) classic, *The Perennial Philosophy*. Huxley defined it as

> the metaphysic that recognizes a Divine Reality substantial to the world of things and lives and minds; the psychology that finds in the soul something similar to or even identical with Divine Reality, the ethic that places man's final end in the knowledge of the immanent and transcendent Ground of all being.

Huxley added,

> Rudiments of the perennial philosophy are found among the tradi-tionary lore of primitive peoples in every region of the world, and in its fully developed forms it has a place in every one of the higher reli-gions. (p. vii)

It is true that ultimate reality figures in one or another way in every spiri-tual tradition. The perennial philosophy and theosophy and other esoteric philosophies see reality as infinite, boundless, and omnipresent. It has to be omnipresent if it is boundless. It can't be apart from us if it is boundless. It can't be only out there. It is here too. It is both transcendent and immanent, as Huxley's definition states. Being boundless, it can't be defined. It is ineffable yet, in an appropriate or meditative state of consciousness, one sees it shining though everything.

Another way of putting this is that transcendent truths are perceived not logically, but directly. Mystics, poets, artists, and scientists of the first rank see transcendent truths directly. For example, William Blake's poem, beginning with the line, "To see the world in a grain of sand," illustrates seeing directly. This line does not come from analysis or from critical thinking. Nor is the poet conveying information. Nor is he expressing merely a socially constructed idea.

If evolution is indeed ongoing, more and more of us should be experiencing intimation of transcendent truths. I believe that is indeed happening. I also believe that by the evidence, this experience, this insight, does not necessarily go hand in hand with knowledge of metaphysics or level of education or even the person's age. It is most often a spontaneous and blissful experience when all boundaries between oneself and everything else dissolve. Incidentally, there are splendid writings today (e.g., Murphy 1993) describing the nature of self-transcendence and the psychotechnologies for developing self-transcendence.

Let me underline that this experience, this expansion of consciousness, has powerful practical consequences—just the kind of impact needed at this juncture in our common journey in consciousness. It vitally affects our relationship to the world. I believe it fosters global mindedness, a sense of being a planetary citizen, irrespective of place of residence. Being a planetary citizen is not at all incompatible with having roots in and love for a particular place. It fosters the sense of the oneness of everything, including planetary affairs: the indivisibility of human rights, world peace, world security, earth's ecology. As planetary citizens we support cooperation and sharing among nations. We appreciate the need for a world coordinating agency such as the United Nations—an agency, too, that can deal with common problems beyond the capacity of any one nation. We much prefer to see the development of world law to continued international anarchy. Above all, a planetary citizen feels that his or her status as a human being takes precedence over every other personal characteristic, including one's sex, color, ethnicity, religion, and ideology.

The awareness of transcendent truths does not depend on a person's age. Jose Macado, an immigrant from El Salvador, wrote a poem, "Life and Me," (Lyne 1997) when he was a 7th grader with limited experience with English.

Life is a mystery of hurt feelings and choices.
It looks like it will never end.
The sky is blue and water is crystal-like.

It's like looking through a glass where you can see but not
    understand.
When the wind blows on my face I feel like my soul *is* that wind
And all my troubles blow away with it.
In the night I feel angels coming and caring for me in the moonlight.
I feel like my fingers are touching God's fingers.
And when this happens I feel I'm an angel myself.
Not a snake or a lion can have this feeling but I can.
It feels so wonderful—the motion of my body
Is so great that tears come to my eyes
And I ask myself what is this feeling.
I feel my soul transforming into a spirit of fire
And at the end of this feeling there is triumph and a beautiful dream.
(pp. 120–121)

Shortly after I discovered this poem, I happened to read the following passage in an essay by the physicist-philosopher David Bohm (1993):

What is spirit? The word is derived from a Latin word meaning "breath" or "wind"—like respiration or inspiration. It is suggested by the trees moving with the invisible force of the wind. We may thus think of spirit as an invisible force—a life-giving essence that moves us deeply, or as a source that moves everything from within.

Soon after reading this, I happened to converse with someone about the Hebrew language. He remarked that the Hebrew word *Ruah* can mean breath or spirit or wind. And he further observed that from the metaphysical to the scientific levels, breath connects us to the world around us. You may notice, he said, that you are breathed as much as you breathe.

Breath is perhaps the ultimate bridge between science and spirituality. As we saw, these two domains are growing progressively more harmonious. I very much like what John White (1990) wrote about the meeting of science and spirit: "It is about the human being as human becoming. We are Spirit materialized, engaged in spiritualizing matter" (p. xiv). Ervin Laszlo (1997), in his excellent recent book on the progress of science, *The Whispering Pond*, states that science is tremendously widening its scope, to the point that it is changing the world outlook and becoming an instrument for the recovery of wholeness. Laszlo added a significant caveat: inasmuch as science does not deal with matters beyond space and time, we will always have need to complement science with wisdom. I myself suggested something very similar in *The Wholeness Principle* (1995/1990).

Let me suggest that our aspiration for holistic learning comes from an inner call, an insistent call of something mysterious, something greater than ourselves.

It arises in the transcendent realm to which wholeness points. It urges us to deepen our understanding, and intimates that we can become more than we presently are.

Together we are embarked on an eons-long learning journey which teaches us to realize increasingly the wholeness of things, the eternal condition. As T. S. Eliot (1971) wrote in "Little Gidding" (*Four Quartets*),

> And the end of all our exploring
> Will be to arrive at where we started
> And know the place for the first time. (p. 59)

REFERENCES

Bohm, D. (1993). Science, spirituality, and the present world crisis. *ReVision*, 15(4).

Eliot, T. S. (1971). *Four quartets*. San Diego: Harcourt Brace.

Havel, V. (1994). Remarks made on July 4, 1994, as he received the Philadelphia Liberty Medal. Reprinted in *Brain/Mind* (August 1994).

Huxley, A. (1970). *The perennial philosophy*. New York: Harper & Row.

Koestlee, A. (1973). *The roots coincidence*. New York: Vintage Books.

Lazlo, E. (1997). *The whispering pond: A personal guide to the emerging vision of science*. Rockport, MA: Element.

Lemkow, A. F. (1995/1990). *The wholeness principle: Dynamics of unity within science, religion and society*. Wheaton, IL: Quest Books.

Lyne, S. (1997). *Ten-second rain showers by young people*. New York: Simon & Schuster.

Murphy, M. (1993). *The future of the body: Explorations into the further evolution of human nature*. New York: Tarcher/Perigee.

White, J. (1990). *The meeting of science and spirit: Guidelines for a new age*. New York: Paragon House.

Whitman, W. (1993). *Leaves of Grass*. New York: Modern Library Edition.

CHAPTER 3

Education and the Modern Assault on Being Human

Nurturing Body, Soul, and Spirit

DOUGLAS SLOAN

Every educational practice implies some underlying image of the human being. When examined, many of our modern educational assumptions and practices imply images of the child and of the adult as essentially other than human—merely an animal to be socialized, a computer to be programmed, a unit of production to be harnessed and utilized, a consumer to be won, and others. The subjection of children to such an education places mighty obstacles in their capacity to develop to the full: the senses become impoverished; thinking is narrowed and becomes incapable of insight and newness; bodily and emotional health are undermined; hope and joy are extinguished; and the development of free, confident, caring, and wise individuals disappears, both as a goal and as a reality.

My intention and hope here is that we can undertake a beginning—and it can only be a sketchy beginning—a beginning exploration of the critical importance for the future of our children and of their earth, both under assault, of an education grounded in an understanding of the whole human being as body, soul, and spirit.

I propose to approach our topic by looking at our four most central soul/spirit functions and asking what, if anything, they imply for our understanding of the human being and for the education of this human being. These four soul/spirit functions include our life of thinking and understanding, our life of feeling and emotion, our life of active initiative and intention, and, finally, our life of sense

Looking Out → Sensing
Looking In → Feeling
Inward look

Choosing — Willing → Adapting
Being with → Thinking!
Wisdom

and perception. Together these functions constitute our most immediate life experience, and they are all involved in our knowledge of the world.

In looking both at thinking, feeling, willing, and sensing on the one hand and at the human as body, soul, and spirit on the other, I want to stress at the outset—and I emphasize this now because I will assume it all the way through, but may not say it again explicitly—that while we can distinguish these as various realms of the human being, we ought not try to separate them. They are all interrelated, interpenetrate, and impinge upon one another. Owen Barfield (1971) once pointed out how important it is to be able to distinguish without necessarily having to separate (pp. 10–12, 18–21, 36 *passim*). He also observed that it seems uncommonly difficult for modern people to do this. Instead, the modern tendency is, on the one hand, to think that if we can distinguish things from each other, then we must take a further step and divide and separate them. On the other hand, we also have the tendency to feel that if we cannot divide and separate, then we cannot, or need not, distinguish. Our dual tendency is toward fragmentation on the one side and monolithic sameness on the other. If, as an example of the latter, we cannot divide body and soul, the modern tendency is not to distinguish them but simply to collapse one into the other, and then to conclude that there is only body or there is only soul. It hardly needs to be said that the overwhelmingly modern propensity is to say there is only body, and that anything smacking of a soul nature is merely an illusory epiphenomenon of body. So in dealing with these various dimensions of the human being we can take as our guiding principle the importance of being able to distinguish without dividing. We can have, in other words, differentiation with interpenetration.

THINKING

Let us begin, then, with our first soul/spirit function, thinking. We have been so subjected in our ordinary education to identifying thinking with a dry, desiccated, and thin academic intellectualism that it has become difficult for us to look upon thinking as a central soul reality, much less look to it as a first and major avenue to spirit. So we often try to bypass thinking, to go around it, in our search for something more real, more substantial, more alive. Both materialists and spiritualists do this—the materialists reducing thinking to electrochemical brain events, spiritualists trying to transcend thinking as mere appearance and maya. Since there is an element of truth in both the one-sided materialist and spiritualist positions, each has ammunition to bring against the other. But in this ongoing battle and polarization between the materialists and the spiritualists, thinking is denigrated by both sides and its full potential in relation to both spirit and matter goes unrecognized and undeveloped.

Nevertheless, some people have recognized and called our attention to the power of thinking. Stanislauf Ulam, the noted mathematician involved in the development of the atomic bomb, once expressed his own amazement at the power of thought. "It is still an unending source of surprise for me," he has said, "to see how a few scribbles on a blackboard or on a sheet of paper could change the course of human affairs" (as cited in Rhodes, 1986, p. 11). Erwin Chargaff, the great biochemist, has observed the power of thinking in penetrating and splitting the two nuclei of matter, the nucleus of the atom and the nucleus of the cell—and in both these instances Chargaff (1986) expressed his deep uneasiness with what thinking had wrought. Finally, to take one last example, the historian John Lukacs has described as the most important fact of our time what he calls "the mental intrusion into the structure of events." In our century this mental intrusion has attained new powers of penetration, capable of what Lukacs (1986) calls, on the one hand, the destructive "insubstantialization of matter" and, on the other, the creative "spiritualization of matter" (pp. 10–12). In other words, he and the others are pointing us to the power of thinking to both create and destroy, right down to the level of the material world itself. If thinking has this power, then we are well advised to pay attention to it, for the quality of our world is going to depend directly on the quality of our thinking.

Let us look at the multiple dimensions and scope of thinking. Our thoughts vary greatly in quality. Much of our thinking is directly related to our sensory perception and the world that opens to us through sense perception. The senses give us the content of much of our thinking, which then creates mental images, pictures, and ideas from the material given by the senses. Probably most of our ideas are based on what comes from the world of the senses. But notice two things of great importance in this experience. First of all, sense experience provides much of the basic content of our ideas, but the idea itself is not sensory. It is a purely nonsensory, invisible reality by which we find the meaning and the real "sense" in sense experience. In the second place, it is the presence of this nonsensory idea in sense perception that gives us our experience of the sensible world as structured, ordered, integrated, and meaningful. If we had only pure perception without the organizing idea, we would have not a world but simply a chaotic barrage of unrelated, meaningless sense impressions. The notion that we have ideas on the one side given in thinking, and facts on the other side given by empirical observation and sense perception cannot be sustained. It won't hold up. This notion of pure facts given in empirical perception the philosophers have called "naive realism," or, better, "naive empiricism." There are no facts apart from ideas that make them facts. If we could separate our thinking from perception, perception by itself would leave us not with a world of pure facts and objects, but with no world at all. Pure perception would be, in William James's phrase (cited in Barfield, 1979, p. 14) "buzzing, blooming confusion." And so we are brought back again to the recognition that the quality of our world depends directly on the quality of our thinking, of our ideas and mental images, that give us a world.

But the interaction of matter and mind, of the world of the senses and thinking, is even more thoroughgoing. Dr. Michaela Glöckler (1999), head of the International Medical Work in Waldorf schools, highlights two further dimensions of the power and presence of thinking in the world.* For one thing, Glöckler points out how all events of the natural world can be described in terms of laws and formulas, mathematical and otherwise—in other words, in terms of thought. These laws, which the natural world obeys, can be discovered, formulated, learned, applied, and further explored. All the aspects of nature—animate, mineral, fluid, gaseous, and so forth—follow their appropriate laws, which themselves are discovered through thinking. The thinking of the human being seems to be met on every hand by a corresponding intelligibility in nature. The vaunted modern dualism between mind and matter seems belied by our act of thinking about and understanding nature herself. One is reminded of Alfred North Whitehead's (1950) observation that modern science itself could not have arisen apart from the early scientists' faith, inherited from the medieval scholastics, that nature can be understood through the exercise of human intelligence because nature is herself intelligent.

In her article, Glöckler goes further, however, to observe that there are other thoughts of an entirely different quality because they are not related to anything in sense experience. Our ideals, she points out, are such thoughts. Goodness, fidelity, truth and truthfulness, courage, love, and so forth are such thoughts. These ideals, to be sure, are expressed in our actions and behavior, which can be perceived, but the ideals themselves are not sense perceptible, they are just that, purely ideal—invisible and essential. And, Glöckler notes further, such ideals, faithfulness, truthfulness, reverence, freedom, only unfold their full power and reality to the extent that we identify with them. In this striving to make these ideals our own we form our deepest identity and are able to express ourselves as beings of soul and spirit in the world.

Several implications for education arise out of these reflections on thinking. I mention two especially because I think they will take us further into our inquiry. The first has to do with what we have seen to be the relation between the quality of our thinking and the quality not only of our world but also of our own self-identity. Emerson once wrote in his journal, "Life consists largely in what a person is thinking of all day." Once we grasp this, then we cannot help asking further, What is the nature and quality of our thinking? What are the sources of life-giving thoughts? How do we tap into them? How do we nourish in our children the capacities of insight, newness, and love in thinking that alone can bring into being new possibilities and new worlds? To speak of insight, creativity, and love in thinking is to speak of the possibility of spiritual transformation, of world and self.

---

*I am greatly indebted to the author for this article.

The other consideration with educational implications that we have touched upon has to do with the interaction that we have seen between the sensible world of matter and nature and the supersensible world of thought. It is becoming increasingly evident that thoughts are realities that have real consequences in the world of matter. We know they have consequences for our social relations. And we have seen how they can penetrate matter. We know that this is confirmed by mind-body-health studies that show the close connection between our thoughts, and the emotions that accompany them, and the strength of our immune system. What is suggested by this interpenetration of supersensible thinking and sensible body and matter is that there is no ultimately impenetrable dualism between them. As Glöckler (1999) put it, "When we begin to understand the nature of thinking, we are quite naturally guided to overcome the dualistic image of the world and perceive it to be one and an integral whole. Here the laws, being spiritual by nature, prove to be the primary principle, governing the world we perceive through the senses and going beyond it" (p. 10). A central educational question that arises from this: Is there a critical relationship between the body, our closest connection to matter and the sense world, and the sources of insight, newness, and a creative, caring living-thinking?

We have some ways of thinking concretely about the mind-body, the spirit-matter relationship that can help us with these questions. I have mentioned the power and reality of thoughts in affecting the body and immune system as established by mind-body-health research. Recently, David Ray Griffin (2000), a leading contemporary process theologian and philosopher, has examined with much rigor the arguments for mind-body dualism and for materialistic monism and has rejected both. We cannot go into his detailed philosophical analysis here, but his conclusion is that mind and matter are different, but they are not, as he himself puts it, ontologically different; that is, they are not fundamentally or substantively different, and, therefore, they are capable of interacting and always are interacting. Owen Barfield (1977) has given us a vivid image for picturing this essential unity of body and mind, matter and spirit. Barfield has reminded us of Leibniz's image of matter as *coagulum spiritus*—a kind of coagulation or concentration of spirit. We could say that matter is frozen thought, that the material is formed from and within the immaterial, rather like ice in water. Barfield also points out that this view was not peculiar to Leibniz but is shared by almost all oriental philosophy and religion.

This image of matter as *coagulum spiritus*, partly because it is almost repugnant in its vividness, can be very helpful. Matter is essentially spirit that has been transformed, concentrated, in such a way that it has become sense perceptible. Yet it remains wisdom filled. It is penetrable by thinking and intelligence because it is itself woven of thought and wisdom. The image of concentration, coagulation, hardening also gives us a concrete way of picturing why matter is at the same time so recalcitrant to our low-level, everyday thought. Our everyday thought does not easily penetrate matter, but requires the high energy focus that we call insight and imagination. However, precisely because matter is coagulated, concentrated spirit, it is susceptible to what John Lukacs (1986) calls "the mental intrusion into the structure of events" (pp. 10–12).

Now we are in position, I think, to really come to grips with the importance of the body in education. Rudolf Steiner expressed this relationship between body and thought and its educational implications as forcibly as anyone I know. He said, "It is of the greatest importance to know that ordinary human powers of thought are refined powers of configuration and growth" (as cited in Glöckler, 1999, p. 11). In other words, the powers that we use in thinking have their source in the same wisdom-filled powers that build up and form the body. Our ordinary powers of thought come from the same powers that give life, form, and forces of growth and regeneration to the body. Because there can be a surplus of these formative powers of growth, some become available for thinking and consciousness. As the young child grows into adulthood, and as the stages of bodily growth and organ development reach maturity, more and more of these growth forces are released and become available for the formative activity of thinking and reflecting. It is this that makes it possible to learn throughout life, and to bring this learning to bear on transforming ourselves and the world, to create anew, which is the essence of spiritual activity.

 In this light we ought not to suppose that the brain produces thoughts. Rather, in a very real way, it is the whole organism that produces thought as it releases its growth forces when, at various stages, their work in building up the body is completed. The surplus of these liberated growth forces makes available structures full of wisdom. The brain reflects these liberated growth forces and structures and brings them to conscious awareness. The brain and nervous system do not produce thoughts, rather, they are our reflecting instruments for bringing to consciousness and working with the deeper thought forces that arise from our entire organism.

The educational implications again are profound, especially for preschool-age children who are in the most plastic and formative stages of their growth. We might expect, for example, that the healthy development of the young child's growing body is not only essential to physical well-being but also lays the indispensable organic foundation for the emergence of powerful, creative cognitive forces later on, as well as providing the basis for healthy social and emotional development. We might also very well surmise from the body-mind interrelationship that a too-early imposition of academic and intellectual emphases upon the young growing child will be harmful. It will be harmful to the physical health of the individual in later life because growth forces will have been siphoned off prematurely into abstract intellectualizing—siphoned off from their first task of building up a sound body. Thus weaknesses can be introduced that may well show up as diseases and disorders much later in the second half of life. And by the same token a too-early imposition of abstract intellectuality upon these early years can actually undercut the development of the creative, insightful knowing that this early emphasis on academics was ironically meant to encourage. A too-early academic and intellectual emphasis short-circuits the child's full experience of living and making one's own the living body-imbedded, thought forms and structures which might later have blossomed as insightful, wisdom-filled cognitive capacities.

Is there evidence for these expectations and surmises? Indeed, there is, much of it coming from mainstream educational research. It is curious to note that mainstream education in practice often ignores it own best research. Consider, for example, what we know about the crucial importance of play in the development of the young child. In play the whole child is engaged. Physically, in the full-bodied large muscle movements of running and jumping, and in the hand-eye coordination of moving objects about in the give-and-take with others, the child is building up its physical body. More than that, however, the child is also engaged in coming to know the world.

In play, the child is actually exercising a way of knowing that will be the foundation for all other knowing. It is a will-directed and will-developing, active, sympathetic exploration and embracing of the world. It can be described as a sympathetic way of knowing, for what the child is doing is reaching out, actively, exercising its own forces of will and attention, and uniting with the world and uniting the world with it. Out of its own active will forces the child is coming to know the world, including its own body, by joining with the world and making the world its own. In this sympathetic experience of knowing, of having a world of its own, the child lays the essential basis for all further knowing, namely, a fundamental sense of well-being, self-confidence, and inner security in the world. It is a cliché of the therapist's office that those persons who never developed this inner security and self-confidence as children are often the persons in later life who are least likely to be able to be adventurous and to take imaginative risks.

Still more than this is taking place in play. If the child is provided an environment that nurtures and provides for the expression of fantasy and imagination, the child is also exploring and creating a thought world of its own. It is becoming at home in the power of creative, imaginative thinking. For this to happen, it is crucial that the child have opportunities for an acquaintance with living nature and an abundance of simple natural objects for play materials, both of which call forth a wealth of open-ended, mobile, and living images and pictures in the child's consciousness. It is also critical for the child to be in the company of others, other children and trusted adults, with whom it can play and give expression to its burgeoning powers of thought and imagination. As thought forces become more and more available to the child's consciousness, they arise first in the child's fantasy life, and are experienced at once by the child both as its own creation and as an illumination of the world without. Toys and play materials for the young child that are themselves simple and open-ended—shells, cloths, stones, logs, ropes, chairs, tables, and so forth—are the kind of objects that allow the child room to make use of its own powers of fantasy. Highly detailed toys and play materials, and, now, computer games, rather than encouraging the child's own fantasy and imagination, can entrap and confine it within the limits of a fixed and second-hand fantasy of someone else—usually a conventional, not very imaginative adult fantasy.

As Joan Almon (1992) has pointed out, in the child nearing the school-age years, fantasy evolves into powers of genuine imagination, imagination now being the ability not only to have a life of inner pictures triggered by objects of the world, but also increasingly to have images and ideas of one's own, no longer tied to objects—ideas and images that now may be talked and acted out, but that may also simply be explored and enjoyed inwardly without objects. In the development of fantasy and imagination, arising out of and grounded in the lived experience of physical activity, the child creatively enters the world of thought and can also make it a world of its own, a world friendly to the child's own being. Then as powers of more abstract conceptuality appear increasingly in later childhood, and begin to flower and bloom in the teen age and young adulthood years, this later abstract conceptuality itself will not be foreign, but can be creatively taken up by the child as also its own.

Abstract conceptuality by its nature is necessarily distancing, for in it we separate ourselves from the world and stand back from the world, in order to reflect upon it. If an abstract conceptuality is imposed too early on the child, before the child has been able to make it its own, this abstract conceptuality can then only be experienced as other, not as the child's own, but as alien to the child, even hostile. It is possible that much of the anger, hostility, depression, and despair expressed by many high school students today has been reinforced, if not caused, by their never really having had the experience from the beginning of being able through play, fantasy, and imagination to know the world as truly their own, to have the fundamental experience of living in a world essentially friendly, sympathetic, and supportive of their own being.

Sara Smilansky (1990) and her colleagues a decade ago brought together the results of a wide range of research on the effect of play, showing that physical-social-fantasy play in early childhood is correlated strongly in later years with enhanced mental, social, and emotional development. In light of its own research on play, it is more than curious that mainstream education continues to impose academic abstractions on children at an ever earlier age, to extend standardized, high-stakes academic testing to all ages, and in many schools in the United States even to eliminate recess and other play periods.

Consider also research that is emerging on the relation between physical movement and human development. Many years ago Jean Piaget stressed that intellectual, social, and emotional development are deeply affected by the quality of a child's mastering his or her physical movements. Current research further substantiates this, indicating that problems in developing bodily balance, for example, are reflected in problems of mental equilibrium, and problems in movement show up in problems of language development. Dr. Peter Struck (1999), a German medical researcher, has written from his own studies:

> Elementary school-age children who have too seldom run and jumped, who have had insufficient opportunity to play on a swing or in the mud, to climb and to balance, will have difficulty walking backwards. They have a corresponding difficulty with counting backwards. They lag behind in arithmetic and appear to be clumsy and stiff. These children cannot accurately judge strength, speed, or distance; and thus they are more accident-prone than other children. (p. 31)

Television viewing, the introduction of early academics, and now, compounding the situation, the introduction of the computer at all age levels, surrounds the child with a physically, sensorially, and emotionally impoverished environment. The opportunities for exercising one's own will and imagination disappear just as physical obesity and disability mount.

In his recent book, *The Hand*, (1998) neurologist Frank Wilson has also demonstrated that ideas are not constrained by brain and formal operations but are intimately related to the interaction of the body with the world, beginning crucially in early childhood, but continuing throughout life. Wilson's main focus is on the hand and the myriad ways in which the interaction of the hand with objects in the world gives rise to ideas. He describes this interaction of the hand with the world as "curious, exploratory, improvisational." This sounds a lot like play, though it would also include more systematic interactions such as handwork, knitting, crafts, carpentry, and so on. In a recent article, Frank Wilson (2000) put it this way: "If the hand and the brain learn to speak to each other intimately and harmoniously, something that humans seem to prize greatly, which we call autonomy, begins to take shape" (p. 9). Autonomy here points to the spiritual reality of the capacity for individual freedom and responsibility through insight and understanding.

Wilson (2000) also examines the currents in modern education that seek to systematize skill and abstract knowledge in misguided efforts to preprogram children for conventional economic and social success. Of these modern educational efforts he comments:

Suppose . . . that it turns out that kids are like free-range chickens with respect to early childhood hands-on experience. It doesn't really matter precisely what they pick up and tinker with, or pull apart and try to put back together, but they actually need to do *something* of that kind, or else they will turn out later to be incapable of grasping not just a screwdriver or a wrench but an idea that comes easily when you can remember what such a tool feels like or behaves in your hand, and doesn't come to you at all if you have never had your hands on anything but a computer keyboard or a mouse or a joy stick. (p. 11)

Perhaps it becomes a little easier for us to understand and have a palpable sense of the body as the spirit made flesh.

FEELINGS

The feelings, our next soul/spiritual function, connect the realms of body and thinking. We experience the feelings more intensely and personally than either of these realms. It is not inaccurate, therefore, to think of the feelings as the center of personality, we could say as "the heart of the soul."

Yet, perhaps just because of the intense personal nature of the feelings, our culture has a long tradition of ignoring and suppressing the feeling life. The proliferation of all manner of feeling therapies today —body therapies, bioenergetics, Gestalt therapies, sensitivity training, primal scream, rolfing, art therapies, and others—may reflect attempts to make up for this developmental deficit. We should be thankful for them for they have arisen to meet a great need. But we also need to be aware that therapies are by definition a little too late. The basic problem is the prior one of failing to provide for the healthy development of the feeling life in the first place.

Modern education, as it reflects and expresses the dominant culture, makes it difficult to pay attention to the care of the feelings. The main emphasis, coming from government, business, universities, and schools of education, is on what is curiously called "the production of knowledge"—theoretical and applied knowledge mainly for economic and technological advance. There is some effort, to be sure, to provide balance through sports and some smattering of social and artistic activities. But in the main, the care of the feeling life does not have a central place in modern education. And students themselves try to make up for the neglect by throwing themselves into whatever feelings are available to them, whether from feelings supplied by the media, by their own emerging sexual energies, or too often in our culture, by drugs, in the last case either to heighten a feeling life which has been thoroughly suppressed by our culture or to dampen feelings which the students have never been prepared to handle.

It is true that increasingly there are signs of an new awareness dawning among many persons of the central importance of the feelings in the act of knowing itself. This awareness is not entirely new. Many years ago the Scottish philosopher John Macmurray (1935) spoke of what he called "emotional rationality." More recently Georg Kühlewind (1988) has described the potential for feelings to become "cognitive organs." And Daniel Goleman (1995) has made popular the notion of "emotional intelligence." So there is a spreading sense that to neglect the care of the feeling life is to damage, perhaps irreparably, one of our major sources of knowledge.

But what kind of knowledge do the feelings, properly educated and developed, make possible? The essential role of the feelings of interest and enthusiasm in inspiring and sustaining any knowledge quest whatever was, of course, a major concern of John Dewey and is alluded to by almost every modern school of educational psychology—but often ignored in practice. It is common knowledge that we all, children and adults alike, learn more easily and remember better those things we are really interested in. But this basic pedagogical principle has all but disappeared in the present craze for standardized testing in every subject at every level.

In addition to providing the interest that drives our knowing, the feelings are also our most important mode of knowing certain important, in many ways the most important, dimensions of the world; namely, for knowing the qualities of the world, qualities such as truth, beauty, goodness, the reality of other persons, and the inner soul of nature. It is in a direct feeling connection and feeling grasp that we apprehend and test such qualities as truth and falsity, beauty and ugliness, goodness and evil, and are able to apprehend the intricate, invisible, nonsensory web of relationships of which all existence is woven. Feelings are food for our souls and they are our direct connection to the soul and spirit of the world.

Feelings such as reverence, gratitude, and devotion are rightly seen not simply as inner states but as indispensable in knowing some of the most important aspects of the world. Owen Barfield (1971) has written, for example, of the foundational role in knowing of the feeling of reverence: "Reverence is not simply a virtue for which we may expect full marks in heaven, or a device for bolstering up the social establishment. It is an organ of perception for a whole range of qualities that are as imperceptible without it as another whole range is imperceptible without an ear for music" (pp. 10–11).

The relation of the feelings to body on the one hand and to thinking on the other becomes important in guiding and supporting a new capacity of thinking that begins to develop in the school-age child. This is the capacity for making judgments. We have seen how the imaging content of thinking has by this time in the life of the child already developed. As the rhythmic system of heart and lungs matures, the aesthetic, feeling life of the child also begins to come into its own. The capacity for judgment is not so much developing new thoughts as it is working with existing thought contents—moving, weighing, comparing thoughts. Aesthetic feelings of the child are intimately involved in this growing power of judgment. The child of this age is intensely engaged in making judgments of good and bad, mean and gentle, fair and unfair, beautiful and ugly, and the child's moods often swing abruptly between the extremes of such polarities as it begins to experience and exercise its aesthetic sensibilities. The careful tending of the aesthetic feelings enables the child to develop sound powers of judgment, which as the child grows can be further informed by the conceptual thinking which then begins to appear in earnest after puberty. But when the aesthetic feelings have been unattended and undeveloped in these years, our powers of sound and discerning judgment always suffer as a consequence.

Finally, the feelings are essential to the development of empathy and care. It is the feeling life that determines the way in which the network of relationships among human and other sentient beings is knitted together and maintained. It is empathy, grounded in the feeling life, that enables us to enter into the situation, needs, and struggles of the other—to understand the other and to care for the other, from the other's point of view. A lack of empathy always brings the danger that human beings will misuse both their intelligence and their capacity for willed activity. Intelligence and action without empathy are reflected in our language. We speak of "cold intellect" and "blind Victorian willpower." Our culture, as we know, is not lacking in either clever intellect or in willful action, but it does suffer grievously from lack of care for and education of the feelings, the heart of the soul.

When we turn to what is required for the education of the feelings one thing particularly needs to be kept in mind: feelings are not all equal. Not just any feelings lead to insight or empathy. In fact, I would hazard that most of the feelings that roil and stream through us, and certainly those that find expression in our dominant conventional culture, are absolute obstacles to knowledge and stand as impenetrable barriers to engagement with anything or anyone other than ourselves. Hate, anger, jealousy, sentimentality, and so on, do not open us either to the world or to the other, but lock us all the more tightly in upon our own obsessive selves. Unless we work to refine and purify our feeling life, we are simply at the mercy of coarse and conventional feelings over which we have little control, and which stifle the highly sensitive but extremely delicate feelings by which we reach out to and enter a world beyond ourselves.

The first prerequisite for the nurture of the delicate cognitive-empathic feelings is that the growing individual be engaged with other human beings in the give-and-take of discovering and exercising the developing feeling life. Of equal importance is the presence of caring adults—parents and teachers—who by their presence and wisdom can provide an environment of nurturing attitudes and feelings. And this, of course, presupposes that the adults are themselves working, meditatively and with others, on the constant care and refinement of their own feeling life.

Also essential to the development of the feeling life is an education that is aesthetic through and through, especially during the school-age years when the aesthetic feelings are coming to the fore. An aesthetic education is one that is rhythmic and rich in qualitative experience. It is rhythmic with a balance between in-breathing and out-breathing, action and rest, remembering and forgetting, receiving and expressing—rhythmic in every lesson and throughout the day, the season, and the year. An aesthetic education is also one in which the growing human being is immersed in the qualities of existence—the qualities of color, sound, movement, relationships, meaning, values, life, and growth. Immersion in the qualities of the world draws forth and strengthens the development of such qualities in ourselves and our feeling capacities for them. Such an education will be rich and overflowing with song, story, fairytale, myth, handwork, painting, modeling, musical instruments, an artistic approach to math and science, and a direct involvement with living nature.

THE SENSES

This brings me to the final dimension of the human being as body, soul, and spirit that I want to explore. This is the domain of the senses. The senses provide the content for our thinking, feeling, and willing. The senses open us to the world beyond, but they also help build up our world of soul within. The senses provide images for thinking to work with, they elicit our feelings, and they open to us the actual field for our activity in the world. Without the soul food provided by the senses—the light, the colors, the warmth, and so forth—we would experience neither the world without nor the world within. Without the proper care and nurture of the senses both our inner life and our experience of the world alike become impoverished, dried up and drab, even distorted and malformed.

The proper care of the senses in daily life, the healing of the senses when they are damaged, and the reenlivening of the senses when they have become dull and atrophied—all are essential to the creation of a world of experience that is itself alive and full of meaning. As the Scottish philosopher John Macmurray (1935) once said, "If we are to be full of life and fully alive, it is the increase in our capacity to be aware of the world through our senses which has first to be achieved" (p. 40).

This points to a mounting problem in our time of direct concern to education, but one which much modern education has largely ignored, probably because it has been complicit in bringing it about. This problem is the massive assault on the senses which comes increasingly from every side. This modern attack on the senses takes three forms, often all at once.

One modern form of disruption of the senses is that of overstimulation, the overwhelming of the senses with sense experiences themselves, but sense experiences that are inharmonious, cacophonous, harsh, disorderly, and brutal: blaring music; the incessant roar of traffic; a constant, all-encompassing, indecipherable cloud of radio and television noise; loud and brutal images on TV and in movies; a bombardment of garish and florid lights and colors; and so on and on. Already in the middle of the 18th century the Frenchman Jean-Jacques Rousseau began to take note of the attack on the senses which modern urban life entails. He wrote in his educational novel *The New Eloise*,

> I'm beginning to feel the drunkenness that this agitated, tumultuous life plunges you into. With such a multitude of objects passing before my eyes, I'm getting dizzy. Of all the things that strike me, there is none that holds my heart, yet all of them together distract my feelings, so that I forget where I am and who I belong to.

And Rousseau also saw clearly the close connection between this overwhelming of the senses and the inability to develop a life of purpose and integrity. Referring to the "constant flux and reflux of prejudices and opinions," he went on to say, "everything is absurd, but nothing is shocking because everyone is accustomed to everything" (as cited in Nord, 1995, p. 23). This was written about 250 years ago as the modern age was just getting under way. Think of what Rousseau might say today.

The second form of the modern assault on the senses is simply a widespread neglect of their proper care and nurture. We ride in cars and planes; we sit all day at our desks, often in windowless cubicles staring at computer screens; we flood ourselves with pollutants in air, water, and food, which add injury to neglect; we impose academic subjects on our children at an age when what they need most is large muscle movements, play, nature, the company of other caring people, and the nourishment of word, color, and music. We could all easily add to the list of neglect.

The third form of the modern assault on the senses—perhaps this is a worst case combination of the first two—is the modern tendency to replace the surrounding world of nature, other people, and concrete human artifacts with an artificial, substitute, virtual world: plastics; synthetic materials of all kinds, recorded voices and music, simulated odors and perfumes that smell "like" the real thing but that actually delude and deceive because they obscure the real thing, artificial flavors, processed foods, air-conditioning, electronically amplified music, telephone, the Internet, and so on. The overwhelming of our senses by an artificial, virtual world handicaps their healthy development and erodes the capacities for sound judgment of reality.

In light of the three-fold assault on the senses, it cannot be surprising that, unfortunately, research is beginning to show disturbing evidence of the decline of the senses. And this research demonstrates vividly that impairments in the sense life are directly connected to disturbances in thinking, in emotional development, and in the ability to act decisively and meaningfully. Researchers at the Universities of Bielefeld and Tübingen in Germany have been discovering that in young people particularly, while the senses are being bombarded with more sense stimuli than ever before, there has been an alarming loss of the ability to respond ("New Health Problems," 1997). With hearing, for example, the researchers have observed that as recently as fifteen years ago Germans could distinguish some 300,000 sounds. Today on average they can distinguish only 180,000, and many children can only attain 100,000. The researchers note that that is enough for rap and rock, but insufficient for the subtleties of a classical concert. Similar results have been observed for the discernment of smells, tastes, and colors. Nothing tastes as good as it once did.

And the Hamburg Center for Child Development reports similarly:

> Today, many children enter school with diminished sensory abilities; their perception and concentration are weak. They are awkward, have difficulty handling materials appropriately, lack language skills, are weak in arithmetic, and are clumsy. They cannot sense when someone is standing behind them. Their field of vision is limited to 70 degrees—the normal range of vision would be approximately 200 degrees. And so on. (Struck, 1999, p. 32)

It is not that we are to avoid living in the modern world and using its technology. But in working with modern surroundings and technology, we can do at least three things to help ensure that the positive potential outweighs the negative. First, it is critical that we try to become consciously aware of the effects of modern culture and technology on our senses, and that we make every effort to provide healing and balancing nourishment to compensate for the damage that otherwise must occur. It is also essential, second, that we become aware of those influences that are irremediably damaging and that are to be avoided. And, finally, above all, we must protect and nurture the healthy sense life of our children during the years of their most plastic, sensitive, and vulnerable growth.

Now, I close with one last thought. Every educational theory and practice implies some image of the human being. So we must ask of every educational endeavor, "What image is implied in it, and what are its consequences?" Unfortunately modern culture is shot through with images of the human being that fix and reduce the human to the less than human, usually to some kind of meaningless mechanism.

Francis Crick (1994), the eminent biologist recently become cognitive scientist, has expressed what is probably the dominant image of the human in most of the natural sciences, and especially in genetic engineering and cognitive science. Crick puts it in this unadorned way:

> You, your joys and sorrows, your memories and your ambitions, your sense of personal identity are in fact no more than the behaviour of a vast assembly of nerve cells and their associated molecules. . . . [Y]ou're nothing but a pack of neurons. (p. 3)

If we give this extreme reductionistic and mechanistic view some closer attention, we can see immediately that it is self-contradictory and, therefore, self-canceling. After all, if what Crick writes is true, then his own words are meaningless, for just as much as yours or mine his thoughts, too, are nothing but the electrical discharges of his neural system. When someone like Crick writes this way, one has to assume that he is making at least one exception, namely for himself, and presumably he is making a second exception so that he can have at least one reader. But if he makes even one exception, the whole thing falls apart—although it wasn't coherent in the first place.

However, lest you suppose that this reductionist view of the human being is simply that of Francis Crick, consider the 1997 statement below of the International Academy of Humanism defending cloning research in higher mammals and human beings. In this statement Crick joins other leading figures, including biologists Richard Dawkins and E. O. Wilson and the humanists Isaiah Berlin, W. V. Quine, and Kurt Vonnegut (I had expected better at least of Vonnegut). In justification of cloning, they appeal to the following image of the human:

> Human nature is held [by traditional cultures and religion] to be unique and sacred. Scientific advances which pose a perceived risk of altering this "nature" are angrily opposed. . . . As far as the scientific enterprise can determine [however] . . . human capabilities appear to differ in degree, not in kind, from those found among the higher animals. Humanity's *rich repertoire* of thoughts, feelings, aspirations, and hopes seems to arise from electrochemical brain processes, not from an immaterial soul that operates in ways no instrument can discover. . . . Views of human nature rooted in humanity's tribal past ought not to be our primary criterion for making moral judgments about cloning. (as cited in Kass, 1999, p. 38)

When examined, this view of the human being is exceedingly incoherent and basically self-canceling, but highly destructive.

Leon Kass (1999), biochemist and medical ethicist at the University of Chicago, has pointed this out recently in writing about this statement put forward by this group of intellectuals:

> They fail to see that the scientific view of man they celebrate does more than insult our vanity. It undermines our self-conception as free, thoughtful, responsible beings, worthy of respect because we alone among the animals have minds and hearts that aim far higher than the mere perpetuation of our genes. It undermines, as well the beliefs that sustain our mores, institutions, and practices—including the practice of science itself. For why, on this radically reductive understanding of "the rich repertoire" of human thought, should anyone choose to accept as true the results of *these* men's "electrochemical brain processes," rather than his own? Thus do truth and error themselves, no less than freedom and dignity, become empty notions when the soul is reduced to chemicals. (p. 38)

Yet in spite of its patent inconsistency and self-canceling nature, this reductionistic, materialistic image of the human being pervades modern culture and education—and even seems to be gaining in strength. It is not difficult to see why.

The reductionistic image of the human being as only a vast assemblage of electrochemical processes serves the purposes of many powerful vested interests. It serves a scientism that is intent upon taking nature and the human being apart and rearranging them for its own purposes of control and manipulation. It offers no checks to what the profoundly humanistic biochemist Erwin Chargaff (1986) has called the "devil's doctrine in science," the doctrine that "[w]e must and will do everything we can do . . . regardless." This reductionist view offers no opposition to those who would homogenize, standardize, and regulate the human being and the environment also for purposes of control and exploitation. And this view, moreover, undergirds the growing global conglomerate of scientists, governments, universities, and transnational corporations that seek to exploit nature and human beings for their own power, prestige, and profit. Unfortunately, this image of the human being permeates modern education from top to bottom.

Over a century ago in an essay on education Ralph Waldo Emerson said that the surest bulwark of all that is sacred in the human being is "not to accept degrading views" (as cited in Perkinson, 1976, p. 123). Our culture and education are full of degrading views and their destructive consequences are great. Nevertheless, the human being is—for a time at least—still human, a being of body, soul, and spirit; a being of interwoven intelligence, emotion, intention, and perception, all capable of infinite growth and development. This, our full human being, contains within itself the resources for countering and transforming all the forces that would reduce the human to the nonhuman. But we must recognize and draw upon this fullness of the human being while it is still possible, while there is still time. Ours is now a critical moment, for ominous signs exist that the time remaining for the fully human is seriously threatened and may be drastically limited. This is why the topic of this book is itself so important.

REFERENCES

Almon, J. (1992, Autumn). Educating for creative thinking: The Waldorf approach. *Revision, Special Issue: Renewal of Thinking in Education and Society, 15*(2), 71–78.

Barfield, O. (1979). *History, guilt, and habit*. Middletown, Conn.: Wesleyan University Press.

Barfield, O. (1971). *What Coleridge thought*. Middletown, Conn.: Wesleyan University Press.

Barfield, O. (1977). Matter, Imagination, and Spirit. In *The rediscovery of meaning and other essays*. Middletown, Conn.: Wesleyan University Press.

Chargaff, E. (1977). *Voices in the labyrinth: Nature, man and science*. New York: Seabury Press.

Chargaff, E. (1986). *Heraclitean fire: Sketches from a life before nature*. New York: Simon and Schuster.

Crick, F. (1994). *That astonishing hypothesis: The scientific search for the soul*. New York: Scribners.

Glöcker, M. (1999). Overcoming mind-body dualism in human development: Identity of vital functions and thinking activity. In *Toward wholeness in knowing: The renewal of thinking, feeling, willing (pp. 106–108)*. Proceedings, Research Consultation, "Toward wholeness in knowing," June 12–15, 1996. Chestnut Ridge, N.Y.: Parker Courtney Press.

Goleman, D. (1995). *Emotional intelligence: Why it can matter more than I.Q.* New York: Bantam Books.

Griffin, D. R. (2000). *Religion and scientific naturalism: Overcoming the conflict*. Albany: State University of New York Press.

Kass, L. (1999, Sept.). The moral meaning of genetic technology. *Commentary, 108*, 38.

Kühlewind, G. (1988). *From normal to healthy*. Great Barrington, Mass.: The Anthroposophic Press.

Lukacs, J. (1986). Preface to *Outgrowing democracy*. Lanham, Md.: University of America.

Macmurray, J. (1935). *Reason and emotion*. London: Faber and Faber.

Center for Research in Childhood and Adolescence, University of Bielefeld, Bielefeld, Germany, "New Health Problems of Children and Youth,"

Research Bulletin, Waldorf Education Research Institute. 2:2. June 1997: 28–33.

Nord, W. A. (1995). *Religion and American education: Rethinking a national dilemma*. Chapel Hill: University of North Carolina Press.

Rhodes, R. (1986). *The making of the atomic bomb*. New York: Simon and Schuster.

Ralph Waldo Emerson, "Education" in Henry J. Perkinson, *Two hundred years of American education thought*. New York: David MacKay Company.

Smilansky, S., and Klugman, E. (Eds.). (1990). *Children's play and learning*. New York: Teachers College Press.

Struck, P. (1999, Jan.). Movement and sensory disorders in today's children. *Research Bulletin*, Waldorf Education Research Institute. 4:1. Jan. 1999: 31–32.

Whitehead, A. N. (1950). *Science and the modern world*. New York: Macmillan.

Wilson, F. (1998). *The Hand: How its use shapes the brain, language, and human culture*. New York: Pantheon Books.

Wilson, F. The real meaning of hands-on education. (2000, Jan.). *Research Bulletin*, Waldorf Education Research Institute 5(1), 9.

CHAPTER 4

Tomorrow's Children

Education for a Partnership World

RIANE EISLER

Today the educational debates center primarily on standards, testing, and other procedural reforms. Unfortunately this debate ignores not only children's real needs but also the real problems children face in our time of rapid economic, social, and technological changes. It ignores questions about education that are critical for both our nation and our world.

As the tragic events of September 11, 2001, highlight, in a world where technologies of both communication and destruction make ours a global village, we need to think of education as much more than just a matter of the three Rs of Reading, Writing, and Arithmetic. There is a fourth R that will determine the kind of future children have: Relationships.

For over two centuries, educational reformers such as Johann Pestalozzi (1781/1976), Maria Montessori (1912/1964), John Dewey (1916/1966), and Paolo Freire (1973) have called for an education that prepares young people for democracy rather than authoritarianism and fosters ethical and caring relations.[1] Building on the work of these and other germinal educational thinkers and on my research and teaching experiences over three decades, I propose an expanded approach to educational reform.

I call this approach *partnership education*. It incorporates many of the contributions of contemporary progressive education, including holistic education. But it provides a new integrated conceptual framework that can help young

Parts of this article are adapted from Riane Eisler, *Tomorrow's Children: A Blueprint for Partnership Education in the 21st Century* (Westview Press, 2000)

people create a future orienting more to what in my study of 30,000 years of cultural evolution I have identified as a *partnership* rather than *dominator* model.

Although we may not use these terms, we are all familiar with these two models from our own lives. We know the pain, fear, and tension of relations based on domination and submission, on coercion and accommodation, of jockeying for control, of trying to manipulate and cajole when we are unable to express our real feelings and needs, of the miserable, awkward tug-of-war for that illusory moment of power rather than powerlessness, of our unfulfilled yearning for caring and mutuality, of all the misery, suffering, and lost lives and potentials that come from these kinds of relations. Most of us also have, at least intermittently, experienced another way of being, one where we feel safe and seen for who we truly are, where our essential humanity and that of others shines through, perhaps only for a little while, lifting our hearts and spirits, enfolding us in a sense that the world can after all be right, that we are valued and valuable.

But the partnership and dominator models do not only describe individual relationships. They describe systems of belief and social structures that either nurture and support—or inhibit and undermine—equitable, democratic, nonviolent, and caring relations. They also describe two different approaches to socialization, and hence education.

Through an understanding of the partnership and dominator cultural, social, and personal configurations, we can more effectively develop the educational methods, materials, and institutions that foster a less violent, more equitable, democratic, and sustainable future. We can more effectively sort out what in existing educational approaches we want to retain and strengthen or leave behind. And we can address goals that are fundamental to education for the 21st century:

- Helping children grow into healthy, caring, competent, self-realized adults.
- Providing them with the knowledge and skills that can see them through this time of environmental, economic, and social upheavals.
- Equipping them to create for themselves and future generations a sustainable future of greater personal, social, economic, and environmental responsibility and caring.

PARTNERSHIP EDUCATION

Partnership education addresses these goals. It consists of three core interconnected components. These are partnership *process*, partnership *structure*, and partnership *content* (Eisler, 2000).

Partnership process is about *how* we learn and teach. It applies the guiding template of the partnership model to educational *methods* and *techniques*. Are young people treated with caring and respect? Do teachers act as primarily lesson dispensers and controllers, or more as mentors and facilitators? Are young people learning to work together or must they continuously compete with each other? Are they offered the opportunity for self-directed learning? In short, is education merely a matter of teachers inserting information into young people's minds, or are students and teachers partners in a meaningful adventure of exploration and learning?

Partnership structure is about *where* learning and teaching take place: what kind of *learning environment* we construct if we follow the partnership model. Is the structure of a school, classroom, or home school one of top-down authoritarian rankings, or is it a more democratic one? Do students, teachers, and other staff participate in school decision-making and rule-setting? Diagramed on an organizational chart, would decisions flow only from the top down and accountability only from the bottom up, or would there be interactive feedback loops? In short, is the learning environment organized in terms of hierarchies of domination ultimately backed up by fear, or is it a combination of horizontal linkings and hierarchies of actualization where power is not used to disempower others but rather to empower them?

Partnership content is *what* we learn and teach. It is the *educational curriculum*. Does the curriculum effectively teach students not only basic academic and vocational skills but also the life skills they need to be competent and caring citizens, workers, parents, and community members? Are we telling young people to be responsible, kind, and nonviolent at the same time that the curriculum content still celebrates male violence and conveys environmentally unsustainable and socially irresponsible messages? Does it present science in holistic, relevant ways? Does what is taught as important knowledge and truth include—not just as an add-on, but as integral to what is learned—both the female and male halves of humanity as well as children of various races and ethnicities? Does it teach young people the difference between the partnership and dominator models as two basic human possibilities and the feasibility of creating a partnership way of life? Or, both overtly and covertly, is this presented as unrealistic in the real world? In short, what kind of view of ourselves, our world, and our roles and responsibilities in it are young people taking away from their schooling?

HUMAN POSSIBILITIES AND CHOICES

One of the tenets of progressive education is to give young people more choices. But much in the curriculum, even in progressive schools, does not really give young people a sense of alternatives. At best it does so in bits and pieces, mostly as an add-on to conventional cultural narratives that we have inherited from earlier more dominator-oriented times. For this reason alternative narratives are a major component of partnership education.

This is particularly important in our time of dominator regression when so much in the mass media, and hence of what young people worldwide learn, still communicates the message that dominator relations are not only normal but fun.

On all sides they see and hear stories that portray us as bad, cruel, violent, and selfish. Video games, action adventure movies, and TV shows present violence as the way to solve problems. Situation comedies make insensitivity, rudeness, and cruelty seem funny. Cartoons present violence as exciting, funny, and without real consequences. As in the journalistic motto, "If it bleeds, it leads," even the stories that make top headlines focus on the infliction and suffering of pain as the most significant and newsworthy human events.

Rather than correcting this false image of what it means to be human, much of what children still learn in schools reinforces it. History curricula still emphasize battles and wars. Western classics such as Homer's *Iliad* and Shakespeare's kings trilogy romanticize heroic violence. Scientific stories tell children that we are the puppets of "selfish genes" ruthlessly competing on the evolutionary stage.

If we are inherently violent, bad, and selfish, we have to be strictly controlled. This is why stories that claim this is human nature are central to an education for a dominator or control system of relations. They are, however, inappropriate if young people are to learn to live in a democratic, peaceful, equitable, and earth-honoring way: the partnership way is needed if today's and tomorrow's children are to have a better future—perhaps even a future at all.

Youth futures are impoverished when their vision of the future comes out of a dominator worldview. But this worldview is our hidden heritage from earlier times when structuring relations into rankings of superiors over inferiors was considered normal, moral, and inevitable.

Rigid dominator ways of structuring relations are still predominant in some cultures and subcultures; for example, so-called religious fundamentalist cultures and subcultures where top-down control in the family and state or tribe; the rigid ranking of the male over the female half of humanity; and the acceptance, idealization, and even sanctification of violence as a means of imposing and maintaining control are considered moral. In Western cultures, these ways of structuring relations were also considered moral in earlier times. People believed in the divine right of kings to rule their subjects and the divine right of men to exert absolute control over the women and children in the castles of their homes. In these much more authoritarian and rigidly male-dominated societies, violence and abuse were socially accepted, as they were required to maintain rigid rankings of domination—whether man over woman, man over man, nation over nation, race over race, or religion over religion.

In contrast to the core dominator template of fear-and-force-backed hierarchies of domination in social institutions—from the family and education to politics and economics—is the core partnership template. It consists of a more egalitarian structure based on linking rather than ranking. Here we see hierarchies of actualization, where power is exercised in empowering rather than disempowering ways—the more stereotypically feminine kind of power we today read about in much of the progressive leadership and management literature.

Indeed, over the last several centuries we have seen many challenges to traditions of domination in politics and economics, in international and intimate relations, in relations between parents and children and women and men. These challenges are part of the movement toward more equitable and caring partnership social structure worldwide.

But at the same time, there has been massive resistance from entrenched beliefs and institutions. There have also been periodic regressions. And much in education still reinforces dominator socialization, keeping many young people locked into a perennial rebellion against what is, but without a real sense of what can be.

CULTURE AND EDUCATION

Our biological repertoire offers many possibilities: violence and nonviolence, indifference and empathy, caring and cruelty, creativity and destructiveness. Which of these possibilities we actualize largely depends on cultural contexts and cues—on what we experience and what we learn is normal, necessary, or appropriate. In short, which human possibilities are actualized or inhibited depends largely on culture. And a major instrument for maintaining or changing culture is education.

Children have an enormous capacity for love, joy, creativity, and caring. Children have a voracious curiosity, a hunger for understanding and meaning. Children also have an acute inborn sense of fairness and unfairness. Above all, children yearn for love and validation and, given half a chance, are able to give them bountifully in return.

But many of these wonderful capacities are distorted and stunted in cultures or subcultures that orient primarily to the dominator model. We need to change this. And we can use partnership education to help us do this.

Children need to understand and appreciate our natural habitat, our Mother Earth. Since partnership education offers a systemic approach, environmental education is not an add-on but an integral part of the curriculum. The same is true of multicultural education, education for peace, and gender-balanced education. All these are integrated into the entire learning tapestry.

Awareness of the interconnected web of life that is our environment, which has largely been ignored in the traditional curriculum, leads to valuing activities and policies that promote environmental sustainability: the new partnership ethic for human and ecological relations needed in our time. Awareness of our interconnection—for example, science classes where children learn of DNA evidence that all of us, no matter what our color or culture, come from a common mother, way back in Africa millions of years ago—leads to a valuing of different races and ethnic groups. The greater inclusion of meaningful material about people from all world cultures, as well as the equal inclusion of materials about women and men, leads to the appreciation of difference, beginning with the difference between the female and male halves of humanity.

In a world connected by technologies of communication and destruction that can span the globe in a matter of minutes, young people need to learn how to solve conflicts nonviolently. Even beyond this, they need to develop their innate capacity for love and friendship, for caring and caregiving, for creativity, for sensitivity to their own real needs and those of others.

If the postindustrial economy is to flourish, we need people who can think for themselves and solve problems creatively, rather than just taking orders from above. The "high-quality human capital" for the postindustrial workplace we hear about cannot be produced by an education that still orients largely to the dominator model, an education where children are constantly ranked by tests into superiors and inferiors and creativity and flexibility are all too often suppressed rather than supported.

But partnership education is not only a matter of more self-directed learning, peer teaching, cooperative learning, more individualized assessment tools, and other partnership pedagogies. It is also a matter of what kinds of behaviors and values are presented as valuable in curriculum narratives. If young people are to develop their essential humanity, they need a view of human nature that grounds their hopes in reality. And this view needs to be reflected in the kinds of behaviors and values the educational structure supports.

These same issues of educational process, content, and structure play a major role in whether democratic institutions are strengthened or weakened. Just talking about democracy in abstractions, or in terms of elections that, as young people cannot fail to notice, are controlled by economic powers, only leads to alienation, cynicism, and doubt about the real possibility of participatory democracy. Partnership teaching and learning process and curriculum content can play a major role here.

If they are to actively participate in political and civic processes, young people need to learn much more about nonviolently achieved social and economic reforms, from the struggle for workplace safety standards and laws prohibiting child labor to the struggle for family planning and the ongoing struggle for the rights of women and children. They also need the opportunity to experience democracy in action through more partnership-oriented school structures.

They need all this not only for themselves but also for their children. Indeed, one of the most urgent challenges today's children face relates to how they will nurture and educate tomorrow's children. Therein lies the real hope for our world.

I passionately believe that if we give a substantial number of today's children the nurturance and education that enables them to live and work in the equitable, nonviolent, gender-fair, environmentally conscious, caring, and creative ways that characterize partnership rather than dominator relations, they will be able to make enough changes in beliefs and institutions to support this way of relating in all spheres of life. They will also be able to give their children the nurturance and education that we are today learning makes the difference between realizing or stunting our great human potentials.

CHILDHOOD, EDUCATION, AND ECONOMICS

People who insist that the best way to teach is to punish are usually replicating their own experiences in dominator families and other cultural contexts. This is why early childhood education is so important and why partnership education includes education for partnership childcare.

Psychologists have long told us that early childhood education is critical. But now this information comes to us with lightning-bolt force from neuroscience. After a baby is born, the brain continues to develop and grow. In the process, it produces trillions of synapses or connections between neurons. But then the brain strengthens those connections or synapses that are used, and eliminates those that are seldom or never used. We now know that what kinds of emotional and cognitive patterns are established through this process are radically different depending on how supportive and nurturing or deprived and abusive the child's human and physical environment is. In other words, these patterns are shaped very differently depending on whether childcare and education orient primarily to the partnership or domination model.

Ironically, the people who today are pushing us back to more rigid dominator pedagogies such as the constant testing, and hence ranking into superiors and inferiors, of children and teachers and schools, argue that this is necessary for the postindustrial economy. But actually the opposite is true. To develop the qualities needed for the postindustrial economy requires partnership rather than dominator pedagogies.

Whether or not we are venturesome and creative, whether we can work with peers or only take orders from above, and whether or not we are able to resolve conflicts nonviolently are matters of key importance for the postindustrial information economy. And dominator pedagogies, beginning in early childhood, produce exactly the wrong results.

By contrast, partnership childcare and education prepares young people for the new information- and service-oriented postindustrial economy. Here, as organizational development and management consultants emphasize, inquisitiveness and innovation, flexibility and creativity, team work, and more stereotypically feminine nurturant or facilitative management styles get the best results (Eisler, 1991, 1994). Whether they reside in women or men, these are all qualities and behaviors appropriate for partnership rather than dominator relations.

Human development is of course first and foremost a matter of access to adequate food and other material resources and good health care. But it is also a matter of the kind of care and education a child receives.

Positive childhood care that heavily relies on praise, caring touch, affection, and lack of violence or threats releases the chemicals dopamine and serotonin into particular areas of the brain, promoting emotional stability and mental health. By contrast, if children are subjected to negative, uncaring, fear, shame, and threat-based treatment or other aversive experiences such as violence or sexual violation, they develop neurochemical responses appropriate for this kind of dominator environment, becoming tyrannical to themselves or others, abusive and aggressive or withdrawn and chronically depressed, defensive, hypervigilant, and numb to their own pain as well as often to that of others. (Perry, Pollard, Blakely, Baker, and Vigilante, 1996).

Children who are dependent on abusive adults tend to replicate these behaviors with their children, having been taught to associate love with coercion and abuse. And often they learn to use psychological defense mechanisms of denial and to deflect repressed pain and anger in violence against those perceived as weak. They learn to bully and scapegoat. They later express their pain and rage in pogroms, ethnic cleansings, and terrorism against defenseless civilians.

Neuroscientists such as Dr. Bruce Perry of Baylor College of Medicine, Dr. Linda Mayes of the Yale Child Study Center, and others have found that regions of the brain's cortex and its limbic system (responsible for emotions, including attachment) are sometimes 20 to 30% smaller in abused children than in normal children. Hence these children often lack the capacity for aggressive impulse control. They also often lack the capacity for long-term planning. And children exposed to chronic and unpredictable stress suffer deficits in their ability to learn (Perry, Pollard, Blakely, Baker, and Vigilante, 1996).

In the same way, more partnership-oriented childcare that depends mainly on praise, caring touch, rewards, and lack of threat not only has a direct influence on emotional development but also on mental development, on the capacity to learn both in school and throughout life (Carlson, 1994; Leach, 1994; Montagu, 1986). This kind of childcare is thus a basis for something else we hear a great deal about: lifelong learning.

Partnership childcare can be learned, as can an understanding of stages of child development, of what babies and children are capable or incapable of understanding and doing, and the harm done to children through some of the traditional punishment-based childrearing. Hence the pivotal importance of teaching partnership childcare and parenting based on praise, caring touch, rewards, and lack of threat through education worldwide.

For optimal results, in addition to parenting classes for adults, the teaching of this kind of parenting and childcare should start early in our schools, as it would in a partnership curriculum. This will ensure that people learn about it while they are still young, and more receptive.

WHAT ARE WE REALLY TEACHING CHILDREN?

But it is all of education, not only early childhood education and education for parenting, that has to be reexamined and reframed to provide children, teenagers, and later, adults, the mental and emotional wherewithal to live good lives and create a good society.

We need an education that counters the old dominator socialization, and with this, the unconscious valuing of the kinds of undemocratic, abusive, and even violent relations that were considered normal and moral in earlier, more authoritarian times.

Through partnership process, teachers can help students experience partnership relations as a viable alternative. Partnership structure provides the learning environment that young people need to develop their unique capacities. But partnership process and structure are not enough without partnership content: narratives that help young people better understand human possibilities.

For example, narratives still taught in many schools and universities tell us that Darwin's scientific theories show that "natural selection," "random variation," and later ideas such as "kinship selection" and "parental investment" are the only principles in evolution. As David Loye shows in *Darwin's Lost Theory of Love* (2000), actually Darwin did *not* share this view, emphasizing that, particularly as we move to human evolution, other dynamics, including the evolution of what he called the "moral sense" come into play. Or, as Frans deWaal writes in *Good Natured: The Origins of Right and Wrong in Humans and Other Animals* (1996), the desire for a modus vivendi fair to everyone may be regarded as an evolutionary outgrowth of the need to get along and cooperate.

Partnership education offers scientific narratives that focus not only on competition but also, following the new evolutionary scholarship, on cooperation. It offers scientific narratives that focus more on love and creativity than on violence and selfishness.

For example, partnership education offers empirical evidence that our human strivings for love, beauty, and justice are just as rooted in our biology as our capacity for violence and aggression. Young people learn how, by the grace of evolution, biochemicals called neuropeptides reward our species with sensations of pleasure, not only when we are cared for, but also when we care for others.

The study of evolution from this larger perspective does not leave young people with the sense that life is devoid of meaning or that humans are inherently violent and selfish—in which case, why bother trying to change anything? On the contrary, partnership education is education for positive social action on all levels, from our communities to our community of nations. If enough children worldwide are given partnership education in our time, a time will come when in reality, rather than just rhetoric, children worldwide are safe and well cared for.

Much of the hopelessness of young people today stems from the belief that the progressive modern movements have failed and that the only possibility is to either dominate or be dominated. There are many factors contributing to this distorted and limiting view of possible futures. But a major reason is that education has not shown young people that, despite enormous resistance and periodic regressions, the movements toward a more just and peaceful world have in fact made great gains.

As the young people in schools that have worked with the Center for Partnership Studies' Partnership Education Institute will attest, partnership education is challenging and exciting. It offers new perspectives. It offers the opportunity to talk about issues that really engage young people. It offers ideas, resources, and social actions that can accelerate the shift from domination to partnership worldwide.

A NEW VIEW OF OUR PAST AND FUTURE

Partnership education offers young people a broader understanding of history, one that is essential if they are to more effectively participate in creating the more equitable, peaceful, and sustainable future that cannot be constructed within the context of social arrangements based on domination and control. It shows that the struggle for our future is not between capitalism and communism, right and left, or religion and secularism, but between a mounting movement toward partnership relations in all spheres of life and strong dominator systems resistance and periodic regressions.

By using the analytical lens of the partnership/dominator continuum, young people can see that along with the massive technological upheavals of the last three hundred year has come a growing questioning of entrenched patterns of domination. The 18th-century rights of man movement challenged the supposedly divinely ordained right of kings to rule, ushering in a shift from authoritarian monarchies to more democratic republics. The 18th- and 19th-century feminist movement challenged men's supposedly divinely ordained right to rule women and children. The movement against slavery, culminating during both the 19th and 20th centuries in worldwide movements to shift from the colonization and exploitation of indigenous peoples to their independence from foreign rule, as well as global movements challenging economic exploitation and injustice, the rise of organized labor, and a gradual shift from unregulated robber-baron capitalism to government regulations (for example, antimonopoly laws and economic safety nets such as Social Security and unemployment insurance) also challenged entrenched patterns of domination. The 20th-century civil rights and the women's liberation and women's rights movements were part of this continuing challenge. So were the 19th-century pacifist movement and the 20th-century peace movement, expressing the first fully organized challenge to the violence of war as a means of resolving international conflicts. The 20th-century family planning movement has been a key to women's emancipation as well as to the alleviation of poverty and greater opportunities for children worldwide. And the 20th-century environmental movement has frontally challenged the once hallowed "conquest of nature" that many young people today recognize as a threat to their survival.

But history is not a linear forward movement. Precisely because of the strong thrust toward partnership, there has been massive dominator systems resistance. We also have over the last 300 years seen resurgences of authoritarianism, racism, and religious persecutions. In the United States we have seen the repeal of laws providing economic safety nets, renewed opposition to reproductive rights for women, and periodic violence against those seeking greater rights. In Africa and Asia, even after Western colonial regimes were overthrown, we have seen the rise of authoritarian dictatorships by local elites over their own people, resulting in renewed repression and exploitation. We have seen a recentralization of economic power worldwide under the guise of economic globalization.[2] Under pressure from major economic players, governments have cut social services and shredded economic safety nets—an "economic restructuring" that is particularly hurtful to women and children worldwide. And we have seen an increase in the use of violence to impose rankings of domination, most recently in terrorist attacks against the United States.

The backlash against women's rights has been particularly violent, as in the government-supported violence against women in fundamentalist regimes such as those in Afghanistan and Iran. We have also seen ever more advanced technologies used to exploit, dominate, and kill, as well as to further "man's conquest of nature," wreaking ever more environmental damage.

These regressions raise the question of what lies behind them, and what we can do to prevent them. Once again, there are many factors, as there always are in complex systems. But a major factor that becomes apparent using the analytical lens of the partnership and dominator social configurations is the need to fully integrate challenges to domination and violence in the so-called public spheres of politics and economics and in the so-called private spheres of parent-child and man-woman relations.

In Europe, for example, a rallying cry of the Nazis was the return of women to their traditional place. In Stalin's Soviet Union, earlier feeble efforts to equalize relations between women and men in the family were abandoned. When Khomeini came to power in Iran, one of his first acts was to repeal family laws granting women a modicum of rights. And the brutally authoritarian and violent Taliban and Osama bin Ladin's alQaida terrorist network have made the total domination of women a centerpiece of their violence-based social policy.

THE IMPORTANCE OF GENDER ROLES AND RELATIONS

This emphasis on gender relations based on domination and submission was not coincidental. Dominator systems will continue to rebuild themselves unless we change the base on which they rest: domination and violence in the foundational human relations between parents and children and men and women.

The reason, simply put, it that how we structure relations between parents and children and men and women is foundational to how we perceive what is normal in human relations. It is in these intimate relations that we first learn and continually practice either partnership or domination, either respect for human rights or acceptance of human rights violations as "just the way things are."

Young people need to understand these still generally ignored social dynamics. They need to understand the significance of today's increased violence against women and children and of a mass media that bombards us with stories and images presenting the infliction of pain as exciting and sexy. If they are to build a world where economic and political systems are more just and caring, they need an awareness that images that normalize, and even romanticize, intimate relations of domination and submission rebuild the foundations for a system based on rankings of superiors over inferiors. At the same time, they need to understand the significance of the fact that child abuse, rape, and wife beating are increasingly prosecuted in some world regions, that a global women's rights movement is frontally challenging the domination of half of humanity by the other half, and that the United Nations has finally adopted conventions to protect the rights of children and women.

With an understanding of the connections between partnership or domination in the so-called private and public spheres, young people will be better equipped to create the future they want and deserve.

Because the social construction of the roles and relations of the female and male halves of humanity is central to either a partnership or dominator social configuration, unlike the traditional male-centered curricula, partnership education is gender balanced. It integrates the history, needs, problems, and aspirations of both halves of humanity into what is taught as important knowledge and truth.

A gender-balanced curriculum that does not reinforce the idea that half of humanity is less important than the other half helps us construct mental maps that do not lead to the devaluing of those who are not like us. It also leads to a greater valuing of traits and activities stereotypically considered feminine, such as empathy, nonviolence, and caregiving.

Indeed, when we talk of stereotypically feminine or masculine traits or behaviors, we are always talking about stereotypes that are our legacy from more dominator-oriented times, and not about anything inherent in women or men. Whether these qualities and behaviors are actualized or inhibited depends largely on the kind of socialization a child receives.

PAIN AND PLEASURE

Another key difference between education for a dominator or partnership way of looking at the world and living in it relates to the two most basic human motivations: pain and pleasure. The dominator model depends primarily on fear of punishment—on pain either here on earth or in some otherwordly realm. The partnership model depends primarily on positive motivations—on the pleasure we humans receive from both being cared for and caring.

Partnership education helps young people learn to regulate their impulses, not out of fear of punishment and pain, but in anticipation of the pleasure of responsible and truly satisfying lives and relationships.

Because in the partnership model difference, beginning with the fundamental difference between the male and female halves of our species, is not automatically equated with inferiority or superiority, children do not learn to see the world in terms of the in-group versus out-group rankings that have made so much of history a bloodbath. And because the gender-balanced partnership curriculum gives visibility and importance to the female half of humanity, it also elevates the status of values such as empathy, nonviolence, and caring that in dominator mental maps are seen as feminine. As a result, boys and girls learn to value these qualities in both women and men. To borrow the words of Nel Noddings (1995), who wrote the foreword to my book *Tomorrow's Children* (2000):

> All children must learn to care for other human beings, and all must find an ultimate concern in some center of care: care for self, for intimate others, for associates and acquaintances, for distant others, for animals, for plants, and the physical environment, for objects and instruments, and for ideas.

But, as she also notes, "Today the curriculum is organized almost entirely around the last center, ideas." And even this "is so poorly put together that important ideas are often swamped," with the emphasis on so-called facts and a very limited set of skills (p. 366). Moreover, as Noddings highlights, the male-centeredness of the curriculum militates against seeing skills of caring as important enough to be included in the curriculum.

Noddings and others have called for a new curriculum design that provides an integrated framework for curriculum transformation. This does not mean that we should discard everything we have been using. But it does mean that out of both old and new elements we need to construct a curriculum that can meet the needs and challenges of our time.

Studies from psychology have long shown that the narratives or stories we internalize as knowledge and truth have a profound effect on attitudes, values, and behaviors. Indeed, one of the basic tenets of Sigmund Freud, Alfred Adler, Karen Horney, and other founders of the field is that how we view ourselves and others is rooted in how we are taught to perceive ourselves and the world.

More recently, studies on the effects of television violence on attitudes and behaviors, not only children's but adults', show how cultural narratives mold attitudes and behaviors. For example, the studies done by George Gerbner and colleagues (Gerbner, Gross, Morgan, & Signorielli, 1994) at the Annenberg School of Communication and by David Loye and colleagues (Loye, Gorney, & Steele, 1977) at UCLA contradict the assertion by some mass media executives that their programs do not affect attitudes and behavior, that somehow only purchasing choices and behaviors are affected by television.

There is also a large body of literature on the power of cultural narratives from anthropology, sociology, social psychology, the study of myth, and other disciplines.[3] The work of scholars such as Milton Rokeach (1973) and Joan Rockwell (1974) show that our values are largely formed through cultural narratives transmitted from generation to generation, and can be changed through new narratives. Rockwell's analysis of how the ancient Greeks used theater to instill dominator values is particularly illuminating when we apply it to contemporary entertainment. Rokeach's work is instructive in that it shows that values can be changed through the introduction of narratives that cause conflict between ostensible or consciously held values such as democracy and equality and latent or unconsciously held values such as biases against people of a different gender, race, or social group. My own research on ancient myths shows that with the shift to a dominator model of organization there was a massive transformation of both religious and secular myths. For example, in *The Chalice and The Blade* (Eisler, 1987) and *Sacred Pleasure* (Eisler, 1995) I trace the transformation of images and narratives showing women in positions of power to images and narratives where they are subordinate to men.

There are studies specifically focusing on education that examine the effect of narratives about gender and race on student attitudes, perceptions, and behaviors. Most of these studies date from the 1960s and 1970s, when there was funding for them, and most deal with only single interventions, or at best of just a few weeks' or months' duration. But, strikingly, many of these interventions had positive effects, indicating that a curriculum informed by gender balance and multiculturalism could indeed have lasting effects (Banks, 1991).

As James Banks writes in "Multicultural Education: Its Effects on Students' Racial and Gender Role Attitudes" (1991), interventions appear "to be most successful with young children, particularly preschoolers and kindergartners" (p. 467). For example, in a 1979 investigation of toy choices and game preferences of nursery school, kindergarten, and 1st-grade children, before they saw a film showing a model choosing non–gender-stereotyped toys, the children displayed high levels of gender stereotyping in their choices. After viewing the film, the students in the experimental groups made fewer such choices. But the older children and the boys still made more stereotyped choices than the girls and younger children. The reading of a picture book to preschool children can also influence the kinds of toys they chose. After children were presented a book with a character that chose stereotypical or nonstereotypical toys, the children who were read the nonstereotypical book chose less stereotyped toys (Banks, 1991, p. 466).

In sum, there is a large body of literature supporting the conclusion that partnership narratives can foster partnership attitudes and behaviors. Moreover, data on educational outcomes from an alternative public school, Nova High School in Seattle, Washington, support the conclusion that the whole-systems approach of partnership education has excellent results.

Nova has not only ranked first among the Seattle area's high schools in educational climate surveys, it can boast that a high percentage of its graduates have the academic accomplishments to get into prestigious universities. These young people (of mixed racial and ethnic origins, many from poor families, and some even from homeless families) also tend to have more awareness, sensitivity, and a greater sense of human possibilities—as teachers at Nova will attest and I observed firsthand during a recent visit to this school, which has worked with the Center for Partnership Studies to develop partnership curricula.

Nova High School not only exemplifies the beneficial results of partnership process and content, it also shows that best results come from an approach that integrates partnership process, content, and structure.

At Nova, the primary governing body that makes school policy and rules is open to both students and faculty. At this school, students also play a key role in formulating and enforcing school rules. This not only encourages responsibility, it also offers them hands-on experience in both democratic process and leadership. And it illustrates that violence is not inevitable in urban schools: Nova High School is violence free.

As noted earlier, the core elements of partnership structure are a more egalitarian rather than top-down organizational structure, gender balance rather than male dominance, and, in contrast to the dominator model requirement of a high level of built-in abuse and violence, emphasis on nonviolent and mutually caring and respectful relations. When educational institutions follow this template, their structure models partnership relations and supports both partnership process and content.

THE PARTNERSHIP LEARNING ENVIRONMENT

If a school, classroom, or home school orients primarily to the dominator model, it will be extremely difficult for either students or teachers to experience and model democracy in action. Nor can they move toward their optimal functioning. This has been demonstrated in the business world by organization development and management research for decades (e.g., Trist & Emery, 1973; Eisler, 1991). Accordingly, many successful corporations have been gradually dismantling top-down hierarchies in what I call "debureaucratization." The same principles apply to educational institutions.

This does not mean a completely horizontal organization. I again want to emphasize the distinction between *hierarchies of domination* and *hierarchies of actualization*. Hierarchies of domination are imposed and maintained by fear. They are held in place by the power that is idealized, and even sanctified, in societies that orient primarily to the dominator model: the power to inflict pain, to hurt and kill. By contrast, hierarchies of actualization are primarily based not on power *over*, but on power *to* (creative power, the power to help and to nurture others) as well as power *with* (the collective power to accomplish things together, as in what is today called teamwork). In hierarchies of actualization, accountability does not only flow from the bottom up, but also from the top down.

In other words, educational structures orienting to the partnership model are not unstructured or laissez-faire; they still have administrators, managers, leaders, and other positions where responsibility for particular tasks and functions is assigned.[4] However, leaders and managers inspire rather than coerce. They empower rather than disempower, making it possible for the organization to access and utilize the knowledge and skills of all its members.

I want to add that partnership structures are not equivalent to consensus structures, although in certain situations this can be appropriate. The consensus mechanism can actually lead to domination by individuals with unmet needs for attention. Although there is emphasis on participatory democracy in partnership structures, following interactive discussions, the individual or team responsible for reaching a goal can proceed to see that it does.

Partnership structures facilitate cooperation among different individuals and groups. But once again—and this too is a critical point—partnership as an organizing template is not equivalent to cooperating or working together. People work together in societies, institutions, or organization orienting closely to the dominator model, for example, to attack other nations, to persecute minorities, in cut-throat competition designed to put competitors out of business, or, as we saw on 9-11, to terrorize and kill defenseless men, women, and children.

There is also competition and conflict in the partnership model. But conflict is not used to select winners and losers, or who dominates and who is dominated, but to creatively arrive at solutions that go beyond compromise to a higher goal. And competition is directed more to striving for excellence and using the achievements of the other person or group as a spur or incentive to likewise attaining our highest potentials.

In partnership structures, young people have responsibilities for determining some of the school rules and for seeing that they are honored. This promotes habit patterns needed for young people to function optimally in the postindustrial information economy, where taking responsibility, flexibility, and creativity are essential. More immediately, it contributes to a mutually respectful, undisrupted, and nonviolent school environment. Despite the assumption that adolescents naturally rebel, we may find that when students feel that they are heard and cared for and have a stake in the functioning of their school, they are less likely to do so, as in this kind of structure rebelling would be rebelling against rules in which they themselves have had a significant input.

Partnership structures require a much higher teacher-student ratio, not only through reduced class sizes but through innovations such as team teaching. This in turn requires far greater fiscal and social support for our schools. While much good teaching goes on, it is despite the fact that our schools are understaffed and underfunded.

THE CHALLENGE AND OPPORTUNITY

I have seen how inspired both teachers and students become once they understand that partnership relations, be they intimate or international, are all of one cloth. And I have seen how they move from apathy to action once they fully understand that there is a viable alternative to the violent and uncaring relations that have for so long distorted the human spirit.

I believe young people really care about their future, and that if their education offers them the vision and the tools to help them effectively participate in its creation, they will readily do so. Through partnership education—process, structure, and content—we can help young people understand and experience the possibility of partnership relations and institutions. We can all use partnership education in our homes, schools, and communities to highlight the enormous human potential to learn, to grow, to create, and to relate to one another in mutually supporting and caring ways.

To create the kind of education that children need, our social and economic policies cannot continue to shortchange education. We must give much greater social recognition to the value of teachers, through both better pay and increased funding for continuing teacher development, education, and support. Teachers need more time for thoughtful preparation and assessments, for curriculum development with other professionals, and for training when new developments in education occur.

We need to pay more attention to how children can develop their unique individual potentials rather than merely focusing on standardized test scores. We need to strengthen and build on the various elements of partnership process and content already being used in many schools. And rather than dismantling our public school system, as some propose, we should debureaucratize our schools, not only making them smaller but restructuring them to more closely approximate partnership rather than dominator organizations.

This means reexamining the old structures and rules and, where necessary, creating new structures and rules appropriate for partnership relations. Are teachers, school counselors, and other staff treated with respect by administrators? Are opportunities created for parent participation? Are there referral systems for parents to access social agencies and other community resources? Are there counseling and educational opportunities for parents and other caretakers that will benefit children and further their development (for example workshops for parenting education where mothers and fathers can share challenges and appropriate solutions)? Are social agencies and other community resources enlisted to support teachers in their growing responsibilities to help children develop not only intellectually but emotionally, to ensure that basic needs such as good nutrition and health care are met, and that each child's unique talents are developed? Are efforts made to bring education into the community to meet community needs?

Greater attention to the interactive relationship of schools to their communities and their natural environment is needed if our schools are to support and model partnership relations, in both their internal and external relations. I would like to see a parent resources center at each school, and social services housed in at least some of the schools in every community. I would like to see small schools—no school larger than 350 students, and where possible less. These are part of my vision for schools that are communities of learning where every child can grow and flourish.

As Sheila Mannix and Mark Harris write, what is urgently needed is a school "that can be an effective antidote to the stress of the street and the hurt of the home, a haven of safety, orderly learning, and personal growth, the school as the guarantor of a child's right to protection, education, and love" (unpublished ms., p. 23). Because schools are increasingly in a position of having to meet these needs, but not equipped to do so, Mannix and Harris call for social investments that will make it possible for schools to become the social hub of the community, a mechanism with which society can reach out to families in trouble and ensure that help is provided.

This may sound like a tall order, but it is part of the vision of the partnership school of the future: a vision to plan and work for. It is, I believe, a vision that can gradually be realized as schools are transformed through partnership education.

Adapted for different regions and cultures, partnership education can be a blueprint for refocusing, reframing, and redesigning education to help all children realize their full humanity and preserve our natural habitat. By exploring, taking creative risks, and holding fast to our partnership principles and vision, we can make partnership education a reality. This is not only necessary, but doable—if we join together and step by step lay the foundations for the education that can make the 21st century a bridge into the better future for which we all yearn.

NOTES

1. These works foreshadow much that is still today considered progressive education. Pestalozzi, for example, already in the 18th century rejected the severe corporeal punishments and rote memorization methods prevalent in his time and instead used approaches geared to children's stages of development.

2. Some readings that contain materials that could be excerpted by teachers are Mander & Goldsmith, 1996; Henderson, 1991; Korten, 1995; Peterson & Runyan, 1993; Eisler, Loye, & Norgaard, 1995; *Human Development Report*, 1995. See also the Center for Partnership Studies' website at http://www.part-nershipway.org to download "Changing the Rules of the Game: Work, Values, and Our Future," by Riane Eisler, 1997.

3. An early classic from anthropology is Benedict, 1934; and from sociology, Weber, 1961. Loye, 1998 shows the power of racially biased narratives and feminist writings, including classics such as Spender, 1983, show the attempts by women over many centuries to contradict sexist cultural narratives.

4. Kurt Lewin (1951), widely considered the father of social psychology, conducted some early experiments showing that laissez-faire structures are not only inefficient but end up by leading to the scapegoating and eventual authoritarianism characteristic of dominator structures.

REFERENCES

Banks, J. (1991). Multicultural education: Its effects on students' racial and gender role attitudes. In J. P. Shaver (Ed.), *Handbook of research on social studies teaching and learning*. New York: Macmillan.

Benedict, R. (1934). *Patterns of culture*. New York: Houghton Mifflin.

Carlson, N. R. (1994). *Physiology of behavior*. Boston: Allyn and Bacon.

deWaal, F. (1996). *Good natured: The origins of right and wrong in humans and other animals*. Cambridge, MA: Harvard University Press.

Dewey, J. (1966). *Democracy and education*. New York: Free Press. (Original work published 1916.)

Eisler, R. (1987). *The chalice and the blade*. San Francisco: Harper & Row.

Eisler, R. (1991, Jan./Feb.). Women, men and management. *Futures, 23*, 3–18.

Eisler, R. (1991). Women, men, and management: Redesigning our future. *Futures, 23*, 3–18.

Eisler, R. (1994). From domination to partnership: The hidden subtext for sustainable change. *Journal of Organizational Change Management, 7*, 32–46.

Eisler, R. (1995). *Sacred pleasure*. San Francisco: Harper Collins.

Eisler, R. (2000). *Tomorrow's children: A blueprint for partnership education in the 21st century*. Boulder, CO: Westview Press.

Eisler, R., Loye, D., & Norgaard, K. (1995). *Women, men, and the global quality of life*. Pacific Grove, CA: Center for Partnership Studies (available at www.partnershipway.org).

Freire, P. (1973). *Pedagogy of the oppressed*. New York: Seabury Press.

Gerbner, G., Gross, L., Morgan, M., & Signorielli, N. (1994). Growing up with television. In J. Bryant and D. Zillman (Eds.), *Media Effects*. Hillsdale, NJ: Erlbaum.

Henderson, H. (1991). *Paradigms in progress: Life beyond economics*. Indianapolis: Knowledge Systems, Inc.

Human Development Report (1995). United Nations Development Program (UNDP). New York: Oxford University Press.

Korten, D. (1995). *When corporations rule the world*. San Francisco: Barrett-Koehler.

Leach, P. (1994). *Children first*. New York: Alfred A. Knopf.

Lewin, K. (1951). *Field theory in social science*. New York: Harper & Row.

Loye, D. (1998). *The healing of a nation*. New York: IUniverse. (Original work published in 1971.)

Loye, D. (2000). *Darwin's lost theory of love*. New York: IUniverse.

Loye, D., Gorney, R., & Steele, G. (1977). Effects of television: An experimental field study. In *Journal of Communication, 27*, 206–216.

Mander, J., & Goldsmith, E. (1996). *The case against the global economy and for a turn toward the local*. San Francisco: Sierra Club Books.

Mannix, S. A., & Harris, M. T. *Raising Cain: Original psychic injury and the healing of humanity*. Unpublished manuscript.

Montagu, A. (1986). *Touching* (3rd ed). New York: Harper & Row.

Montessori, M. (1964). *The montessori method*. New York: Schocken Books. (Original work published 1912.)

Noddings, N. (1995, Jan.). A morally defensible mission for schools in the 21st century. *Phi Delta Kappan,* 366.

Perry, B. D., Pollard, R. A., Blakley, T. L., Baker, W. L., & Vigilante,D. (1996). Childhood trauma, the neurobiology of adaptation, and "use dependent" development of the brain: how "states" become "traits." *Infant Mental Health Journal, 16,* 271–291.

Pestalozzi, J. (1976). *Leonard and Gertrude.* New York: Gordon Press Publishers. (Original work published 1781.)

Peterson, S., & Runyan, A. S. (1993). *Global gender issues.* Boulder, CO: Westview Press.

Rockwell, J. *(1974). Fact in fiction: The use of literature in the systematic study of society.* London: Routledge & Kegan Paul.

Rokeach, M. (1973). *The nature of human values.* New York: Free Press.

Spender, D. (Ed.). (1983). *Feminist theorists.* New York: Pantheon.

Trist, E., & Emery, F. (1973). *Toward a social ecology.* London & New York: Plenum Press.

Weber, M. (1961). The social psychology of the world's religions. In T. Parsons et al., (Eds.), *Theories of Society.* New York: Free Press.

CHAPTER 5

Emancipatory Hope

Transformative Learning and the "Strange Attractors"

EDMUND O'SULLIVAN

INTRODUCTION

Educators at all levels of teaching and learning today need the "Big Picture." And let me say quite emphatically, at the outset, that the Big Picture is not the global-market economy. The Big Picture comes as a result of depth encounters with the sacred. It is a deep encounter with the natural economy of the living universe in which we have the privilege to be participant with all our relations. It is a real struggle to have a sustained encounter with the sacred in our contemporary market-driven world. There is great difficulty in the world economy governed by the profit motive for the cultivation and nourishment of the spiritual life. Leisure, contemplation, and silence have no value in this system because none of these activities are governed by the motivation of profit. People who attend to their spiritual life are seen as nonproductive, and more pejoratively underdeveloped. Our world economy is geared toward total emphasis on material wants and needs and there is an eclipse of the hunger that people have called the hunger of the spirit.

From an educational point of view, our present state is in need of transformation. We in the minority world (first world) must confront and come to terms with the quality of life that we have created for ourselves and also assume responsibility for how that manner of living has diminished the manner of living of countless peoples in the majority world and in our own (O'Sullivan, 1999). The bottom line, in the global-market economy, is profit. The singular major goal is economic growth indexed in the gross national product (GNP). We have sold

69

this dream of profit to our world by commodity fetishism. Our Western labor force has bought the notion of standard of living but this is only a comparative phrase to tell you if your buying power has increased or decreased in wage potential to buy market commodities. But standard of living does not add up to quality of life. Our economic market vision has left our whole culture with a crisis of meaning and a felt sense of hopelessness. Michael Lerner (1996) maintains that we hunger more for meaning and purpose in life in the final analysis. Our cultural values, fixated on the market place, have caught us up in a deep cynicism that makes us question whether there is any deeper meaning and higher purpose to life beyond material self-interest. The bottom line of all this materialism and glorification of self-interest is that we find ourselves impoverished morally and spiritually.

Our first and foremost task in life is to take hold of our spiritual destiny. "Spiritual destiny" or "vocation" are not words that are encountered often in educational circles. Nevertheless we are beginning to see a concern in education that opens up the possibility of considering education as a spiritual venture. The indigenous peoples of the Americas, both in the past and in the present, have something to teach us on these matters. One of the traditions of indigenous cultures is the vision quest (Brown 1988), in which individuals must take hold of a vision for their life that allows them to follow their vocation and destiny. May I say that the vision quest does not focus on economic destiny. With this in mind, we see how important it is to have a community life that recognizes the importance of the growth of our spirits.

The contemporary market-driven world has trivialized wonder and we have ended up attempting to reinvent it in Disneyland or through virtual reality (Mander 1991). The sense of awe that could be experienced by looking at the sky on a starry night is receding as we now look into the skies as a challenge to our industrial and military imagination. Our Western drive that propelled our exploitation of the planet now fuels our ambition to explore the stars and the further reaches of outer space. Nevertheless, we continue to return to the sacred and the sense of awe that the universe invites. We have, I believe, what Rudolf Otto (1969) once called the sense of the "holy." It is a sense of the numinous dimension of all reality. It is a sense that when experienced leaves us breathless. It is a sense that is frequently coupled with gratitude, a thankfulness for being a part of a great mystery.

This sense of wonder and awe seems to be part of our response to the real and is present from birth. We certainly see it in the gaze of the young and certainly in the young at heart. The sense of the numinous is present and activated at all levels of life. It is not confined to any one organ of the senses and it is activated in sight, sound, touch, and all manner of sensing. In education we must let our sense of awe direct us in our understanding and we must resist being restricted by the shallowness of the market mentality. It has had a unique manifestation with the native peoples of the Americas. Thomas Berry (1988) observes that aboriginal peoples of the Americas have a special type of nature mysticism. Awareness of the numinous presence throughout the entire cosmic order establishes among these peoples one of the most integral forms of spirituality known to us. Berry ventures that the grand vision of Black Elk is one of the most breathtaking visions of the cosmos and the human place in the circle of life. We see this in a very compelling way in the reflections of the astronauts and cosmonauts who ventured into outer space. These men (they were almost all men) left the earth to go into outer space as creatures of the cold war and they came back as creatures of the planet. The reflections of the astronauts about their journeys into space moved from militarism to mysticism. The sense of awe evoked by the pristine beauty of the planet earth seemed to transcend the sense of nation state consciousness (O'Sullivan, 1999). All seemed to be earth-identified creatures at the end of their incredible journey. Brian Swimme (1996) in his reflective work *The Hidden Heart of the Cosmos* reflects on the scope and magnitude of what I am saying with eloquence:

> Unless we live our lives with at least some cosmological awareness, we risk collapsing into tiny worlds. For we can be fooled into thinking that our lives are passed in political entities, such as the state or a nation; or that the bottom-line concerns in life have to do with economic realities of consumer life-styles. In truth, we live in the midst of immensities and we are intricately woven into a great cosmic drama. (p. 60)

My sense of the Big Picture is this larger cosmological context.

EMANCIPATORY HOPE

We have entered the 21st century having experienced over twenty years of the cyclonic effects of market globalization and its political side kick, neoliberal politics. It has been disastrous to the biosphere, the human community at large, and our brothers and sisters of the animal and plant kingdom. It has created cynicism and hopelessness in its wake. Anthony Giddens (1990) likens economic globalization to a juggernaut, an ancient Hindu festival vehicle that had the propensity to be erratic and go out of control. Like the juggernaut, globalization, seemingly following a steady path by its own conceits, veers erratically in all directions and is very destructive.

We are all aware of the profound destruction that the forces of globalization are visiting on this planet. My argument attempts, in a small way, to address the necessary energy and vision that we must hold educationally if we are to turn back the destructive forces that seem to move at such a furious pace in our time. I take it as a given that the global market forces need to be subject to profound criticism. But critique without vision leads to despair. The long-term survival of our species, and of other species that share our living planet, depends on under-standing the depth of what is happening to the planet at present. It is essential to admit that what is occurring is nothing less than biocide, genocide, and eco-cide. This situation can potentially break our hearts and our spirits and lead us to despair. This is where hope is absolutely necessary. The great Brazilian educa-tor Paulo Friere commences one of his final works with a clear understanding that hope is an absolutely essential feature in our lives and essential for a criti-cally conscious and visionary education in our critical historical moment. In the *Pedagogy of Hope* (1996) he explains:

> I do not understand human existence and the struggle needed to improve it, apart from hope and dream. Hope is an ontological need. Hopelessness is but hope that has lost its bearing, and become a dis-tortion of the ontological need. . . . When it becomes a program, hope-lessness paralyzes us, immobilizes us. We succumb to fatalism, and then it becomes impossible to muster the strength we absolutely need for the fierce struggle that will re-create the world. . . .
>
> Without a minimum of hope, we cannot so much as start the struggle. But without the struggle, hope as an ontological need dissi-pates, loses its bearings, and turns into hopelessness. And hopelessness can become tragic despair. Hence the need for a kind of education in hope. Hope, as it happens, is so important for our existence, individual and social, that we must take every care not to experience it in a mis-taken form, and thereby allow it to slip toward hopelessness and despair. (pp. 8–9)

We must simultaneously dream as we hope. Hope is needed for survival but along with surviving we need critical vision. The prologue of Transformative Learning has the title *The Dream Drives the Action* (O'Sullivan, 1999). Thomas Berry attributes this phrase to Carl Jung (cf. O'Sullivan, 1999). The dream is the visionary-utopian side of hope. In our own time it will encompass rekindling a relationship between the human and natural worlds that is far beyond the exploitative relationships of our current transnational global-market economy. A different kind of prosperity and progress needs to be envisioned which embraces the whole life community. All our human institutions, professions, programs, and activities need to function now in this wider life community context.

HOPE AND THE "GREAT WORK:" TRANSFORMATIVE VISION AND THE "STRANGE ATTRACTORS"

We are living in a momentous period of human and earth history whose scope and magnitude we can barely imagine because it is so daunting. We are living in a period of history that involves the necessity of deep transformations at both the personal and communal levels of our lives. The deep work of transformation that I am speaking of is only just starting. This century must be one of deep transformation if there is to be a next century. We as educators must situate ourselves in a "great work." I take this term from Thomas Berry, who uses it to describe this transformational project. In his book titled *The Great Work: Our Way into the Future* (1999) Thomas Berry describes the great work in the following manner:

> History is governed by those overarching movements that give shape and meaning to life by relating the human venture to the larger destinies of the universe. Creating such a movement might be called the Great Work of a people. There have been great works in the past: the great work of the classical Greek world with its understanding of the human mind and creation of the Western humanist tradition; the Great Work of Israel in articulating a new experience of the divine in human affairs; the Great Work of Rome in gathering the peoples of the Mediterranean world and of Western Europe into an ordered relation with one another. So too in the medieval period there was the task of giving a first shape to the Western world in its Christian form. The symbols of this Great Work were the medieval cathedrals rising so graciously into the heavens from the region of the old Frankish empire. There, the divine and the human could be present to each other in some grand manner. (p. 1)

We have to situate and envision ourselves in the great work of this new century. We are in a period of history that Jean Houston (2000) characterizes as a "jump time":

> The Earth is a hothouse now. Six billion members of the human family and rising, congregated together on a spinning ball, in stress, in ferment, caught between what was and what is yet to be. . . . It is a time to ask great questions: How can we make a better world? What must we do to serve the larger story? These questions help us to clarify and define our objectives. They prompt us to articulate goals lofty enough to lift us out of petty preoccupations and unite us in pursuit of objectives worthy of our best efforts. . . . The world is hungry for vision. At a time when whole systems are in transition and global forces challenge all authority, there is an insistence in the mud, contractions shiver through the Earth womb, patterns of possibility strain to emerge from the rough clay of changing social structures. (p. 116)

These patterns of possibility are what I would call the "strange attractors," a very important concept in modern chaos theory (1984) first formulated by Prigogine and Stengers in the physical sciences and further developed in the social spheres of evolutionary process. The strange attractors are basically those features in a rapidly transforming system suffused in chaos and dissipation that hold creative edge in the transformation of that system. The strange attractors are those systems of possibility that will help the system to move to a higher level, saving it from total destruction and disintegration. From my point of view, hope must be embedded in those strange attractor possibilities.

Let me explain by examples from North America and around the world. I will start by summarizing some survey research recently summarised in *Yes Magazine: A Journal of Positive Futures*. The article that I am citing is one entitled "A Culture Gets Creative." In this article, two U.S. survey researchers are interviewed about their work on emergent trends in a population they call the "Cultural Creatives." This is a subculture which they label as a core group of people who are active in living their values and are socially engaged. This group is simultaneously concerned about consciousness issues and personal growth, are very strong on the ecological front, and are strong on women's issues. The group constitutes about 12% of the U.S. population, roughly 25 million adults, and consists of twice as many women as men. It shades imperceptibly into a circle that can be called "the greens," who don't have as many personal growth concerns. These people support slowing business growth in order to save the planet. The researchers found that the typical Cultural Creative cares intensely about the issues raised by post–World War II social movements. These movements include those focused on civil rights, the environment, women's rights, peace, jobs and social justice, gay and lesbian rights, alternative health care, spirituality, personal growth, and now, of course, stopping corporate globalization. These concerns are now converging into a strong concern for the whole planet.

Paul Ray, one of the researchers interviewed, made the following observation about the Cultural Creatives:

> This seeking for authenticity is part of what links each person's own personal and spiritual growth with a concern for the big picture, including a concern for social justice. What Christopher Lasch says about a culture of narcissism—that the people who are concerned about personal growth don't care about social justice and vice versa— is flat out not true. Our research shows that the more a person is engaged in social activism, ecology, and social justice, the more likely they are to be engaged also in developing their spiritual lives and in personal growth. (p. 16)

In Canada the Council of Canadians is also trying to forge a politics of hope. They are attempting to help Canadians build a bold and visionary social movement to provide an alternative to the fragmenting effects of market globalization. They are attempting to help Canadians forge an education for responsible, active citizenship. The council labels this movement "The Citizens' Agenda," which envisions the following goals:

> We shall not entrust our future to the supremacy of the market. Instead we shall build a new politics of hope. . . . A better world is possible. Alternatives to the rise of corporate rule and the decline of meaningful democracy do exist. They can be found in communities across this country. A powerful and creative Citizens' Agenda is needed to bring these alternatives together into a vibrant and effective program for change. . . . We extend this invitation to all Canadians, in the fullness of our diversity as peoples and cultures, to join together in a transformative project for the social good. (Creating a New Politics of Hope, p. 5)

These patterns of possibility are global. All regions of the world have these seeds of transformative hope. Examples from the majority world are also seen.

Recently I visited the city of Porto Alegre on the west coast of south central Brazil and, as a city, it is a strange attractor indeed. This is the city that has hosted the First and Second World Social Forums, the major-world-movement-oriented forum that is the alternative to the yearly meetings of the market-oriented economic summits. (i.e., the G8). This is a city that has a participatory process that involves all Porto Alegran citizens in the decision making and voting. Cities from all over the world come to see how this city conducts such a process. The mayor of Porto Alegre is a Marxist who has been democratically elected for three straight terms. The city's school system has a priority commitment to help its young citizens to become proficient in systems of democratic and participatory living. They are therefore committed to cooperative learning strategies that model democratic learning. A very strong emphasis is made on universal access to literacy, an essential component to democratic living and the cultivation of democratic citizens.

Many of the current trends in education do not qualify as strange attractors in my system of accounts. The tide toward standardized achievement testing in education is not an attractor and the very procedures and priorities created tend to work against originality and creativity. The emphasis is on good grades, paper and pencil, and multiple-choice testing which fosters conformity and stifles creativity. Worse than the testing is the cutting back of subjects and educational concerns in the curriculum that are not covered in the testing priorities. Such integrative subjects as drama, the arts, physical and outdoor education, ecology, and media literacy are cut back or eliminated from the curriculum. We need to forge a presence in the curriculum for the very subjects that are being ignored, bypassed, or eliminated. We need to identify areas of education that foster new creative and transformative energy and pursue them even as we live through the neoconservative educational reforms to which I have just alluded. My examples of strange attractors, I would hope, gives a sense that there are much wider purposes in this world than market competitiveness and the lean and mean strategies for living. Wherever these strange attractors are, they are the emergent creative edge of a new transformative vision for living in this century.

EXPANDING THE BOUNDARIES
OF TRANSFORMATIVE LEARNING

At the *Transformative Learning Centre* located within the Ontario Institute for Studies in Education (OISE/UT) we have created a working definition of transformative learning on our Web site (http://www.tlcentre.org.) that is as follows:

> Transformative learning involves experiencing a deep, structural shift in the basic premises of thought, feelings, and actions. It is a shift of consciousness that dramatically and permanently alters our way of being in the world. Such a shift involves our understanding of ourselves and our self-locations; our relationships with other humans and with the natural world; our understanding of relations of power in interlocking structures of class, race and gender; our body-awarenesses, our visions of alternative approaches to living; and our sense of possibilities for social justice and peace and personal joy.

Our centre, which we call the TLC, has just recently published a volume of essays written by our members and associates entitled *Expanding the Boundaries of Transformative Learning: Essays on Theory and Praxis* (Sullivan, Morrell, & O'Connor, 2002). The overall intent of these essays is to argue that transformative learning requires new educational practices consistent with the content of education. Arts-based research and teaching and learning practices are examples of such new educational practices. Education for the soul, or spiritual practices such as meditation, modified martial arts, and forms of teaching and learning of indigenous peoples, is another example. Each essay in the collection presents a model of these new practices. The fascinating thing for me, as one of the editors, is how differently each of the contributors comes at his or her own work, and how they take our learning and teaching in so many creative new directions. The various authors in this volume were prepared to engage educational questions in terms of new ways of being, of deep structural transformation, and all sorts of hitherto unimagined possibilities arise. And this is a key point for the distinction between OISE's approach to transformative learning and the approaches taken elsewhere. We are most interested in the generation of energy for radical vision, action, and new ways of being. If humans are going to survive on this planet, we need new connections to each other and to the natural world.

Changing political and economic relationships is part of the larger project of reconstituting and revitalizing all of our relationships. Our purpose in transformative learning is not to delineate abstract principles about education and learning, and we are not interested in theoretical generalizability—at least not in the sense in which this term is ordinarily used. We are asking ourselves why transformative learning matters. And when we speak of transformation, we need to know *from* what *to* what? These essays collectively expand upon and problematize the purposes of transformative learning.

At the same time, these questions also require us to understand the content of learning in ways that other approaches to transformative learning have shied away from. As reflected in this collection, the aim was to leave a much more open space for the marginal, the liminal, the unconscious, and the embodied. The essays in this book are a collection of strange attractors. They have an expansive diversity that is sorely needed in the educational great work of the 21st century. I consider the collection by imagining the rainbow. At the manifest level we see the diversity and color of many sites and locations. At the core is the white beam of deep transformation. Thus transformative vision will have many hues. In this volume that we have just compiled, we have diverse examples of potentially transforming education. Such an array of topics includes critical global education, arts-based education, education for spirituality, antiracist and diversity education, decolonizing education, peace education and education that fosters nonviolence, and holistic ecological and planetary education. *Let a thousand flowers grow but make sure they are attractive, strange or otherwise.*

Finally, although the great work of this century will involve many critical struggles, we must always seek out the celebratory events of life to give us the energy for our efforts. This is a task that will involve the dimension of the sacred. I will end this chapter as I end my work on transformative learning (O'Sullivan, 1999) by emphasising the essential need for celebration:

> We find cause for celebration around significant core events such as the solstice, equinox, births and wedding and funeral rituals that include a multiplicity of friends and relations. The loss of our sense of place in the cosmos and the corresponding loss of ritual concerning our participation in the great mystery of life is significant. The inability to express our sense of ecstasy and gratitude for the *gift of life* constitutes a loss of meaning about our vocation and place in the larger life processes. We live in an incredible time in Earth history and we must capture the sense of our purpose through celebrating the fullness of our existence in both time and space. Celebration is an essential part of the ritual of existence. For creatures of the millennia, we must remind ourselves that we are about a great work. It is a joy to be part of this grandeur. (O'Sullivan, 1999, p. 281)

REFERENCES

Berry, T. (1988). *The dream of the earth*. San Francisco: Sierra Club.

Berry, T. (1999). *The great work: Our way into the future*. New York: Bell Tower Books.

Brown, T. (1988). *The vision*. New York. Berkley Books.

Creating a new politics of hope: Citizens Agenda declaration. (2001, Winter). *Canadian Perspective; The Council of Canadians*.

Friere, P. (1996). *Pedagogy of hope: Reliving the pedagogy of the oppressed*. New York: Continuum.

Giddens, A. (1990). *The consequences of modernity*. Stanford, CA: Stanford University Press.

Houston, J. (2000). *Jump time: Shaping your future in a world of radical change*. New York: Jeremy Tarcher/Putnam.

Lerner, M. (1996). *The politics of meaning*. Reading, MA: Addison-Wesley.

Mander, J. (1991). *In the absence of the sacred: The failure of technology and the survival of indian nations*. San Francisco: Sierra Club.

O'Sullivan, E. (1999). *Transformative vision for education in the new century: Educational vision for the 21st century*. New York: St. Martins Press.

O'Sullivan, E. V., Morrell, A., & O'Connor, M. (Eds.). (2002). *Expanding the boundaries of transformative learning: Essays on theory and praxis*. New York: St. Martin's Press.

Otto, R. (1969). *The idea of the holy*. New York: Oxford University Press.

Prigogine, I., & Stengers, I. (1984). *Order out of chaos: Man's dialogue with nature*. New York: Bantam.

Ray, P., and. Anderson, S. (2001). *The cultural creatives: How 50 million people are changing the world*. New York: Harmony Books.

Ray, P., and. Anderson, S. (2001, Winter). A culture gets creative. *Yes Magazine; A Journal of Positive Futures*.

Swimme, B. (1996). *The hidden heart of the cosmos*. Marynoll, NY: Orbis Books.

CHAPTER 6

Teilhard de Chardin and Holistic Education

BOK YOUNG KIM

Humankind, as an integral part of the whole process that is called Earth, has evolved, is evolving, and will continue to evolve. The latter half of the twentieth century marks a very significant point on the spiral of evolution, for it was then that human beings fully discovered the complex and unfolding nature of their own evolution. This awareness was first cited as important by the Jesuit priest, Pierre Teilhard de Chardin, whose major thesis was that as the human mind has been changing and evolving through time, it has finally reached that critical point of discovery of its own evolution (Smith, T. E., Roland, C. C., Havens, M. D., Hoyt, J. A., 1992, p. 114).

Some of his ideas were so controversial that he was deprived of his teaching position and his works were banned by Catholic Church authorities. He spent almost twenty years doing research as a geologist and palaeontologist, carefully observing the world from the viewpoint of the evolutionary anthropologist, working the nature of the relationships between evolution, the nature of religious experience, the human personality, and the totality of the universe.

In times of global crisis, it is reasonable to revisit Teilhard's tenets of holistic philosophy. In this chapter I will focus on the impact of evolution on holistic philosophy of Teilhard de Chardin and implications for holistic education.

THE IMPACT OF EVOLUTION ON HOLISTIC PHILOSOPHY OF TEILHARD DE CHARDIN

Teilhard is an evolutionist. British scientist Charles Darwin's (1809–1882) theory of biological evolution and fellow Frenchman Henri Bergson's (1859–1941) philosophy of creative evolution greatly influenced his thinking (White, 2002, p. 115).

It is argued that his controversial work, *The Phenomenon of Man*, first published in 1955, after the death of Teilhard, may be one of the most important and influential books written in the 20th century, representing as it does the most intelligent interpretation of evolution still existing. The only other work similar to Teilhard's insights into the evolutionary process is Smut's *Holism and Evolution*, originally published in 1926.

According to Settanni (1990), both of these men seem to have been aware of the impact of contemporary physics on the background of their worldviews concerning evolution. They share an awareness of the fact that evolution is a process, a process that becomes an integral phenomenon in the whole universe. The phenomena of biological evolution should lead in reflection to the realization that the world is not a mere collection of static entities, but rather a world of change and interrelationships. The Darwin-Mendel Theory of Evolution fails to grasp the implications of evolution for a new worldview (p. 115).

This 19th-century theory regards the world as a collection of static entities. For instance, mind, life, and matter are all separate, discrete, unrelated entities even though biological evolution implies that life and mind arose from matter. Nineteenth century physics held that space, time, matter and motion were discrete and separate entities.

In comparison, 20th-century physics has revealed that space, time, matter, and motion are not discrete, separate entities—but are dependent upon motion. There are no discrete entities for contemporary physics. From this viewpoint, the world is the natural result of interrelated events, which imply process and change.

What is true in physics is also true in biology as long as living organisms are observed with unclouded vision. The world may be observed as an inanimate machine in which all parts are moved by other mechanical parts external to them. Evolution may be seen as a special application of this mechanistic worldview, assuming that mechanisms are moved by external forces, the forces of the natural environment and the cosmic rays of the sun.

The mechanistic worldview must assume that matter, life, and mind, in some sense, are separate entities, accustomed, as we are to think in this way. Many empirical philosophers from John Locke in the 18th century onward have thought of matter as totally inert, lacking in the power of self-motion. This seems self-evident if nature is observed anew from the revolutionist and process perspectives.

Since life and mind arise from matter, it becomes improbable that there is a rigorous cutoff point below which life and mind cease to exist. On the other hand, paralleling physics, if life, mind, and matter interpenetrate, this should constitute a different worldview. Upon the foundations of this new worldview a more appropriate theory of the evolutionary process could be constructed.

The construction of just such a new worldview is the accomplishment of Teilhard. In his book, *The Phenomenon of Man*, biology, physics, sociology, and theology are integrated with true artistic intuition. The world is perceived as unity by him: "The age of nations is past; the task now is to build the earth" (p. 5). This quotation from another of Teilhard's books, *Building the Earth* (1965) is the social core of his new vision, from which theology, biology and physics are derived.

Perhaps there is no other work in the 20th century that does more to replace the mechanistic view of the world with a holistic view than does Teilhard's central work on evolution, *The Phenomenon of Man*. Holistic philosophy goes back to the ancient world. In this continuum it is probable that *The Phenomenon of Man* will serve as key for opening up patterns of thought for the 21st century.

As a French-Jesuit priest, who had an early interest in the natural sciences, Teilhard headed an expedition team later in his life to investigate the remains of prehistoric Peking man in China. This scientific experience lead to his reflecting on the meaning of evolution. Although his first works were scientific in nature, all of Teilhard's later writings were philosophical speculations on biological evolution.

Throughout his life, he questioned if evolution was able to provide a key to human nature. Years of reflection bore fruits in the publication of *The Phenomenon of Man* in 1955. "Fuller being is closer union; such is the kernel and conclusion of this book." is a statement in his foreword of *The Phenomenon of Man* that summarizes the holistic vision of reality.

Holism, coined by the South African philosopher and statesman Jan Christian Smuts, is equivalent to interconnectedness, and this interconnectedness was for Teilhard the culmination of the long process of change known as evolution. Humanity, in the new world view, should be seen as one of the significant phenomena of the total universe, a delicate part of the whole process (Settanni, 1990, pp. 117–118). All of the evolutionary processes, including the phenomena of humanity, are processes which cannot be described solely in terms of their origins. They must also be defined in terms of their directions, their inherent capabilities, and their unfolding potentialities.

Evolution endows human beings with an even greater dignity than they possessed in the old mechanistic view of the world. Man has a task; that of growing and developing in the process of change. The future of humanity is a holistic future; the future of increasingly integrating and interconnecting reality and human society within himself. The goal of his future, perhaps millions of years away, is to be the Omega Point, the culmination of history. Human beings at the Omega Point will arrive at a full sense of integration with society and the entire earth (Settanni, 1990, p. 118).

Individuals will look upon themselves, not as members of an immediate neighborhood, state, or nation but as true citizens of the earth. Their sense of identity will consist of an intimate sense of interconnectedness with all reality. The part that is the individual, will be necessary for the whole and tightly interlinked with it.

This future pacified earth will be more intricately organized than the one that we are familiar with today because it will be more of an organism. The holistic perspective will be in the ascendant over the mechanistic view. The earth as a whole will be more important than each of its parts.

It is Teilhard's central assertion that as human beings are the product of biological evolution in the past, they will evolve socially in the future. Modern human beings do not in reality identify with the earth as a whole, but in the future they will. In Teilhard's thinking, future communal consciousness will replace our present sense of individualism and alienation.

The holistic consciousness Teilhard pictured is actually the ramification of evolution because it is broader, more truly integrated, and more complex than the present form of consciousness. Teilhard holds that evolution is essentially aspiring to organisms increasingly more integrated and more complex than their relatively simple ancestors. He attempts to illustrate the central truth of this reflection through examination of the process of biological evolution.

Life has advanced from simplicity to complexity, from disorganization to organization, and for Teilhard this is the fundamental law of evolution. The operation of this law will continue into the future. The more complicated and sophisticated the organism is on the biological level, the more complex the organism becomes biologically. While the simple one-celled organism contains one cell; humans are composed biologically of several million cells. Between those two extremes it is generally the case that the more cells the organism contains, the more complex it is.

IMPLICATIONS FOR HOLISTIC EDUCATION

Holism is often defined as a functional, integrated and generalized model of education that focuses on the whole teaching-learning situation, and varies the teaching learning strategy to meet the needs of the learner, the teacher, and the situation in an effort to attain educational outcomes greater than the sum of their parts.

Based on this philosophy, holistic education provides for a broad range of strategies and curriculum formats. Holistic education is also founded on the belief that human beings are moving toward transcendence of the narrow worldview of science and technology. Such a change in perspective demands a new design and ideas for education.

Rinke (1985) noticed that essential and implied characteristics of holistic education are as follows:

1. Holistic educators vary their strategies to meet the needs of the learner, the educator and the situation.
2. Holistic educators assist learners to reach unique potential, and they promote learning as a lifelong process.
3. Holistic educators structure learning environments to promote the creative and insightful potential of the human mind.
4. Evaluation strategies include all individuals involved in the teaching-learning process (pp. 67–68).

In an age of fragmentation Teilhard saw life as a whole, and crossed the boundary line of traditional academic disciplines. Here is a man who in a lifetime was theologian, biologist, and physicist as well as social theorist and who saw no essential differences among these disciplines. Like the study of evolution which he pursued, all of these fields are interrelated perspectives on the process of an interrelated, dynamic world.

For instance, MacDonald (1973) observes that Teilhard provides a holistic picture in the various areas of epistemology, such as the possibility of knowledge, the origins of knowledge, the methods of knowledge, the structure of knowledge, the kinds of knowledge, and the problem of truth (pp. 68–139).

Regarding the possibility of knowledge, Teilhard acknowledges that human beings are not only capable of knowing, but that it is necessary that they do so in order to direct and control the process of change. In viewing the origin of knowledge, Teilhard accepts that it is a union of precepts and concepts in the formulation and testing of hypotheses.

Agreeing that the origin of knowledge is in the active unity of the a priori and posteriori, Teilhard sees the scientific method as the method for knowing. He goes further and advocates that after analysis, synthesis must follow. Remaining consistent with the analysis of the scientific method, he views the structure of knowledge in the constancy of recurrence, the order of change.

Having established his progressive view, he discussed the kinds of knowledge he would accept. He also argued for rational, empirical, and authoritative knowledge. As concerns revealed knowledge, Teilhard, acting in faith, accepts it and attempts to reconcile it with his process position. Finally, he defined truth as a result of specific verifications.

In her dissertation, Ryan (1981) shows the aesthetic dimension of process philosophy in Teilhard. She concludes that the aesthetic is integral to the lifelong educational process as well as to formal education. Process aesthetics supports the generic notion that we can experience the aesthetic dimension of life only if we are educated in our wholeness, that is, educated to become a fully experiencing self (p. 235).

It also supports those who propose that only in aesthetic education can one achieve what has been set as the goal for all education: the growth of the whole person through responses to our total environment. Only in aesthetic education is the total person involved in the educative process, for only in informed aesthetic perceptions are the centers of sense, affectivity, conceptualization, and imagination brought to focus in a single experience. Nowhere else can we have such a clear notion of the experiencing self. Nowhere else is it possible to experience more fully and integratively.

CONCLUDING REMARKS

As Teilhard mentioned above, the consciousness of humankind of the future will be more centralized as well as more complex, and he explains how the emergence of a new consciousness takes place. He argues that the earth is shrinking. There will continue to be more and different cultures, and different ways of life. Our increasingly more advanced consciousness will integrate these different ways and different cultures. Through increased complexity and centralization, we are driving toward the Omega Point, the zenith of complexity and centralization in which humans will completely identify themselves with the earth as a whole.

An example of the awakening of this kind of consciousness can be identified in that of the worldwide ecological movement with its image of Spaceship Earth. Ecological consciousness demands an integrated effort on a global basis. It demands that individuals be able to reconnect their consciousness, their goals, and their aims toward the betterment of the whole.

In this context, there is much evidence that this new form of consciousness is coming to realization. A good example is the growth and development of technology itself, especially the growth of information technology. The advancement of the IT industry has made this planet Earth to be a smaller world than it was before.

In Teilhard's optimistic opinion, growth in awareness leads to tolerance and sympathy and heralds our beginning the process of becoming citizens of the Earth. As we becomes increasingly interconnected through the development of technological communications, consciousness becomes ever more centralized up to the Omega Point. The goal Teilhard posited for evolution, in a nutshell, was unity. It reminds us that fuller being is closer to union. Being and reality are one. In other words, unity is the interconnectedness of things on the biological level and change on the psychological level. Together these constitute the holistic vision of education.

In a way, Teilhard's cosmology is parallel to "dependent co-arising" in Buddhism. This will be this writer's future project in holistic education.

REFERENCES

Mac Donald, M. A. (1973). *Epistemological dimensions of process philosophy in John Dewey and Pierre Teilhard de Chardin: Implications for education.* Unpublished doctoral dissertation, University of Pennsylvania.

Rinke, W. J. (1985). Holistic education: An answer? *Training and Development Journal, 39*(8), 67–68.

Ryan, J. (1981). *The aesthetic dimension of process philosophy in Alfred North Whitehead and Pierre Teilhard Chardin and its significance for education.* Unpublished doctoral dissertation, New York University.

Settanni, H. (1990). *Holism: A philosophy for today anticipating the twenty first century.* New York: Peter Lang.

Smith, T. E., Roland, C. C., Havens, M. D., & Hoyt, J. A. (1992). *The theory and practice of challenge education.* Dubuque, IA: Kendall/Hunt.

Smuts, J. C. (1961). *Holism and evolution.* New York: The Viking Press. (Original work published 1926.)

Teilhard de Chardin, P. (1955). *The phenomenon of man.* New York: Harper and Row.

Teilhard de Chardin, P. (1965). *Building the earth.* Wilkes-Barre, PA: Dimension Books.

White, S. R. (2002). Organization model of a constructivist learning community: A Teilhardian metaphor for educators. *Journal of Educational Thought/Revue de la Pensee Educative, 36*(2), 111–128.

CHAPTER 7

Minding the Soul in Education

Conceptualizing and Teaching the Whole Person

DEBORAH ORR

INTRODUCTION

Holistic education means that we strive to teach the whole person as a human soul which includes mind, body, emotions, and spirit. This is the orientation so creatively engaged by the other chapters in this book. However, the idea of bringing spirit or soul into education can be difficult for some to accept, especially where there is a strict "separation of church and state," or a concern that addressing the soul will involve religious proselytizing. Holistic education cannot avoid coming to terms with this issue if it is to live up to its name, to teach the whole person.

In this chapter I address this issue in two ways. The first is to outline some philosophical reasons why a concern with a nonreligious concept of the soul is a valid one for educators (the first two sections). The second is to draw out some of the implications of this concept of the person as soul for educators and to illustrate this with an example drawn from anti-oppressive pedagogy (the third and fourth sections).

In making the first point I explore the ordinary-language concept "soul" to show that the word "soul" in its nonreligious uses is a linguistic marker for human being holistically understood. I also argue that it is logically primary in that the concepts of mind, body, and so forth are dependent upon it. These are conventional and provisional ways of speaking about aspects of the human, and not names of independent and separate entities which are somehow conjoined to form a person. If we accept the validity of the holistic notion of the soul for which I argue, then many implications for teaching and learning will follow since it now becomes apparent that all learning necessarily involves the whole person—it is not something which happens solely in the mind, as the still-dominant ideology would have it. In this chapter I focus on only one aspect of this to show that teaching the acceptance of difference, which antioppressive pedagogy strives for, must involve teaching the whole person. Simply teaching a more acceptable set of ideas to replace discriminatory ones will not suffice if that teaching fails to address the emotional, bodily, behavioral, and spiritual aspects of those ideas in a student's life.

Because of the ineluctable engagement of the full range of a student's lived experience by the ideas the student encounters, I will propose that mindfulness techniques can be a valuable adjunct to holistic teaching and learning. A wide range of yoga and meditation techniques have been perfected over millennia specifically for the purpose of developing awareness of and holistic change in the conceptual structures which help to define and guide human life. Western researchers in many fields, such as psychology and medicine (Butler, 2002; Kabat-Zinn, 2000; Ornish, 1990; Watson, Batchelor, & Claxton, 2000), have begun to discover their power and usefulness and they promise to be as fruitful in the field of education (Emavardhana & Tori, 1997; Miller, 1994; Orr, work in progress). The aim of holistic teaching—to facilitate a more fully integrated learning experience, rather than the fractured and alienated leaning experience and consequent life experience produced by much modern Western pedagogy—can be facilitated and enhanced in a multitude of ways through the use of mindfulness techniques; only one of them is explored in the last section.

A PHILOSOPHICAL INVESTIGATION OF "SOUL": WITTGENSTEIN

The 20th-century Western philosopher Wittgenstein and the 2nd-century Indian Buddhist philosopher Nagarjuna share a surprising range of affinities (Gudmunsen, 1977; Streng, 1967), including similar insights into the holistic nature of human being and the extent to which all learning implicates the whole person. For that reason both will be drawn upon to develop the themes of this chapter. Unlike Wittgenstein, however, Nagarjuna had the advantage of being situated in a culture which provided him with the therapeutic techniques to address the "diseases of the understanding" which his philosophical insights enabled him to diagnose. Both philosophers showed that language acquisition and use involve the totality of human experience rather than simply the mind as an isolated entity; both argued that conceptual frameworks structure and organize human life; both examined in detail numerous concepts which make up those conceptual frameworks to show how they can mislead and confuse language users and so produce diseases of the understanding which distort their lives; and both believed that their philosophical methodology of close conceptual analysis had therapeutic value in that it could help to cure diseases of the understanding. However, while Wittgenstein looked for "new ways of thinking" (1980, p. 48) which would help establish a different, better way of living (p. 61), only Nagarjuna fully appreciated the deep emotional, bodily, behavioral, and spiritual connections people have to ideas, and only he had the cultural resources necessary to address those connections holistically. Whether students are doing formal philosophical analysis, or exploring racist or sexist ideas, or attempting to develop fresh, new responses to a work of art (Burack, 1999), bringing Nagarjuna's insights into the current context shows how yogic and meditation techniques can be useful in effective pedagogy. As we will see, they can be used in the classroom first to develop mindful awareness of the full range of experience evoked by an idea, and then to facilitate change as students watch patterns of response emerge, peak, and die away. This mindful watching but nonengagement with the experiential process is what enables students to control, rather than be controlled by, ideas. Since Wittgenstein more directly addresses the philosophical presuppositions of contemporary Western pedagogy, we will begin with a brief overview of his work and then turn to Nagarjuna to explore the role mindfulness can play in teaching the holistic human soul.

In order to investigate the concept of soul Wittgenstein employed both positive lines of argumentation, in which he attempted to foreground natural-language uses of concepts and negative lines, in which he investigated a wide range of problematic philosophical, theoretical, and religious uses. He argued that these latter types of uses, whether philosophically questionable or not, are logically dependant on conceptually primary natural uses. As with his treatment of all concepts, in his negative arguments he attempted to show the ways in which a particular theoretical position or use of the concept had the potential for "bewitching" the understanding and thus misleading people in their thinking and consequently in their life. As he famously has said, he did not want to solve, but rather to dissolve, philosophical problems, to expose the confusions and illogicality inherent in them so that they lost their power to mislead. It is well beyond the scope of this work to explore Wittgenstein's philosophy in any detail, but a brief look at his treatment of a paradigmatic example of mind/body dualism as exemplified by Descartes will be useful since some form of this view still undergirds much practical and theoretical pedagogy, and it is a model Wittgenstein dealt with in detail.

Descartes' *Meditations* (1989) is deeply rooted in Western philosophy and cultural ideology and it continues to exert a massive influence on both cultural production and personal experience (Taylor, 1989). In order to establish a ground for certainty, in his *Meditations* Descartes introduced a radical distinction between his mind, which he deemed to be his essential self, and his body, which was only contingently and far less certainly a part of him. "Thought [which happens in the mind, the cogito] is an attribute that belongs to me; it alone is inseparable from my nature" (Descartes, 1989, p. 26). A cogito, a thinking being, is one who doubts, understands, conceives, affirms, denies, wills, rejects, imagines, and perceives (p. 27). In Descartes' view any subjective experience, for instance the phenomena of sensation (color, sound, taste, pain), which comes to the mind via the body shares the body's uncertain status and is inessential to the self (p. 6). Thus in his view, cognitive processes are radically alienated from bodily or emotional experience and can proceed in isolation from the rest of personal experience.

Brief though it is, this sketch encapsulates the germ of numerous philosophical problems inherent in Descartes' work, and they are reproduced in subsequent work and thinking influenced by him. These include the mind/body problem (how can an incorporeal mind influence a material body?); the problem of other minds (If mind is inner and private, that is, sequestered in the body and only accessible to its possessor, how can it be shown that other beings, who are only perceptible as outer bodies, are not, as Descartes suggested, mere mindless automata?); the problem of solipsism (How can the cogito know anything whatsoever outside of itself); and the private language problem (a family of problems around language acquisition and use which result in the logical impossibility of language acquisition or even its solipsistic use) (see Malcolm, esp. 1963b and 1971).

Given the still pervasive influence of Cartesian mind/body dualism and the central role of language in teaching and learning, the latter set of issues is of particular interest to us. Implicit in Descartes' theory is a referential model of meaning; since thinking and cognate processes happen in the mind, in order to be communicated to others they must be correctly connected with the words of a public and shared language. On this model the meaning of a word is the inner idea or experience it refers to (Wittgenstein, 1968, 1). Thus, in one of Wittgenstein's key examples, the criterion of correct usage of the word *pain* is that it be actually connected with an inner experience of pain or the idea of pain. First-person uses must make such a connection, and understanding third-person uses requires that one know that such a connection is being made. To deny these consequences is to dispense with the role of an inner mind and thus to undermine Descartes' model. Among his many lines of response to this, Wittgenstein showed that, owing to the privacy of mind, it is logically impossible to know what inner object another person has connected with a particular word and so, on this model, language is solipsistic in that only the speaker can know what connections are being made. Further, since this model is criteriological—the appropriate connection between word and object is the criterion of correct usage—it is impossible to be certain that any first-person use is ever correct either. This is because the only plausible criteriological connection available to the linguist between "pain" and a particular inner experience is a memory which itself requires a further criterion of correctness. This is an infinite and vicious regress that reduces language to incoherence; people can never know, with certainty, what they mean, that is, what their words refer to. In fact, it is impossible to teach language on this model since mothers and other teachers have no way of knowing what is going on in a child's mind and consequently what inner object they are connecting with a given word.

The way out of this impasse, Wittgenstein (1968) suggests, is to abandon Descartes' dualistic model of the person with its referential model of meaning, and to look instead at the multitude of ways in which language is interwoven with holistic human experience in language games (7). In a famous metaphor he compared language to a tool box containing many types of tools with which people can perform a multitude of tasks. The words in some language games, like some tools, perform a wide range of functions. They are woven into human lived experience in a multitude of different ways which may have nothing at all in common with each other (23). But taken as a group, the instances of general concepts, like the members of a family, share a variety of similarities among themselves and so Wittgenstein replaced referential and essentialized theories of meaning with the notion of their "family resemblance" (67). He has shown that language may be used referentially, but this is relatively rare and its possibility depends upon nonreferential uses (10). So rather than seeking to teach language by establishing connections between words and things, we can best understand, for example, the acquisition of the word *pain* as learning a new form of pain behavior: "A child has hurt himself and he cries; and then adults talk to him and teach him exclamations and, later, sentences. They teach the child new pain-behaviour" (Wittgenstein, 1968, 244). In this example there is neither an inner nor an outer criterion of usage; rather, the language is woven into natural, pre- and nonlinguistic pain behaviors and human interactions which are "the prototype of a way of thinking and not the result of thought" (Wittgenstein, 1970, 541). This understanding of language as language games shifts our focus from Descartes' radically dichotomized model of human being to a holistic one in which language acquisition and use engages the whole person.

This holistic model of the person is reinforced by Wittgenstein's response to Descartes' worry that other human beings might be automata since their cogito is not directly perceptible. Wittgenstein (1968) writes, as a point of logic and not as an autobiographical remark, "My attitude towards him is an attitude towards a soul. I am not of the opinion that he has a soul" (p. 178). Here the word "soul" is a marker for the prelinguistic, holistic concept of the human out of which language games are formed. This concept is rooted in the natural and relational experience of human beings. It is not the result of ratiocination which would result in an opinion about which, like Descartes with his automata, one might be mistaken. It is this natural attitude of one human to another, along with the behaviors and responses which it involves, which enables an adult to teach a child the word *pain* in the example above. In the pain-language example language use involves "a primitive reaction to tend, to treat, the part that hurts when someone else is in pain" (Wittgenstein, 1970, 54) into which language is interwoven. Thus a mother, say, responds to the totality of her child's experience and expression of pain and in the course of this response teaches language. It is never an open question for her whether or not her child has subjective experience, whether she is an automata as Descartes' model would suggest; rather she responds to her child holistically, as a human soul. At the same time, the child is not occupied with connecting words with mental objects, but is learning new, more refined ways of self-expression and interaction with its Mother. Here we can also see that language is relational in the sense that its acquisition and use necessarily involve interactions with others.

Wittgenstein's work is replete with examples drawn from all linguistic domains which show the nonreferential and noncriteriological nature of natural uses, which foreground the multitude of ways in which they are woven into the patterns of nonlinguistic human life, and which highlight their public, communal nature. Much of what he does revolves around the question of how a child might learn language, and he shows repeatedly that that question can not be answered if we understand learning as something which happens in the mind. Learning involves the whole person. A major consequence of this for our concerns is that who and what humans are as persons is intimately tied up with the language games they play. As we learn to play different games, we change as persons and thus to change language games is to change the human soul. While Wittgenstein argued for the logical primacy of the concept "soul," while he demonstrated its holism throughout his mature philosophical work, and while he believed that misunderstandings about the nature and role of language had deeply damaged both individual and communal human life, he failed to work out the full implications of this for effecting change. For this I propose to turn to the work and culture of Nagarjuna, the primary philosophical voice of Mahayana Buddhism.

A PHILOSOPHICAL INVESTIGATION OF SOUL: NAGARJUNA

As noted above, the striking affinities between the work of Wittgenstein and Nagarjuna are well detailed in the literature. Like Wittgenstein, Nagarjuna was concerned with the problems generated by referential and essentialist theories of meaning, and like Wittgenstein he realized that these problems were not confined to formal philosophy. We all frequently make the mistake of believing that the words we use refer to permanent essences, for instance that the soul or mind is self-subsistent, or, like Descartes with his mind/body distinction, that the conceptual boundaries we draw reflect a hard-and-fast reality which exists independently of language. The problems here are twofold: they lie in assuming that (1) words have meaning by virtue of their referential function, and (2) that the things they refer to exist independently and eternally. Again like Wittgenstein, Nagarjuna rejected both of these propositions by showing their incoherence. His concept of "emptiness" encapsulates the result of his negative dialectic, argumentation which he employed against referential theories of meaning and reified concepts to demonstrate the dilemma that we can not say of things either (1) that they exist, or (2) that they do not exist, or (3) that they both exist and do not exist, or (4) that they neither exist nor do not exist. Nagarjuna shows, however, that this does not mean that we can not use the word *exists* to talk about all sorts of particular things, for example, pains or cats on mats to use examples favored by Western philosophers. His point was that we cannot draw any metaphysical conclusions about essences or isolated and independent entities from these everyday uses. Nagarjuna (1967) argued, "you deny all mundane and customary activities when you deny emptiness [in the sense of] dependent co-origination" (24:36). One aspect of his expression "dependent co-origination" is that language can only function within the context of a web of language games, to use Wittgenstein's phrase. It is the mundane and customary activities of human beings—their pains and joys, experiences with others, plans and calculations, search for the cat—together with the conventional relationships between words that give language meaning. Again like Wittgenstein, Nagarjuna (1967) tests and rejects the positions that the human is composed of an inner self (which could contain thoughts, ideas, and so on) housed in a corporeal body (18:3–4), and that the human soul is a substantive entity. Rather, the human soul is conceptualized as fluid, ever changing being (emptiness) which exists in a complex web of relationships with other souls and the nonhuman world (dependent co-origination). In rejecting the dualistic view of human ontology and the referential theory of meaning which it calls for, and in placing language squarely in the context of human life, Nagarjuna, as Wittgenstein was to do millennia later, showed that the human soul is formed by the language games one plays. If those language games are in any way diseased, perverse, or corrupt, or if a person is confused about their nature, then the person's life will likewise be disordered. Thus gaining clarity about the true nature of our concepts and thoughts, and so being able to disengage from undesirable language games, was of paramount importance to Nagarjuna, as it was for Wittgenstein.

In his major work, *Mulamadhyamakakarikas* (1967), Nagarjuna speaks of two forms of truth, the "world-ensconced," which has to do with mundane activities—yes, the cat is on the mat—and truth in the "highest sense" (24:8–10). The highest sense, he holds, "is not taught apart from practical [i.e., mundane, world-ensconced] behavior" (24:10). Truth in the highest sense has to do with having clarity about and a healthy relationship with our thoughts and ideas so that they do not control our lives. Commenting on this distinction between types of truth one scholar has said that it is not one that refers to specific characteristics or a unique essence. Rather, it is a difference of attitude or awareness about oneself in relation to existence. It is foremost an epistemological difference, which becomes an ontological difference insofar as knowledge determines what one becomes. (Streng, 1967, p. 145)

Or, in Wittgensteinian terms, we are the language games we play. "World-ensconced" truth refers to the forms of truth produced by different language-games, such as those of science or of everyday life activities, and truth in the highest sense is that possessed by the individual who remains firmly grounded in the activities which produce world-ensconced truth. Such a person is not misled by belief in a third type of truth, the type which philosophers have believed for millennia that metaphysics can give access to. This, for example, is the type of truth about human ontology which Descartes believed he had revealed. Since this type of truth, as exemplified by the Cartesian mind/body dichotomy, is grounded in deep linguistic confusions, and since such confusions have the power to perturb human life and relationships, a pedagogy rooted in it will be likewise misleading for students and ineffective in addressing such issues as those that anti-oppressive pedagogy seeks to engage. These pedagogies contest forms of oppression which are often rooted in conceptual schema which not only alienate the student's mind from other aspects of the self but which posit radical distinctions between self and other. But before addressing this in more detail, let us turn to some of the concerns most frequently raised when proposals are made to address the soul or use mindfulness techniques in the classroom.

ISSUES AND RESPONSES

The above points from Nagarjuna's philosophy are all consistent with Wittgenstein's work, up to and including the position that humans suffer from "diseases of the understanding" and that overcoming these will enable a better, more fully human life. Their difference lies in the fact that Nagarjuna's work was situated in and developed to serve Buddhism.

The core four noble truths of Buddhism hold that life is characterized by suffering, which is caused by craving (desire or attachment), that by overcoming craving suffering is reduced and eventually eliminated, and that there are specific ways to do this (the eightfold path) which include having correct views and being mindful in speech, thought, and action (H. H. The Dalai Lama, 1997). Nagarjuna's work, through showing what it did and did not make sense to believe, could help one achieve correct views and greater mindfulness. In this it was efficacious not simply in providing more correct intellectual positions but in helping to heal the existential diseases which deluded beliefs created by challenging the attachments one forms to incorrect beliefs. At the same time, owing to their understanding of the empty and codependent nature of the human soul, neither Nagarjuna nor his tradition in general hold that simply changing one's mind, that is, dropping one position to espouse another, would be likely to effect real change in the person. Thus a range of yogic and meditation practices were developed to go beyond simply changing minds and to help to root out the delusions created by attachment to erroneous views by breaking those very attachments.

It is, of course, at this point that some might object that we have slipped from doing philosophy or teaching to engaging in religious activity, for, after all, doing yoga or meditation are practices which form a part of religious traditions. This is a complex issue which can not be fully explored here but a few points may prove helpful. First, as we have seen, however sketchily, the philosophy of Wittgenstein and Nagarjuna are mutually consistent in their findings regarding the nature of language, their view of the human soul, the role of language in creating the human soul, the ill effects on life of mistaken understandings about thoughts and ideas, their call for a "therapy of the understanding," and their belief that cures can be effected which in turn can open the possibility of a fuller and healthier life. The philosopher Chris Gudmunsen (1977) has argued that "a good deal of what would universally be called 'religious' in Madhyamika texts can also . . . be found in Wittgenstein's work" (p. 115), although no none would call Wittgenstein a "religious" philosopher. Aside from the role of cultural institutions and practices in a religion, the major difference which Gudmunsen points to here is a Foucauldian one, it lies in cultures (roughly those of the West in contrast to those of the East) with radically different views as to what constitutes religious activity and human salvation. The mindfulness practices which we will explore below were not designed to effect salvation as that is understood by the dominant Western religions, nor is the concept of the human soul, as revealed by the philosophy of Nagarjuna, consistent with that to be found in most of their mainstream theology. An additional relevant point is that the Hindu and Buddhist traditions in which the meditation practices to which I wish to turn were developed themselves recognize both their nonreligious uses and the simply preparatory or supporting religious uses for them (Fields, 2001, pp. 122–123); they are not necessarily religious practices per se even in those traditions. Finally, we must also take into account the multitude of nonreligious uses to which the family of practices which comprise yoga and meditation are now being put in the West. The argument of this chapter is that they also have important pedagogical roles to play.

A different type of objection to utilizing yogic meditation practices in formal education might be that they take education well beyond what is currently mandated, to form the minds and academic or vocational skill sets of students. In answer to this both Wittgenstein and Nagarjuna have shown that the belief that we can and do deal with minds in isolation from the rest of human being is simply mistaken. Education already involves the soul, the holistic human being, whether we acknowledge that or not; however, in recognizing this fact we can educate more effectively. Thus the second point of this chapter is that any effective pedagogy, and most especially antioppressive pedagogy, can only effect real learning when it consciously and deliberately addresses the whole person.

AN EXAMPLE OF MINDFULNESS IN THE CLASSROOM: ANTIOPPRESSIVE PEDAGOGY

Let me illustrate this with a specific example. Antioppressive pedagogy calls for ways of unlearning sexism, racism, classism, homophobia, religious intolerance, ableism, and other forms of discrimination. These forms of social discrimination are grounded in a binaristic cultural logic which creates radical differences on the basis of such categories as sex, race, and so forth. Thus education must enable the student to understand the dualistic forms of thinking and the logic of domination (Warren, 1988) which ground oppression, at the same time that it confronts and changes the behaviors and internalized attitudes which make up the language games of oppression (hooks, 1994). Here we must bear in mind that discrimination does not only disadvantage its target group; it works by internalizing attitudes which harm the members of dominant groups themselves, for instance by leading boys to believe that they must conform to unattainable and dehumanizing ideals of masculinity, such as learning the language game "boys don't cry" (Kaufman, 1987). While a Wittgensteinian analysis of the language games of oppression which exposes their roots in dualistic and essentialized thinking is extremely useful, it does not provide techniques for engaging the noncognitive experiential elements of language games. For this we must turn to other philosophical traditions and it is the mindfulness meditation techniques of Nagarjuna's culture which have proven their efficacy over time.

Space does not allow for even a cursory survey of the many yoga and meditation techniques, let alone a discussion of the multitudinous ways in which they might be developed for application in the classroom. For illustrative purposes I will take an example drawn from feminist pedagogy and briefly discuss how the mindfulness techniques of vipassana meditation might handle it. Feminist teachers often introduce a work, for instance a novel, in order to uncover, discuss, and deconstruct its sexist content. This pedagogy can prove highly effective and produce real changes in the views of students. In some instances it may even change behavior. At the same time a holistic concept of the student suggests that the student will retain levels of sexism which remain untouched by such a purely abstract approach (Orr, 1993). Vipassana practices can be used here to facilitate a mindful awareness of other experiential manifestations of sexism. Guided by their teacher, and eventually working on their own, students can work progressively through levels of associated thoughts, attitudes, emotions, and bodily sensation which are evoked by the novel and the ideas it contains. Mindful attention to these experiences allows them to become fully conscious, while simply watching them as they arise, rather than engaging with them, allows their energy to crest and dissipate. Thus their power to form the soul will be dispelled as the student is able to disengage from them.

There are two types of positive outcomes from this pedagogy. First, it follows from our holistic concept of the human soul that addressing the experiential aspects of sexism which are associated with its purely cognitive content is pedagogically more salutary and deeper than simply dealing with ideas which are held at a quite superficial level of understanding. Second, the process of meditation itself, in addition to helping clear the soul of unwanted and harmful formations which impede interpersonal understanding, can enable a more open and richer relationship with others, as Nagarjuna's relational concept of dependent co-origination and Wittgenstein's picture of the human soul embedded in a web of nonlinguistic relationships both suggest. Both of these results are widely endorsed by feminist and other antioppressive teachers, but all too often not achieved in spite of their best efforts.

Holistic teaching means that we must mind the soul, that we as teachers must take into account the student as a holistic being. This calls for pedagogical techniques which can address much more than isolated and alienated minds. Indeed, a philosophical investigation of human being such as that undertaken by Wittgenstein and Nagarjuna shows that the very notion of an isolated mind is radically mistaken and logically untenable.

I have hardly been able to hint here at the promise which the yogic and meditation technologies of the self drawn from Nagarjuna's culture holds for us. My attempt has been rather to begin to make the argument that understanding the holism of the human soul shows not simply that mindfulness meditation, and more broadly yogic techniques, might have a role to play in education, but that they must.

REFERENCES

Burack, C. (1999, September/October). Returning meditation to education, *Tikkun, 14*(5), 41–46.

Butler, K. (2002, Spring). On the borderline. *Tricycle, 11*(3), 47 ff.

Descartes, R. (1989). *Meditations on first philosophy.* (Laurence J. Lafleur, Trans.). New York: Macmillan.

Emavardhana, T., & Tori, C. (1997). Changes in self-concept, ego defense mechanisms, and religiosity following seven-day vipassana meditation retreats. *Journal for the Scientific Study of Religion, 36*(2), 194–206.

Fields, G. P. (2001). *Religious therapeutics: Body and health in yoga, ayurveda, and tantra*. Albany: State University of New York Press.

Gudmunsen, C. (1977). *Wittgenstein and Buddhism*. London: MacMillan.

H. H. the Dalai Lama. (1997). *The four noble truths*. (Thupten Jinpa, Trans., Dominique Side, Ed.). London: Thorsons.

hooks, b. (1994). *Teaching to transgress: Education as the practice of freedom*. New York: Routledge.

Kabat-Zinn, J. (2000). Indra's net at work: The mainstreaming of dharma practice in society. In G. Watson, S. Batchelor, & G. Claxton (Eds.), *The psychology of awakening: Buddhism, science, and our day-to-day lives* (pp. 225–249). York Beach, ME: Samuel Weiser.

Kaufman, M. (1987). The construction of masculinity and the triad of men's violence. In M. Kaufman (Ed.), *Beyond patriarchy: Essays by men on pleasure, power, and change* (pp. 1–29). Toronto: Oxford University Press.

Malcolm, N. (1963a). Wittgenstein's philosophical investigations. In *Knowledge and certainty: Essays and lectures*. Ithaca: Cornell University Press.

Malcolm, N. (1963b). Knowledge of other minds. In *Knowledge and certainty: Essays and lectures*. Ithaca: Cornell University Press.

Malcolm, N. (1971). *Problems of mind: Descartes to Wittgenstein*. New York: Harper & Row.

Malcolm, N. (1982). Wittgenstein: The relation of language to instinctive behaviour. *Philosophical Investigations, 5*(1), 3–22.

Malcolm, N. (1986). *Nothing is hidden: Wittgenstein's criticism of his early thought*. Oxford: Basil Blackwell.

Miller, J. P. (1994). *The contemplative practitioner: Meditation in education and the professions*. Toronto: OISE Press.

Nagarjuna. (1967). Mulamadhyamakakarikas: Fundamentals of the middle way. (F. J. Streng, trans.), in F. J. Streng, *Emptiness: A study in religious meaning*. Nashville: Abingdon Press.

Ornish, D. (1990). *Dr. Dean Ornish's program for reversing heart disease*. New York: Ballantine Books.

Orr, D. (1993, Summer). Toward a critical rethinking of feminist pedagogical praxis and resistant male students. *Canadian Journal of Education/Revue canadienne de l'education, 18*(3), 239–254.

Orr, D. (2002). The uses of mindfulness in anti-oppressive pedagogies: Philosophy and praxis. *Canadian Journal of Education, 27*(2), 246–267.

Streng, F. J. (1967). *Emptiness: A study in religious meaning*. Nashville: Abingdon Press.

Taylor, C. (1989). *Sources of the self: The making of the modern identity*. Cambridge, MA: Harvard University Press.

Warren, K. J. (1988). Critical thinking and feminism. *Informal Logic, 10*(1), 31–44.

Watson, G., Batchelor, S., & Claxton, G. (Eds.). (2000). *The psychology of awakening: Buddhism, science, and our day-to-day lives*. York Beach, ME: Samuel Weiser.

Wittgenstein, L. (1968). *Philosophical investigations*. (G. E. M. Anscombe, Trans.). Oxford: Basil Blackwell.

Wittgenstein, L. (1970). *Zettel*. (G. E. M. Anscombe & G. H. von Wright, Eds., G. E. M. Anscombe, Trans.). Berkeley: University of California Press.

Wittgenstein, L. (1980). *Culture and value*. (G. H. von Wright, Ed., P. Winch, Trans.). Chicago: University of Chicago Press.

CHAPTER 8

Nourishing Adolescents' Spirituality

RACHAEL KESSLER

How do educators make a place for soul in the classroom? What does a classroom look like in which soul is vital to the enterprise of education? What are the experiences that nourish spiritual development of adolescents in secular schools? And why should schools even consider addressing this terrain?

The Passages Program is a curriculum for adolescents that integrates heart, spirit, and community with a strong academic program. This curriculum of the heart is a response to the mysteries of teenagers: their usually unspoken questions and concerns are at its center.[1]

Like other comprehensive health and social and emotional learning programs, Passages deals with a broad range of issues: friendship, communication skills, stress management, diversity, study skills, problem solving, health, and personal and social responsibility. But unlike most programs, it also addresses spiritual development.

WHY ADDRESS SPIRITUAL DEVELOPMENT IN SCHOOLS?

It has been considered dangerous for educators to address the question of spiritual development in schools. But we in the Passages Program dared to do so because after decades of headlines about "a generation at risk," the void of spiritual guidance and opportunity in the lives of teenagers is still a rarely noticed factor contributing to the self-destructive and violent behavior plaguing our nation. Drugs, sex, gang violence, and even suicide may be, for some teenagers, both a search for connection, mystery, and meaning and an escape from the pain of not having a genuine source of spiritual fulfillment.

But it is not only the violence of youth culture that calls us to their spiritual development. The exquisite opening to spirit at the heart of the adolescent experience also inspires Passages. During adolescence, energies awaken with a force that many dismiss as "hormones." The larger questions of meaning and purpose, about ultimate beginnings and endings begin to press with urgency and loneliness.

CLASSROOMS THAT WELCOME SOUL

To achieve the safety and openness required for meaningful exploration of spiritual development, students and I work together carefully for weeks and months. We create ground rules—conditions that students name as essential for speaking about what matters most to them (Elias et al., 1997). Games help students become fully focused, relax, and become a team through laughter and cooperation. Symbols that students create or bring into class allow teenagers to speak indirectly about feelings and thoughts that are awkward to address head-on. We work with a highly structured form of discourse called Council. With everyone sitting in a circle where all can see and be seen, the council process allows each person to speak without interruption or immediate response. Students learn to listen deeply and discover what it feels like to be truly heard. Silence becomes a comfortable ally as we pause to digest one story and wait for the other to form, when teachers call for moments of reflection or when the room fills with feeling at the end of a class.

Since "we teach who we are," teachers who invite heart and soul into the classroom also find it essential to nurture their own spiritual development. This may mean personal practices to cultivate awareness, serenity, and compassion as well as collaborative efforts with other teachers to give and receive support on the challenges and joys of entering this terrain with their students. In addition, staff development can increase our capacity to open our hearts while also providing firm guidance and the problem-solving skills that will protect our students from disrespect.[2]

When we can cocreate with our students this climate of honor and respect, stories emerge about what matters most to young people, what has moved them deeply, what has nourished their spirits. I listened to these stories for years. Then a pattern began to emerge—a map to the territory of soul.

A MAP OF ADOLESCENT SPIRITUAL DEVELOPMENT

Based on students' stories and questions, I have mapped spiritual development in adolescents who may or may not have a religious tradition or other beliefs about the true nature of spirituality. This mapping comprises seven interrelated yearnings, needs, or hungers. Just as the child's body grows when the hunger for fuel and air is fed, and the child's emotional life grows when the hunger for love and guidance is met, meeting these spiritual yearnings supports, strengthens, and fosters the development of the spirit of a young person.

Following are the domains of adolescent spiritual development.

1. Search for Meaning and Purpose. This concerns the exploration of existential questions that burst forth in adolescence. "Why am I here?" "Does my life have a purpose? How do I find out what it is?" "Is there a meaning to life?" "Why should I live?" "What is life for?" "What does my future hold?" "What is my destiny?" "Is there life after death?" "Is there a God?" I've read these questions time and again when students write anonymously about their personal mysteries—their wonder, worries, curiosity, fear, and excitement.

This domain of meaning and purpose not only is crucial to motivation and learning for students but also is paradoxically simple and uncomfortable for teachers to deal with. Purpose is primarily taught in the curriculum through goal setting and decision-making, often with strictly rational techniques. But if this spiritual dimension is omitted or if the inner life of the adolescent is not cultivated as part of the search for goals or careers, they will most likely base their decisions on external pressures, from peers, parents, and teachers. One student wrote:

> So many of my friends are so clueless. They don't know what they want to do; they know what they're supposed to do. They don't know how they feel; they know how they're supposed to feel. And here I find myself in a group of people going through all my same stuff, and although I don't have the answers to all questions, I find myself feeling like everything is perfect and right. . . . I have this "community" that gives me a home base and a sense of security.

Throughout the curriculum, teachers can create a safe environment where students can reveal and explore these existential questions. Because our profession predicates most authority on our ability to "know," or to have the "right answer," many teachers are profoundly uncomfortable with questions that appear to have no answers.

Yet educators can provide experiences that honor the questions. They can also allow students to give their gifts to the world through school and community service, creative expression, or academic or athletic achievement. In the way we teach, we can help students see and create patterns that connect learning to their personal lives.[3]

2. Longing for Silence and Solitude. This can lead to identity formation and goal setting, to learning readiness and inner peace. For adolescents, this domain is often ambivalent, fraught with both fear and urgent need. As a respite from the tyranny of busyness and noise that afflicts even our young children, silence may be a realm of reflection, calm, or fertile chaos—an avenue of stillness and rest for some, prayer or contemplation for others. Another student wrote:

I like to take time to go within myself sometimes. And when I do that, I try to take an emptiness inside there. I think that everyone struggles to find their own way with their spirit and it's in the struggle that our spirit comes forth.

3. *Urge for Transcendence.* This describes the desire of young people to go beyond their perceived limits. It includes not only the mystical realm, but also secular experiences of the extraordinary in the arts, athletics, academics, or human relations. By naming this human need that spans all cultures, educators can help students constructively channel this urge and challenge themselves in ways that reach for this peak experience.

4. *Hunger for Joy and Delight.* This can be satisfied through experiences of great simplicity, such as play, celebration, or gratitude. Educators can also help students express the exaltation they feel when encountering beauty, power, grace, brilliance, love, or the sheer joy of being alive.

5. *Creative Drive.* This is perhaps the most familiar domain for nourishing the spirit of students in secular schools. In opportunities for acts of creation, people often encounter their participation in a process infused with depth, meaning, and mystery.

There is something that happens to me in pottery class—I lose myself in the feeling of wet clay rolling smoothly under my hands as the wheel spins. I have it last period, so no matter how difficult the day was, pottery makes every day a good day. It's almost magical—to feel so good, so serene.

6. *Call for Initiation.* This refers to a hunger the ancients met by rites of passage for their young. As educators, we can create programs that guide adolescents to become conscious of the irrevocable transition from childhood to adulthood, give them tools for making transitions and separations, challenge them to discover the capacities for their next step, and create ceremonies with parents and other faculty that acknowledge and welcome them into the community of adults.

7. *Deep Connection.* This is the common thread in the stories I have heard from students over the years. Ron Miller (1995), historian of holistic education, observes:

spirituality is nourished, not through formal rituals that students practice in school, but by the *quality of relationship* that is developed between person and world. We can, and must, cultivate an attitude of caring, respect, and contemplation to replace the narrow modernist view that the world is a resource to be exploited. (p. 96)

Whether students are describing deep connection to themselves, to others, to nature, or to a higher power, this seventh domain describes a quality of relationship that is profoundly caring and resonant with meaning, and involves feelings of belonging and of being truly seen or known.

Through *deep connection to the self*, students encounter a strength and richness within that is the basis for developing the autonomy central to the adolescent journey, to discovering purpose and unlocking creativity. As teachers, we can nourish this form of deep connection by giving our students time for solitary reflection. Classroom exercises which encourage reflection and expression through writing or art can also allow a student access to the inner self while in the midst of other people. Totally engrossed in such creative activities, students are encouraged to discover and express their own feelings, values, and beliefs.

Connecting deeply to one other person or to a meaningful group, they discover the balm of belonging that soothes the profound alienation which fractures the identity of our youth and prevents them from contributing to our communities. To feel a sense of belonging at school, students must be part of an authentic community in the classroom—a community in which students feel seen and heard for who they really are. Many teachers create this opportunity through morning meetings, weekly councils, or sharing circles offered in a context of ground rules that make it safe to be vulnerable. The teacher must continue to support the autonomy and uniqueness of the individual while fostering a sense of belonging and union with the group. The more that young people are encouraged to strengthen their own boundaries and develop their own identity, the more capable they are of bonding to a group in a healthy, enduring way.

Connecting deeply to nature, to their lineage, or to a higher power, they participate in a larger, ongoing source of meaning, a joy that provides them with perspective, wisdom, and faith. "Is there life after death?" "How did life start?" "Is there a God?" "What makes people evil?" "What is the meaning of life?"

When students know there is a time in school life where they may give voice to the great comfort and joy they find in their relationship to God or to nature, this freedom of expression nourishes their spirits. My students have expressed themselves through this freedom in many ways:

"When I get depressed," revealed Keisha to her family group members in a school in Manhattan, "I go to this park near my house where there is an absolutely enormous tree. I go and sit down with it because it feels so strong to me."

"It was my science teacher who awakened my spirit," said a teacher about his high school days in Massachusetts. "He conveyed a sense of awe about the natural world that would change me forever."

"I try to practice being present—that's what Buddhism has given to me that I really cherish. It's really the most important thing to me now."

"I became a Christian a few years back. It's been the most wonderful thing in my life. I can't tell you what it feels like to know that I'm loved like that. Always loved and guided. By Jesus. And it's brought our family much closer."

Students who feel deeply connected don't need danger to feel fully alive. They don't need guns to feel powerful. They don't want to hurt others or themselves. Out of connection grows compassion and passion—passion for people, for students' goals and dreams, for life itself.

EDUCATION FOR WHOLENESS

Defining the "moral meaning" of democracy, John Dewey (1957) wrote that "the supreme task of all political institutions . . . shall be the contribution they make to the all-round growth of every member of society" (p. 186). If we are educating for wholeness, citizenship, and leadership in a democracy, spiritual development belongs in schools. But because we have concerns about separation of church and state, because we often confuse spiritual development with religion, and because we fear reprisal from "the other side" in a decade of culture wars, educators have been reluctant to develop a methodology and curriculum to directly address this aspect of human growth.

In a pluralistic society, educators can give students a glimpse of the rich array of experiences that feed the soul. We can provide a forum which honors the ways individual students nourish their spirits. We can offer activities which allow them to experience deep connection.

Perhaps most important, as teachers, we can honor the quest of all students to find what gives their life meaning and integrity, and what allows them to feel connected to what is most precious for them. In the search itself, in loving the questions, in the deep yearning they let themselves feel, young people will discover what is sacred in life, what is sacred in their own lives, and what allows them to bring their most sacred gift to nourish the world.

NOTES

1. The Passages Program has three roots: the Mysteries Program at Crossroads School for Arts and Science in Santa Monica, California, where core methods for high school seniors were expanded into a curriculum for grades 7–12 by a team of teachers; teacher-training programs that I have offered over the last decade through the Passage Ways Institute in Boulder, Colorado (www.passageways.org) and the Collaborative for Academic, Social, and Emotional Learning (CASEL) with colleagues from a broad range of approaches to social and emotional learning.

2. I have written more extensively about the question of how teachers cultivate their own capacities for teaching safely in this arena in a chapter called:

"Soul of Students, Soul of Teacher: Welcoming the Inner Life to School," in Linda Lantieri, 2001.

3. See writers on recent brain research such as Caine and Caine (1997); also see Parker Palmer.

REFERENCES

Caine, R. N., & Caine, G. (1997). *Education for the edge of possibility.* Alexandria, VA: Association for Supervision and Curriculum Development.

Elias, et al. (1997). *Promoting social and emotional learning: Guidelines for educators.* Association for Supervision and Curriculum Development.

Lantieri, L. (2001). *Schools with spirit: Nurturing the inner lives of children and teachers.* Boston: Beacon.

Miller, R. (1995/96, Winter). The renewal of education and culture: A multifaceted task. *Great ideas in education,* 7(5).

Palmer, P. (1998). *The courage to teach.* San Francisco: Jossy Bass.

CHAPTER 9

Won Hyo's One Heart-Mind and Meditation on One Heart-Mind as Part of Holistic Education

YOUNG-MANN PARK AND MIN-YOUNG SONG

INTRODUCTION: WAR AND PEACE

After the terrorist attack on the United States in September 2001, concern for peace has become more serious than ever. How can we conduct peace education and establish peace in the global village?

Won Hyo was a Korean Buddhist scholar (617–686). His concept of *One Heart-Mind* (or One Mind-Heart, hereafter OHM) is a gate to peace, truth, compassion, and wisdom. OHM might mean our true and original self. To meditate on OHM and to be awakened to OHM should be a part of holistic education. As the UNESCO charter says, war starts from the human mind and peace also starts from the human mind-heart. So we need to find the original, peaceful OHM, which can help overcome conflict and establish harmony among people and cultures.

ENLIGHTENMENT EXPERIENCE OF ONE HEART-MIND

Won Hyo was a leading thinker and one of the most energetic evangelists in the history of not only Korean but also Asian Buddhism. The literal meaning of *Won Hyo* is "dawn." Won Hyo's enlightenment experience of OHM transformed his life and thoughts, and impelled him to become a prolific scholar and evangelist.

Won Hyo's mystical experience of OHM is somewhat parallel to St. Paul's mystical experience of the resurrected Christ. After this experience St. Paul became a passionate evangelist and wrote letters to churches and individuals. Ancient Won Hyo also resonates with modern Gandhi who said, "Turn your spotlight inward."

While traveling to China to seek the truth (dharma), Won Hyo spent one night in a cave. He awoke in the middle of the night to drink water. The next morning he discovered that the water dipper he had drunk from the night before was a human skull. He thought, "Yesterday the water was so sweet, now I'm vomiting it. Aha! All depends on mind-heart. All things are created by mind-heart." In that very moment, he was enlightened to OHM and the relative kinship of all things.

Won Hyo did not study abroad as he had originally intended. In Silla, one of the three kingdoms of ancient Korea, he did not belong to a particular Buddhist denomination. He studied widely under several scholars and participated in the Popular Buddhism Movement. He showed that diverse Buddhist teachings and practices are part of a single, comprehensive path to enlightenment.

Won Hyo wrote commentaries on most of the known Mahayana scriptures and summaries of the teachings of the Chinese scriptural schools. He explained the Vinaya texts and explored Buddhist philosophy, epistemology, and psychology. Furthermore he wrote assorted synthetic works and tried to harmonize all forms of Buddhism into a single system of holistic Buddhism.

PEACE MAKING THOUGHTS AND ACTS BASED ON ONE HEART-MIND

Two Tasks Won Hyo Faced

Won Hyo faced two cultural and sociopolitical tasks: 1) how to harmonize the different Buddhist teachings, and 2) how to help bring enlightenment to the common people in the indigenous system of social stratification in Silla known as the "Bone-rank system." He wanted to bring peace to the Unified Silla people composed of the Silla, ex-Koguryo, and ex-Baekche people.

Won Hyo was born into a nonelite family. He saw different Buddhist denominations and experienced the disastrous war among Silla, Koguryo, and Baekche. He tried to respond to these difficulties through Buddhism, especially based on his enlightenment experience of OHM.

Hwajaeng

According to Won Hyo, all the Buddhist teachings are footnotes to OHM. Won Hyo said, "People see the sky through the hole of a straw." This is similar to a proverb which says, "No one's mouth is big enough to say all the truth."

Won Hyo's knowledge of Buddhism was encyclopedic, for he studied all aspects of Buddhism then known to China, including Prajna, San Lun (Three Treatises), Tathagata-garbha, Vijpapti-vada, Hua-yen, Vinaya, Pure Land, and

Son (or Ch'an in Chinese, Zen in Japanese). Through his philosophical concept of Hwajaeng, meaning "the reconciliation of doctrinal controversy," Won Hyo harmonized different Buddhist denominations, based on his practical and personal experience of OHM.

OHM can be supported by the Sradhotpada Sutra (Treatise on the Awakening of Faith), the Vajra-samadhi Sutra, and the Hwa-yen Sutra, among others. According to the concept of OHM, the heart-mind is the origin of all objects, transcending nonbeing and being. The universe or any one thing are not objective entities, but products of OHM. When one completely purifies OHM, one becomes Buddha.

The heart-mind of people is defiled by three poisons: desire, hatred, and ignorance. One should purify the poisons and return to the original state and function of heart-mind to be an Awakened One (Buddha).

Though there are limitless ways (upayas) to achieve Buddhahood depending on the individual situation, one must return finally to OHM. All people are equal with respect to OHM, which is the source of compassion, wisdom, peace, and loving kindness. OHM clears obstacles between noumena and phenomena, even between phenomena and phenomena.

Holistic Buddhism for all kinds of Buddhists— Common People as well as the Nobility

When Won Hyo, a nobleman, took his monastic vows Buddhism was very popular in the Silla royal house. There was mutual support between Buddhism and the Silla royal house. The Buddhism of this time was for the nobility. The common people were discriminated against religiously as well as sociopolitically. However, in the 7th century monks from nonaristocratic backgrounds began to criticize aristocratic Buddhism. They started preaching Buddhism to the common people. This was the beginning of the Popular Buddhism Movement.

Won Hyo had special concern that the common people saw OHM in themselves and he became an important person in the Popular Buddhism Movement. He caught the attention of the ruling elite of Middle Period Silla (654–780). Silla's policies showed more concern for the common people than before. In this matter, Won Hyo worked with the national leaders. Won Hyo taught the common people Yumbul, which is meditative recitation of Buddha's name and was a popular practice in Amitabha, Pure Land Buddhism. A latter-day historian mentioned, "Thanks to Won Hyo even poor and illiterate people could recite the name of the Buddha."

Won Hyo's social status reached a peak when he married Princess Yosuk, through whom he obtained the patronage of the Silla royal house. In this way, he embodied the ideal of the nondualism of the monkhood and the laity, of the noble and the common people.

Based on OHM, Won Hyo practiced Conduct of Nonobstruction as it is found in the Hwa-yen or the Avatamsaka Sutra. OHM goes beyond the dualism of the secular and the sacred. To find OHM is far more important than to have a good family line or geographical affiliations. Won Hyo democratized Buddhism to a great extent and to some extent the society in which he lived. In fact the OHM idea has ultimately become a basis for democracy in modern Korea.

Won Hyo's Holistic Buddhism and Popular Buddhism became the common spiritual foundation for the Unified Silla people, and brought peace to the three formerly separate groups (the Silla, ex-Koguryo, and ex-Baekche people). It is interesting to make a comparison between the role of Christianity in the unification of the Roman Empire under Constantine and the role of Holistic Buddhism in reconciling the people in Unified Silla.

Won Hyo's Influence

Won Hyo's influence went beyond his time and place. His scholarship and personality have influenced people around the world especially in Korea, China, Japan, and India.

In the Koryo dynasty that came after the Silla, Won Hyo was revered by the four Buddhist sects as their patriarch, and was compared with Asvaghosa and Nagarjuna of India. Won Hyo's *Commentary on the Awakening of Faith* influenced Fa Tsang (643–712) to formulate the Hua-Yen philosophy. In subsequent centuries Won Hyo's works continued to guide Chinese Buddhist philosophers.

Won Hyo's works were also transmitted to Japan and guided Japanese Buddhism of the 8th century. He was considered a reincarnation of Dignaga (480–ca. 540). Disciples of Dignaga brought Won Hyo's famous book, *Simmunhwajaengnon* ("Exposition to Ten Gates to Reconciliation of Doctrinal Controversy") to India. The book was translated into Sanskrit.

Recently Rev. Kim Jin-Hong, a Korean Presbyterian pastor, was asked by a newspaper reporter who had influenced him the most. Rev. Kim answered, "Won Hyo influenced me most." Rev. Kim is very famous for his passionate and compassionate pastoring to common people in Korea and China. It seems that Won Hyo's OHM is transmitted by Rev. Kim today beyond the differences of time and religion.

ONE HEART-MIND, "GATES," AND HERMENEUTICS

Gates (Paths) to OHM: The Source of Peace and Harmony

OHM is the source of good, including peace and harmony, compassion and wisdom, happiness and freedom. How can we reach OHM and then follow Won

Hyo's exemplary life and thoughts? There are many gates (or paths) to OHM. All gates root in (converge into) OHM. OHM in turn branches out (or diverges) to all the gates. So one can practice to awaken the OHM through any gate or path.

Let us draw a mandala to explain Won Hyo's understanding of OHM and gates.

FIGURE 9.1
Mandala: One Heart-Mind as the center of gates.

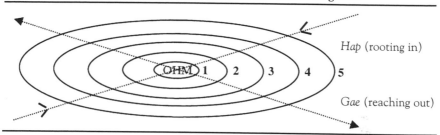

Gae literally means "to open up." Hap literally means "to combine."

According to Won Hyo we may awaken and nurture OHM through diverse gates such as the following:

- Single gate = One Heart-Mind
- Double gate = suchness-gate & life-death gate—Seeking truth from above, teaching people down
- Triple gate = precepts, meditation, and wisdom
- Fourfold gate = the Four Great Vows:
  1 vow to save all beings
  1 vow to end all sufferings
  1 vow to learn all dharma teachings
  1 vow to attain enlightenment
- Fivefold gate = 5 practices
  the Dana Paramita (giving out)
  the Silla Paramita (precept)
  the Ksanti Paramita (patience)
  the Virya Paramita (effort)
  the Dhyana-Prajna Paramita (meditation and wisdom)

Regarding wisdom (Prajna), Won Hyo maintained that wisdom seekers (or truth seekers) need to abide by triple wisdom (or triple learning): wisdom of listening, wisdom of critical thinking, and wisdom of cultivation/practice. This triple wisdom can be compared to John Miller's concept of *transmission, transaction, and transformation.* This comparison waits for further research.

TABLE 9.1
Rooting In and Branching Out

Hap (rooting in)	Gae (branching out)
OHM	many or all things
one gate	many gates
essence	various teachings
Holistic Buddhism	various Buddhist denominations

OHM and Hwa-Yen Sutra

Truth is all in all. So all points to truth. All gates are summarized within OHM. OHM can develop into many gates, and it is the gate to all. OHM is the contraction of the whole world, and the world is the expansion of OHM. OHM as a microcosmos corresponds to the macrocosmos. OHM is related to all elements of the universe.

Woh Hyo's thoughts are supported by many Buddhist sutras (scriptures). The Hwa Yen Sutra is a good example of this. Let us look at the famous formula of Hwa-Yen Sutra:

One in all, all in one.
One is all, all is one.

This shows mutual coarising and interpenetration of all. OHM is the source of all and conclusion of all.

OHM and Hermeneutics

OHM was the content of Won Hyo's enlightenment experience, and was the basis of his life and thoughts. It also served as a foundation for his hermeneutics.

According to Won Hyo, from OHM all branches out, to OHM all roots in. Won Hyo used the hermeneutics of branching out/rooting in (or analysis/synthesis) to expound the text in most of his teachings. Branching out is to unpack the vast array of teachings in a text. Rooting in is to explain how the diverse teachings can be harmonized, how they complement one another, and how they can be synthesized into one root, OHM. Gae/Hap reveals the diverse teachings and essence of the text. Diverse teachings pointing to one essence, OHM.

Won Hyo uses the Gae-Hap approach, for example, in his two largest works. In his *Daesunggisinlonso* (Commentary on the Awakening of Faith), Won

Hyo says, "If the meaning of this treatise 'branches out,' then it has immeasurable, limitless meanings and teachings. If it 'roots in,' then it has as its essence the OHM." In his *Gumgangsammaegyongnon* (Commentary on the Diamond Meditation Sutra), Won Hyo also says,

> The teachings and essence of this scripture have both analytical (or branching out) and synthetic (or rooting in) aspects. Discussed from the standpoint of hap, [the scripture's] essential point is the contemplation practice that has a "single taste" of OHM. Explained from the standpoint of Gae, its fundamental doctrine involves ten types of approaches to Dharma. . . . But even if this scripture is explained in Gae, its ten approaches to Dharma do not add to the "one taste"; even if it is interpreted in Hap, it does not detract from those ten. Neither increase nor decrease is the diverse teachings and essence of this scripture.

Using the Gae/Hap hermeneutical approach, Won Hyo shows both forest (the whole) and trees (parts or details) in his works. Won Hyo typically starts with showing a forest (a general view of the text) and the essential themes of the text. He then goes on to work on his detailed exegesis, chapter by chapter.

CONCLUSION

Won Hyo's life flowered from the root of OHM, and his writings were the footnotes of OHM to which he was enlightened in the cave. Based on his own enlightenment experience and study of OHM, Won Hyo could help bring the same enlightenment to people, and peace to the world.

OHM is our ultimate and universal source of peace and hope and compassion and wisdom as we face our global village in terror and turmoil. OHM-centered meditation, study, and life, as an essential part of holistic education, can transform people to be fully human and to bring peace to their inner and outer world, and to history.

REFERENCES

Note: In addition to the following, there are many books on Won Hyo available in Korean.

Park, Young-Mann. (1999). *Holistic meditation.* Seoul: Eun Sung.
Park, Young-Mann. (2000). *Dr. Park's soul-body discipline.* Seoul: Gyung Sung.
Song, Min-Young. (2001, Sept.). Holistic education and Korean traditional thoughts. *New Education.*

Won Hyo. (1994). Daesunggisinlonso: Commentary on the Awakening of Faith. In *A Collection of Korean Buddhist Books*, vol. 1. Seoul: Dong Guk University Press.

Won Hyo. (1994). Gumgangsammaegyongnon: Commentary to the diamond meditation sutra. In *A Collection of Korean Buddhist Books*, vol. 1. Seoul: Dong Guk University Press.

Won Hyo. (1994). Simmunhwajaengnon: Commentary on ten gates of harmonizing disputes. In *A Collection of Korean Buddhist Books*, vol. 1. Seoul: Dong Guk University Press.

PART 2

Practices

Integrating Self, Soul, and Spirit in the Classroom

CHAPTER 10

Caring Classroom Relationships Take Time and Commitment

One School's Vision of a Holistic Learning Community

GARY BABIUK

INTRODUCTION

Our fast-paced technological society with its focus on the economic aspects of our lives has lost sight in many ways of our human need to develop meaningful relationships with others in our communities. The current approach to business and manufacturing has taken on a tough-minded, global, competitive fervor and this corporate mentality has influenced governments and their social agencies, causing them to try to raise themselves to corporate or business standards. In the last decade our schools have tended to marginalize the humanistic qualities of education for the efficient, back-to-the-basics, bottom-line goals of the corporate agenda. The increase in standardized testing, competitive rankings, and downsizing has placed less emphasis on the caring relationship between teachers, students, and parents so vital to the ultimate goals of education in a democratic society.

Currently most secondary schools are structured like factories, hindering the creation of long-lasting and committed relationships. The building architecture, the yearly passing of students to new teachers, the movement of students through subject specialist teachers, and the division of subjects all tend to keep teachers and students from developing significant relationships. It is the structure and organization of schools, not the individuals in them, which impede the development of caring relationships.

Roland Barth states (1980), "If we want good things to happen in our schools we must start with people—children and teachers—not ideology or minimum competencies" (p. 25). I agree that we need to not only concentrate on teaching our young people the intellectual skills and academic qualifications that are sought after by governments and business but balance this with the development and modeling of caring relationships. After 23 years of experience teaching and administering junior high schools in Alberta, I have concluded that it is the caring relationships among teachers, students, and their parents that are the foundation of the education process.

Over a six-year period (1993–1999) at Jubilee Junior High School[1] in Edson, Alberta, the staff developed a holistic model (Miller, 1993) of a school structure and organization. I was the principal of the school and we worked to develop a school that challenged the traditional hierarchical structure in order to nourish the development of significant relationships and mirror the interconnected and interdependent aspects of society and nature. We developed teams of teachers and students in a way that allowed caring, committed relationships to develop and flourish in order to form a learning community.

The development of long-term relationships would be the key to the creation of a caring learning community. We felt that a change in the structure and organization of the school was needed to provide the time for relationships to be nurtured. Sapon-Shevin (1995) writes:

> Communities don't just happen. No teacher, no matter how skilled or well intentioned, can enter a new classroom and announce, "We are a community." Communities are built over time, through shared experience, and by providing multiple opportunities for students to know themselves, know one another, and interact in positive and supportive ways. (p. 256)

The following is the story of one school's attempt to achieve its vision of a caring learning community.

It all began as I was established as the new principal. In my first year we worked on team building in an atmosphere of ongoing school-based collaborative professional development that was encouraged by the school division. As a result of the trust developed in that first year two teachers came forward with an idea. The foundation of their vision was to organize the school into teams of three teachers and 70 students together in one large classroom. Each team of three teachers was self-chosen. The teachers and students remained together for three years (Grades 7, 8, and 9), also known as "looping." The teachers were responsible for all six core subjects (mathematics, language arts, science, social studies, health and physical education) and they taught them in an integrated style as a "true" team (Babiuk, 1996). "True" means that all three taught together all day long in the same room. Each was responsible to each other and to all of the students. Student evaluation moved away from a grade orientation toward student portfolios and teacher assessments of skills and attitudes presented in a student-led parent-teacher conference. The school jurisdiction had an inclusive policy so all students were integrated. The vision was to build a community of learners in the school that connected with the outside community.

Over a six-year period this team format saw four cohorts work successfully through the complete three-year loop. A story of these teams was the focus of my research (Babiuk, 2000).[2] The changes made to the structure and organization of the school, which centered around giving each team more time together over three years[3] provided a milieu for trusting relationships to grow among the teachers, students, and parents with a resulting increase in caring, commitment, communication, continuity, and collaboration and the nurturing of a community of learners.

CARE AND COMMITMENT

Caring, as explained by Noddings (1984), is characterized by "the commitment to act in behalf of the cared-for, a continued interest in his reality throughout the appropriate time span, and the continual renewal of commitment over this span of time" (p. 16).

Demonstrations of caring by all members of the large-group classroom increased over the three years as there seemed to be time for serious attention to relationships that are more difficult to develop in a few minutes a day in a traditional classroom. Incidents of students assisting and standing up for each other were more evident than in the teachers' previous experience. Students were more willing to share ideas and provide academic assistance, and emotional support increased. Teachers saw the student learning in many subjects and situations and observed both strengths and weaknesses, in a way not possible in the single-subject classroom. This provided a holistic perspective of each student. The development of personal relationships between students and teachers was not seen as possible sources for problems but as a natural and supportive component of a caring classroom. Learning became more personal for students and teachers and the school more inviting for parents as the three years together provided time to get to know each other.

Commitment to the students was developed by the teachers from the beginning as they prepared for three years together, not just one term or year. Teachers endeavored to keep students in the program even through difficult disciplinary situations as they took ownership of this extended relationship. The team had time to develop an in-depth understanding of each student, which impressed parents. As parents observed the teachers' caring and commitment to their children, they reciprocated in kind. Students also sensed their teachers' commitment and took greater responsibility for their actions. Incidents where students acted out or said derogatory things to adults, made easier when they were together for only a few minutes a day, were reduced. All were now part of an extended community and would not be able to leave behind classmates or teachers at the end of the class period or at the end of the year. The students and teachers were now relating with others daily over three years.

The fact that students and teachers were in a classroom for three years allowed them to create and develop their own space. They came to see this classroom as a home base, a safe haven. This was much different from traditional junior high schools, where students move from class to class throughout the day. Even if they have a homeroom or a home group, the relatively short time together each day (20 to 30 minutes) does not permit the deep feelings of safety and comfort that developed in the three-year teaming setting.

Care and commitment for each other formed the foundation for this learning community. Learning and teaching together over the successful three-year period allowed for individuals to take more time to express themselves and to listen to each other. The increased opportunities to share feelings and points of view allowed all to express their individualism but also to see their common beliefs and visions. Modeling of community actions such as problem solving and decision making was an important part of learning about the democratic process. The flexible schedule allowed teachers and students to create their own learning environment at their own pace both in the classroom and in the general or outer community.

Entering the general community and having members of it visit their classroom was expedient as all day, every day was available for presentations by visitors and for students to be involved in community service projects and work-studies. Students could enter the extended community at a moment's notice, as the day was guided by the participants' (both teachers' and students') objectives and in the control of the community of learners. The classroom moved toward what Moffett (1994) called the "Universal Schoolhouse": "Seeing school as the community and the community as a school is the best way to realize all the aims of education, whether these are practical and intellectual or moral and spiritual" (p. 311). There was a sense of belonging by all in the large-group classroom.

COMMUNICATION

All forms of communication improved. Over three years students and parents came to feel more at ease talking with teachers about academic and social problems. Many students began to see their teachers as counselors and guides. Teachers could take individuals or small groups aside to discuss issues, concerns, and problems without disturbing the larger classroom process and could take the time needed to plan for appropriate action. If parents arrived during the day because that was the only time they were free, one team member could meet with them and not leave the remaining students alone. As all three teachers knew each of the students it didn't matter which teacher was free to meet with the parent at that time.

The addition of direct phone lines to the classroom provided instant connection to home and community. Students and teachers could connect with parents whenever necessary and parents could communicate with the classrooms.[4] Each classroom had at least four computers connected to the Internet. This allowed for immediate use of the "Information Highway" and also connected the classroom to the wider community.

Communication also improved with the implementation of student portfolios. The portfolios were more than a collection of the students' best work. It allowed them to outline challenges, areas in need of improvement, gains, celebrations, and goals. Teachers provided anecdotal feedback of each student's progress in becoming effective communicators, competent problem solvers, critical and creative thinkers, collaborative team members, and socially responsible students.[5] Homework, assignment completion, and other social goals were also discussed. In the student-led conference format, students took control and direction of the discussion and ultimately responsibility for their education. The teachers were facilitators and supporters of the student instead of the dispenser of grades. Parents were delighted with their adolescents' involvement in their education. One parent stated with tears in her eyes, "This is the first time I have had a real conversation with my child about school. It's the first time that when I asked her what she was doing in school, she didn't just say, 'nothing.'"

Communication at the staff level improved. This was accomplished by doing away with the hierarchical structure of principal, vice principal, and teacher. We moved into an administrative team format, made up of one principal and one administrative representative from each of the six teams. This administrative team met every two weeks. The administrative representatives (a teacher self-selected from each team) were responsible for the discipline of their students and the supervision of their team. They also took on project portfolios that involved them in activities that were schoolwide (the school newsletter, for example). The total school staff met in alternate weeks.

CONTINUITY

Continuity was ensured with increased daily, weekly, monthly, and yearly contact between teachers and students. Teachers found benefits to this as they did not have to restart at the beginning of every school year—there wasn't the usual first few months of "feeling each other out." Student skills and attitudes were worked on over extended periods of time. Education was viewed as a three-year project. The team of teachers taught all subjects so lessons could extend as long as needed and teachers could complete other lessons or projects at their discretion. There were no more science labs or student presentations left half finished or interrupted by the bell that ended the period. Classroom activities dictated the use of classroom time, not a preset school schedule.

Consistent expectations for student behavior and quality of work lead to greater improvement in both and a feeling of reassurance for teachers, students, and parents about what needed to be done. The three teachers had common classroom observations and experiences during the day, which not only allowed for immediate action to be taken, but also provided a common base of information on which lessons and student interventions could be planned.

COLLABORATION

Built-in collaboration was a result of the three-year experience in teamwork. Professional development was continuous and immediate as lessons were critiqued, planned, and revised, sometimes instantly, as the day unfolded. Each team had common preparation time created while students took optional subjects. The rapport built by teachers with students and parents over the three years allowed them to work collaboratively on solving students' personal problems and planning future educational goals.

There were stresses in the teachers' relationships, but as professionals they were able to work them out and grow from the experience. The modeling to students of teachers participating as a team and problem solving together was a daily occurrence. All teachers widened their experience with different subject matter, as mathematics teachers taught social studies and language arts teachers worked in science. Professional development was ongoing with personal support, they didn't have to occur after school or on weekends. The team was constantly meeting to develop lessons, consult with parents, and create exciting learning opportunities.

OTHER BENEFITS

There were many other benefits from this arrangement. One was flexibility to plan the length and venue of lessons. It was not necessary to check with other teachers, who in the traditional situation would be expecting the students next period. When teachers were ill, the substitute was not left alone but became a member of the existing team. The regular program continued without the possible lost time of having a "fill-in" lesson. The ill teacher was not burdened with creating lessons while not feeling well. If a student needed to be removed from class because of an emotional or discipline problem, one teacher took the student out of the class and dealt with the problem immediately and got the student back to class as soon as possible, unlike the traditional situation where a student was sent to the principal's office to be dealt with at a later time. Again the rest of the students were not left alone but carried on with the lesson. Students who were absent for a while or were new to the school were tutored and caught up by one teacher while the rest of the class carried on. Flexible grouping was possible in all subject and skill areas.

Academic results did not suffer. The results of Grade 9 students in the large group were compared with those of the students in the traditional classrooms on the Provincial Achievement Tests (PATs).[6] During the first four years the results for the large group students were equal or better than the traditional classroom students, and significantly higher for the second team. The relationship between the teachers and students after three years seemed to affect the students' commitment to do well on the tests, even though tests had not been a central part of their studies. On the whole, the large group Grade 9 students seemed to try harder as observed by the teachers in relation to previous traditional classrooms. The large group teachers saw an improvement in the overall quality of student work compared to their previous students' classroom work. When the high school teachers received the graduates of the large group, they commented on the improved skills and attitudes toward learning in comparison to previous students.

CONCERNS

Things did not always work out neatly and quickly. It was a process, a journey into developing a new kind of classroom. The change distressed some parents. Some did not wait long enough to see the caring and committed relationships develop between students and teachers. Some parents had difficulties with the change process and felt the perceived confusion and noise of the large classroom was not beneficial. They felt their child would be lost in the large group format, though the opposite was usually true.[7] It was difficult to outline the varied benefits to these parents as their classroom experience was gained in a traditional teaching situation from the student's point of view.

In the third year of the implementation process, a group of parents lobbied the school board for a return to a traditional junior high school format. In the ensuing turmoil, the town hall meeting was the usual form of communication, which exacerbated the lack of dialogue and tended to disintegrate into shouting matches. However, after a few months a compromise was developed. A dual track school was created, with parents choosing between a large-group classroom and three traditional-style classrooms.[8] As well—and this was probably the main reason for the turmoil—grades were partially reinstated. Student evaluation became a combination of portfolios presented in student-led conferences and graded report cards.

The dual-track system of traditional or large-group classrooms was in effect for the last three years of the six in which large-group classrooms were present in the school. However, it was a challenge to operate the school because of the different underlying philosophies and visions of the large group team format and the traditional classroom. But for those parents and students who remained in the large-group classroom, the three years of junior high were less traumatic and the caring and commitment allowed for trust to develop, for the ultimate benefit of students.

The increase in caring, commitment, communication, continuity, and collaboration in the large-group classroom built trust and support for all involved. The use of extensive looping (three years), block timetabling (full day together), team teaching (three teachers in the same room, working together with one group of students), an integrated curriculum, alternate student assessment such a student portfolios, and community building both inside and outside of the classroom contributed to the development of supportive relationships. It was an attempt "to educate community-builders—people who will be faithful to each other—people who will have a sense of efficacy, a belief that their own effort coupled with that of others can achieve something" (Noddings, 1986, p. 500).

I believe the insights gained in developing a caring learning community during this large-group team teaching at Jubilee School must become a priority for public education in order to prepare our students to meet the societal challenges of the new millennium.

NOTES

1. Jubilee had a student population of approximately 500 in three grades, and a staff of 25 teachers and 9 paraprofessionals. It served the needs of an extended community of approximately 12,000.

2. The results are a synthesis of my lived experience as principal for eight years and three years of taped interviews with teachers, students, and parents. It is also the subject of my unpublished doctoral thesis at the Ontario Institute for Studies in Education of the University of Toronto, 2000.

3. No extra time or money was added and the student/teacher ratio was the same as before the changes.

4. Incoming telephone calls are directed through the main office to help reduce disruption in classroom activities.

5. A community-based strategic planning team established these district-wide student exit outcomes in 1994.

6. PATs are standardized Province of Alberta exams based on the curriculum in social studies, science, mathematics, and language arts. They are administered in Grades 3, 6, and 9 each June.

7. Students who move from class to class, teacher to teacher, every 50 minutes or so, moving through crowded hallways to and from their lockers can get

lost in the movement and it is difficult to track their schoolwork across subjects on a daily basis.

8. Jubilee Junior High School is the only junior high school for the seven elementary schools in the community. The typical yearly enrollment in Grade 7 was 150 students, or six classes of 25 students.

REFERENCES

Babiuk, G. E. (1996). The turbulent waters of change. Journey through integrated curriculum. *Orbit, 39*(1), 4–7.

Babiuk, G. E. (2000). *Holistic changes in school structure and organization.* Unpublished doctoral thesis, University of Toronto, Ontario.

Barth, R. S. (1980). *Run school run.* Cambridge, MA: Harvard University Press.

Miller, J. P. (1993). *The holistic curriculum.* Toronto: OISE Press.

Moffett, J. (1994). *The universal schoolhouse: Spiritual awakening through education.* San Francisco: Jossey-Bass.

Noddings, N. (1984). *Caring: A Feminine approach to ethics and moral education.* Berkeley: University of California Press.

Noddings, N. (1984). Fidelity in teaching, teacher education, and research for teaching. *Harvard Educational Review, 56*(4), 496–510.

Sapon-Shevin, M. (1995). Building a safe community for learning. In W. Ayers (Ed.), *To become a teacher: Making a difference in children's lives.* New York: Teachers College Press.

CHAPTER 11

Interface of Holistic Changes in Japanese Schools and Waldorf Education

ATSUHIKO YOSHIDA

INTRODUCTION: BETWEEN THE WEST AND THE EAST

The main theme of the 2nd Holistic Learning conference (1999, Toronto) was "Interfaces of the Outer Work and the Inner Work in Educational Practice." Rudolf Steiner (1983), founder of the Waldorf schools, described this interface in the context of Western civilization and Eastern life as:

> Looking at the East, Western man—the man of recent civilization in general—receives the impression of dream-like spiritual life. Modern spiritual life is used to sharply delineated concepts, closely linked to *external* observation; in contrast . . . [the Eastern] concepts were not gained by examining external data, that is analytically, but emerged from an *inwardly* experienced and apprehended spiritual life. (p. 67)

With my experience in the holistic education movement in Japan and with Waldorf education in Toronto, I would like to explore this theme of the interface between the West and the East. The central questions here are:

- In general, how can Waldorf education developed in central Europe be adapted to other cultures?
- More specifically, how can I bring some practical experiences in Waldorf Education from a multicultural city, Toronto, into a Japanese context to transform education?
- Can Steiner's theory of human development and evolution be applied to education in the East (Japan)?

129

AT THE TURNING POINT:
THE CURRENT STATE OF JAPANESE SCHOOLS

Balancing Inward Cultivation with the Outward Schooling

It is said that traditional native values in the East, including Japan have been connected with inwardly experienced spiritual life. On the other hand, in general, the modern school system imported to Japan from the West can be characterized by the "outward" economical and political values that are directly useful in modern industry. Japanese schools in the 20th century were effectively organized to catch up with Western Europe and the United States as quickly as possible.

But the important point here is that education can only be effective when formal school systems have been balanced with the informal spiritual education traditionally supported by family and community culture. In other words, the imported Western school system has been balanced with traditional Eastern culture. If you look only at the school system, you will fail to see the whole picture of education in Japan. It is only a half-truth that Japanese education has been intellectual, judgmental, and competition centered. This is true of schooling but it is not true of Japanese education as a whole, including informal education rooted in a cooperative and spiritual culture. It can be said that inward spirituality in Japanese education has been working in an invisible, informal way.

The End of Modernization Aimed at Catching up with Western Civilization

Education was previously effective in Japan because the formal school system was balanced with informal education (cultivation) within family and community culture focusing on inward spiritual and soulful development. However, since modernization, education has lost this balance. These days family and community culture is decreasing and is less influential in modern society. Since the late 1980s, when industrialization was achieved and informal cultural and spiritual cultivation became less and less influential, serious problems have arisen in the school system. For example, the number of school dropouts was over 120,000 in 1999. Therefore, Japanese schools in the 21st century need to take a different role: they need holistic change to integrate soulful, inward values as part of the core curriculum.

Nowadays not only holistic teachers but also administrators in the Japanese ministry of education seem to be becoming aware of this need. In 2002 the ministry of education decreed that the new curriculum would emphasize integrated learning and whole-person activities that include the hands, heart, and head.

The three key words of the government reform plan of 2002 are *kokoro-no-kyoiku* (education for the heart and soul), *sogo-gakushyu* (integrated learning), and *tokushyoku, koseika* (the uniqueness of each school as well as of the individual person). Each individual school will be given more latitude to decide its own curriculum.

These three concepts support the development of holistic and Waldorf education in Japan. Indeed, from the holistic point of view, so-called integrated learning is not enough and Japanese educators would like to include more spiritual elements, but this is still a good opportunity to develop holistic education in Japan. Although it is impossible to introduce any specific religion in public schools in Japan, we can develop soulful schools by reviving and sustaining our spiritual folk culture. For instance, we can connect with spiritual events in communities. We are now at a turning point, moving toward holistic changes, and this entails both great risk and opportunity.

Increasing Interest in Waldorf Education

Interest in Rudolph Steiner and Waldorf education is expanding in Japan. A large number of books by Steiner have been translated into Japanese, including several on education. There are 58 books by Japanese authors on anthroposophy and Waldorf education (38 on education), and Japanese translations of 62 books on these topics (31 on education).

Powerful initiatives for Waldorf education are increasing. The Anthroposophical Society was founded in Japan in the mid-1980s. There is a Steiner school in Tokyo and some initiatives for starting Waldof schools in Kyoto, Hiroshima, and Hokkaidou. The Center for Promoting the Establishment of Steiner Schools in Japan was founded in 1998. There are many Waldorf-inspired teachers in public education in Japan.

However, there have also been quite a few problems in the development of Waldorf education in Japan due to the complexity of political, economical, and cultural issues. Indeed, the political and economic situations are still big problems, but at least there have been gradual changes toward a more supportive environment, as mentioned above.

WALDORF EDUCATION: CULTIVATION IN TUNE WITH THE ESSENCE OF CULTURE

I think the most important issue today for Waldorf education is cultural especially the difference in cultural and spiritual backgrounds between the West and the East. In other words, it would be impossible to import Waldorf without adapting it to the local culture. However it is very difficult to identify the universal principals underlying cultural differences.

Practical Experiences in a Waldorf School in a Multicultural City

In this sense, it is very interesting to witness multicultural challenges in the Waldorf school in downtown Toronto, the Alan Howard Waldorf School, where I have been taking part as a parent, assistant, and researcher. The following are examples from Grade 2–3 classes.

The school holds many kinds of celebrations and rituals from different cultures—Chinese Moon festival, Irish Halloween, Advent (Christianity), Japanese New Year celebration, Ukrainian Easter, Hebrew harvest festival, and so on—without emphasizing only Christianity, for example, changing the word *Maria* into *Gaia* in a Christmas verse. Students also explore the universal significance of each celebration, for example, they celebrate Halloween as the communion with souls of the dead, as well as Bon Festival from Japan and other Buddhist cultures. Students share fairy tales from different cultures in relation to integrated learning. For example, the Japanese fairly tale "Crane Wife" is told as a story, followed by writing impressions, crafts (origami), and painting cranes. Finally, the school teaches the creation myth of the Old Testament in Grade 3 along with dancing eurythmy in three languages, Hebrew, English, and Japanese. Other creation myths such as the ancient Japanese myth of *Kojkiki* are introduced.

Through such experiences in Waldorf education in Toronto, I rediscovered the significance of Japanese spiritual and cultural values. I had not been fully aware of their meanings, but thanks to Waldorf education, I have become more aware of these values. I realized that we are not too late to revive the cultural and spiritual ways which have been devalued in modern civilization.

REDISCOVERING THE INNER SPIRITUAL ROOTS IN EACH CULTURE

I appreciate Steiner and Waldorf education for the insights they bring in seeing the spiritual core of different cultures. I have already asked, How can the Waldorf education developed in Central Europe be adapted to other cultures? Now I would like to answer in general: through rediscovering the inner spiritual roots and their expressions in one's own culture with the essential insights that Waldorf education and anthroposophy offer.

More specifically, how can I bring practical experiences in Waldorf education into the Japanese context to transform our schools? First, inspired by Waldorf education, we need to discover the Japanese ways within our rich traditions to cultivate the body-mind-spirit. Second, we should try to revive the spiritual and cultural ways by bringing them into integrated learning. Then, what are these cultivation ways? I believe that they include "the Way of Art"(in Zen tradition), fairy tales, folk crafts, myths, rituals, folk songs, dances, and so on. The art of calligraphy is one of the best examples of this type of cultivation, as shown below.

An Example: The Art of Calligraphy

In Waldorf 1st grade education, the letters of the alphabet are taught through artistic experience (Steiner, 1919/1997). To learn the letters it is not only important to memorize the form of characters, but also to experience how the characters were created in human history, and to learn that characters have a life in those who are writing them. The way that Japanese approach calligraphy, especially for writing Chinese characters, is very similar to the Waldorf way of teaching letters. Here I would like to share my experience of the art of calligraphy.

In the 1998 fall term, I enrolled in a Japanese calligraphy course at the Rudolf Steiner Center in Toronto. Through this experience I learned what it means to write letters or characters in depth. The process was as follows.

First of all, we make black ink by scraping an ink stick on a stone dish. In a quiet room, we are scraping and pulling the ink stick very slowly. The sound of the stick is rhythmical. The aroma of ink rises. We pay attention to it. We are getting relaxed, without thinking. Simply, I devote myself to this movement, just like meditation.

One day in the course, I was writing the character for river, *kawa* in Japanese. I cannot forget my experience of that day. *Kawa* is made with three vertical lines. One stroke, two strokes, three strokes. When I finished the third stroke, I recognized a strong feeling that remained in my body. I stopped and put the brush down, and went into that feeling. It was similar to a feeling in my palm which I remembered from canoeing in the wildness north of Toronto a month earlier. The beautiful scene came back. I closed my eyes with this image. And again I wrote *Kawa* with a brush as if I was paddling with the flow of the river. In the left sidestroke the water flows with a paddle (brush). In the middle stroke, I hold the water and stop the brush. For the third, I sink the paddle deep down, holding the heavy water for the longest stroke. I push it all the way down.

I felt the *Kawa* character written in this way came alive, as if flowing in front of me. I encountered the vital life of the *Kawa* character in this way. Since that, the experience of writing *Kawa* has become totally different for me. The character is no longer an object outside myself, it is something living within. In other words, a loving connection was born between the character and myself. After this event occurred, I wrote the letter for "fire," after gazing at a fire for a long while. And I wrote the character for "mountain" by remembering the beautiful mountains in my hometown that I had looked at every day in my teens.

Through these experiences I started to learn how powerful it is to write a character. As soon as the characters unfold their life, they unfold the soul, not only in me, but also in all the souls of the people who lived and wrote this character throughout Japanese history. Through the handwriting, you can connect to all the souls that have existed in the past or, in other words, folk souls.

In the process of forming a character throughout folk history, so many various people wrote and used the character with their love and soul. That is why the character was created and why it has survived. Every time somebody writes the character, it can express their own spirit and culture.

The characters and the handwriting are one form of the culture, a way of expressing the spiritual and cultural. There is so much depth in each culture. The important point is whether we have insight to see the inner depth.

That is what Waldorf education is trying to support and nurture. This is the most important idea to adapt from Waldorf education to other cultures, including those of the East. And this example also suggests how to develop Waldorf-inspired education in Japan.

FURTHER QUESTIONS: EXPLORING THE THIRD WAY BETWEEN THE WEST AND THE EAST

> Yet it would be wrong to say that the Oriental did not observe nature. His organs were finely attuned to its observation. For him, however, from everything that he faithfully observed and lovingly honored as a replica, something of the spirit shone. Nature revealed spirit to him, shone spirit upon him at every turn. And this spirit was his reality. (R. Steiner, 1927/1983, p. 74)

As the experience with the river and calligraphy has shown, I appreciate Steiner's insight in helping me to understand my experience. I have been enjoying these valuable practices and insights through Waldorf education. On the other hand, one big question has been troubling me. While Waldorf education was founded to such an extent upon a Western view of human development and evolution, (R. Steiner, 1919/1996), I wonder if these theories of human development are useful in the East.

Specifically, I feel difficulty in accepting the theory which suggests that the independent ego (or I) must be established before further spiritual development. Steiner (1919/1943) wrote:

> The Eastern view is exactly the opposite. The Oriental remains, in a sense, at the level of childhood, not allowing his astral body and ego to plunge down into the physical and etheric bodies although at the present epoch it is fore-ordained that humanity should do so. (p. 85)

It is true that ego (or I) in the East (or at least in Japan) is very unique, we might say weak, but I am not sure that we should say it is at the level of childhood. We know very wise elders without I-Ego who are very respected. The Eastern ego develops through a different process from the Western idea.

For instance, the word *I* can be translated into many words in Japanese (*watashi, boku, ore, shyousei,* and so on) depending on the various relationships or context. The concept of "I" is very contextual and is not independent. During the process of modernization to catch up with the Western world, many Japanese people, including myself, thought that this showed a weakness because "I" does not have strong independence. But nowadays I do not believe in the necessity of lessening dependence on others in order to develop as an individual human being with freedom. Is it necessary to be totally independent first to develop as a mature human being? Is it possible to be free of any relationships without interdepending on each other? Steiner (1927/1983) writes:

> But the experience of such a world would never have created in human development the impulse to freedom. When man feels closely linked to the spiritual world, he feels at the same time inwardly determined by and dependent on it. Therefore he and his conciseness had to move out of it and, for a passing phase of history (in which we now are), to turn to a world of mere fact. . . . This was necessary for man's experience of freedom, which is something that has only been attained in the West and in recent civilization. (p. 76)

What do "independent" or "freedom" mean, exactly? I can not answer this here. What seems sure is that they mean different things for the cultures of the West and East. We can learn from each other, both West and East; we can explore a third way between East and West for our future evolution. It might be very good to conclude this exploration with the following quotation from Steiner (1927/1983):

> If we are to reach an understanding of these [East and West] two diametrically opposed world-pictures, we need a philosophy that combines them and not just adds them together mechanically, one that will develop through its own inner life, not from the one or the other, but in a spiritual progression from human substance itself. (p. 78)

REFERENCES

Steiner, R. (1927/1983). *The tension between east and west*. New York: Anthoroposophic Press.

Steiner, R. (1919/1943). *The problems of our time*. New York: Anthoroposophic Press.

Steiner, R. (1919/1997). *Practical advice to teachers*. New York: Anthoroposophic Press.

Steiner, R. (1919/1996). *The foundations of human experience*. New York: Anthoroposophic Press.

CHAPTER 12

Remembering the Past, Celebrating the Present, and Imagining the Future

The Storytelling Project at Lord Dufferin Public School

MARNI BINDER

INTRODUCTION

The stories people tell have a way of taking care of them. If stories come to you, care for them. And learn to give them away where they are needed. Sometimes a person needs a story more than food to stay alive. That is why we put these stories in each other's memories. This is how people care for themselves.

—Barry Lopez, *Crow and Weasel*

The Storytelling Project was presented at the Holistic Conference: Breaking New Ground, 2001 in Toronto. Stories were read, artwork was shown, resources were displayed and discussions were held. This retelling reflects the spirit of my original presentation at the conference.

Lord Dufferin Public School is in the inner city of Toronto, in a neighborhood called Regent Park. There are approximately 600 Junior Kindergarten–Grade 8 students from diverse backgrounds and cultures (e.g., Chinese, Vietnamese, Tamil, Somali). Non–English-speaking students comprise 70% of this school. Issues of poverty and at times violence intrude into the life of the community. It is also a community that has tremendous pride and is becoming empowered to take back the neighborhood.

Lord Dufferin is an extremely busy school, with a hard-working staff that looks for a variety of ways to provide a creative, challenging, and inclusive environment for learning. When the idea for the Storytelling project was brought forth to the staff, much excitement was generated. At the time I was teaching a Senior Kindergarten, Grade 1, and Grade 2 class. For me, it was a wonderful journey. I watched children gain confidence and feel pride when telling their personal stories. The talk in the classroom was rich and extended into the students' drawings, writing, and reading. As their teacher, I gained tremendous insight into the personal worlds of these children.

This storytelling project allowed participating students, staff, and parents to share their personal stories with others, honoring the diversity and commonalities that lie within us all. By remembering the past, we all were able to celebrate the present. This union of spirits allowed us to imagine a future for all where understanding the texts of experience provides a sense of hope and harmony.

STORYTELLING AND SPIRITUAL LITERACY

Historically, telling stories has been socially and culturally embedded around the world. Stories were and are told to teach a lesson and make meaning of the world and life's very existence in the universe. The desire to tell stories is innate and tantamount to our existence. We share and reshare our life's experiences and understandings. Knowledge is constructed, often through the stories we tell and retell.

Frederic Brussat and Mary Ann Brussat (1996) define spiritual literacy as "the ability to read the signs written in the texts of our own experience" (p. 1). Spiritual literacy is meaning making and at the core of our existence in defining our place at a local, global, and universal level. Our meaning making is embedded in stories. These stories arise from our inner landscape and shape who we are, where we came from, and where we may go.

The Storytelling Project at Lord Dufferin deepened my understanding of the importance of meaning making for children and extended this knowledge into a larger vision of community. Sanders (1994) states that "stories spring from emotional roots that grow as large underground as the stories we hear above. Everytime a child rattles one off, he taps deep into those emotional roots, for the stories get told from the inner senses out" (p. 46).

THE STORYTELLING PROJECT

Booth and Barton (2000) write, "We humans are storytelling animals. The drive to story is basic in all people and exists in all cultures. Stories shape our lives and our culture—we cannot seem to live without them" (p. 7). Through the Storytelling Project, students, staff, and parents at Lord Dufferin were reawakened to the essential need for personal stories to be heard and honored. For the teachers, insight was provided into the world of the students they taught and the community they worked in. The students attained an understanding of themselves and of each other. For the parents of our community, there was an inclusive and celebratory feeling through the sharing and resharing of the stories.

The project itself took place over two years. Approximately 10 to 12 classes from JK-8 participated. It took a tremendous amount of commitment and work. The experience was beyond our expectations.

Phase 1 (1997–1998)

A series of stages led to a storytelling festival. Professional development was significant in assisting teachers in understanding the importance of storytelling and how it could be used in the classroom. Presentations using First Steps,[1] children's books, and a storytelling package composed by our vice-principal, Helen Bryce, provided a comprehensive curriculum foundation. A visit from Bob Barton, a professional storyteller who works with educators, provided staff with a wealth of information and ideas on how to initiate and implement storytelling in the classroom.

Professional storytellers visited the classrooms. Each participating class had at least two storytellers come in and share stories with the children. This provided role modeling for staff and students.

The next step was where we, as a staff, took a risk in developing our own skills. We each chose a story (for example, a legend) and practiced it. We then went into another classroom to tell the story. Again this provided role modeling for the students. The most important fact was that the students saw us telling stories. If we could take risks, so could they.

A letter was sent home to the parents in a variety of languages to discuss the project and the storytelling component. There was a session for parents on the importance of storytelling in learning. The parents were asked to tell their children a story to memorize, or the student could choose a favorite tale to retell.

The storytelling festival lasted a whole day. To begin the festival, a Grade 4/5 class had written an integrated arts story combining the visual arts, drama, movement, and music. They performed their work for participating classes. Afterward, the children, who had been divided into small heterogeneous groups ranging from JK–8, rotated through participating classrooms telling their stories.

I can remember how frightened some of my SK/1/2 students were about going into other classrooms but they rose to the occasion and were wonderful. Many retold favorite fairytales and a few actually told stories from home. I remember a particular Grade 2 child's story entitled, A *Story about My Parents*:

In January 1987, my dad left Sri Lanka to come to Canada. When he came to Toronto, he lived at 142 Wellesley St. My dad had two jobs, one in the day and one in the night. During the day he worked at a car company. At night he worked in a knitting factory making socks. My dad met my mom in the sock factory. She worked there too. On August 28, 1989, my dad and my mom got married. On April 12th, 1990, I was born. That was a happy day for my mom and dad.

Phase 2 (1998–1999)

In this next phase, oral stories were extended into writing. The staff was provided with professional development again. David Booth came to talk about storytelling, writing, and literacy. He validated what we were already doing and inspired us to move further, delving deeper into our practice.

The students went home and brought back family stories to tell. Many of the stories were written in their first language and had to be translated into English. An important piece was the illustration process. Mark Thurman, an artist and illustrator of children's books and a graduate of our school, worked with a representation of students from Grades 2–8. These amazing illustrations provided the aesthetic complement to the written work and extended the stories into what I call "visual literacy." *Family Stories from Lord Dufferin* was published in June 1999.

Following are some of the published stories.

Why My Family Came to Canada

When my mother was in Cambodia, she was only a little girl. My mom lived in a big house in Cambodia and she would work very hard to buy food for her mother and father. My dad lived in Cambodia too, but when he was 4 years old he moved to Thailand with his family.

In 1971, in Cambodia, there was a war between Vietnam and Cambodia. People were killed and people were hurt badly during the war. My dad's and my mom's family moved to Canada in 1983 to get away from the war.

My mom and dad went to different highschools when they were only 16 years old. My mom liked sports and my dad also liked playing sports. When my mom was 19 years old and my dad was 23 years old they got married and had 3 beautiful kids named Joanne, the oldest, Johnnie, the second oldest and Alex the youngest. We live very happily together.

—Grade 7 student

Me and My Sisters

Me and my sisters do our homework. Then sometimes we could watch TV. Sometimes we are nice to each other. Sometimes we don't like playing Barbie dolls. When we are done our homework, we look at the stars. We would say together, "In the sky, in the sky."

The stars look like they are a window so all the people who died in my family are looking down at us, like my sister Dannila, my great grandmother and grandfather and people too.

When we eat grapes and we find a baby grape, we would say this one is for Dannila and throw it up to the sky. We would never see the grapes come down, so we think she grabs them and eats them up.

I love my sister Dannila and so does Leasha. We believe in God and that's the end of my story.

—Grade 2 student

The Hungry Alligator

Many, many years ago, when my grandfather was still alive, he used to work in the canals near the sugar cane fields in Guyana. He and his partner used to work very hard cleaning weeds and grass out of the canals.

No people lived back in around the fields and there was no access to transportation or anything else. So every morning, trucks would come around to take everyone to work and then take them all back home in the evening.

One day, my grandfather went to work with the other men as usual. He worked all day and when it was almost time to go home, he had just a small area left in the canal to clean out. The rest of the workers were finished their jobs and were getting ready to head for the trucks when they heard my grandfather screaming in fear and pain.

They rushed to water and found an alligator attacking him. As they pulled him out, the angry alligator pranced around. My poor grandfather nearly died that day. He was bleeding alot from all his wounds. When the truck arrived, he was taken to the hospital.

Grandfather couldn't walk for weeks and he was scared for a long time from his experience but he was thankful to be still alive.

—Grade 4 student

The Four Seasons

SPRING: My grandma and my great grandma plant seeds to grow Chinese vegetables.

SUMMER: My grandma brings my cousins and I to swimming lessons. My mommy and daddy take us on vacations to places like Canada's Wonderland, the CNE, Centre Island and the park.

FALL: I look forward to school and my birthday. I have a birthday party at school and at home.

WINTER: My aunties take me skating and tobogganing. Christmas is usually at one of my auntie's houses. Christmas presents are opened at midnight on Christmas Eve. My seven aunties always buy me a lot of presents.

—SK student, as told to her mother

The Gulf War

When I was about 6 years old there was a war in Saudi Arabia. The war's name was the Gulf War.

One night when my family was sleeping, somebody called in our home and told us a war was going on and they are going to shoot bombs at our house if the lights are on. Then we turned off our lights. We put this stuff in our windows because if they shoot the bomb, the gas will come inside the house. Then the next morning my dad went to his job and he called us and told us to take the stuff out of the window.

—Grade 5 student

My Story

In 1990 there was a war in my country Somalia. For the first time I saw war and heard guns. One day I was in school and our house was blown up. My brother, my mom and I were lucky because we weren't in there. But my aunt and one of my friends were in there and they died. So when our house blew up, we had to move to Kenya and it was peaceful there. The last time I heard a gun was when I left my country.

After one year we came to Canada and we were lucky. But our dad was even more lucky because he didn't see the war or hear the guns. I hope they stop the war and it gets peaceful like in Canada, so we could go back and see our family.

—Grade 7 student

Meguido Zola (1999) tells us:

To story in the teaching-and-learning exchange, is thus to create a space. By space, I mean at once the tone of the classroom, the framework that the teacher scaffolds around the children and what they are learning, the ethos of the learning community. (p. 4)

The ethos of our learning community at Lord Dufferin was extended beyond the classroom. The stories became a transformative and empowering construct of the community's lived experiences.

Phase 3 (1999)

This was an unexpected phase of the project. The owner of a local art gallery heard about the artwork and wanted to show the pieces with the students' stories. We had a gallery opening and showing! The opening night was very special and meaningful.

The students whose stories and artwork were represented came with their parents and siblings. Staff and students and other parents attended. There was much excitement and pride.

The coordinator of visual arts and the director of accountability from the Toronto District School Board were also invited to this opening. This led to phase 4.

Phase 4: The Video (2002)

The board wanted the project documented on video so that other schools could use our experience to do similar work in their schools. The video is entitled, *The Storytelling Project: Our Community Speaks.* I had the privilege, with a few other key professionals involved in the project, to take part in the final stages, giving input for content, style, and editing. This short video is an educational piece that reflects the passion and commitment of all who were involved. The community voice of students, parents, and teachers emerges strongly, as do the eloquent words of the professionals who supported the project. Visually moving and artistic, this video reflects the importance of storytelling as a significant curricular piece for educational practice.

REFLECTIONS

This experience was one of the most rewarding times in my teaching career. It was truly a holistic experience, as a true sense of community was formed. The stories in many cases reflected the struggles of immigrating to a new land. Some were of violence in the neighborhood. There were also stories of joy.

Whatever the story, there was a transformation in the personal and social growth of many of these students through allowing their voices to be heard and honored. One story relayed to me was of a Grade 8 student who really did not want to partake in the art aspect of the project. He felt that he couldn't represent his story in visual images. Through support from his teacher and a resource staff member, this student forged ahead with the art and produced an amazing piece of work. His teacher observed a significant change in the student after. He was more confident and felt appreciative that he was able to tell his family story. This student's inner landscape emerged. This is spiritual literacy.

There was a change for all who took part in the project. Teachers continued to use storytelling in the classroom. Students were eager to share their stories. A sense of spirit and union unfolded between staff and the families. The pride that was felt by the school was significant and strengthened our ties to each other.

I observed the children I teach exude such joy and confidence. The telling of stories had always been an important part of my classroom program. This project gave it a deeper dimension.

The storytelling project is an excellent model for holistic practice in education. All areas of holistic learning were touched: intellectual, physical, emotional, and spiritual. It also allowed teachers to understand that the expectations of a standardized curriculum can be addressed in a creative and soulful way. A "curriculum for the inner life" (Miller, 2000, p. 49) develops spiritual literacy. The storytelling project shaped this process.

Storytelling is the oldest form of education. This project was a way of preserving, sharing, and celebrating the wisdom of all members of our learning community. All who took part cherished this moment in time. We continually retell our stories from the experience and relate to the stories of others. As Larry Swartz (1999) would say, "The best response to a story is another story" (p. 14).

NOTES

I would like to acknowledge and thank Helen Bryce and Dinny Biggs who allowed me to share this special project at the conference and in this chapter. I would also like to thank the staff, students, and parents of Lord Dufferin who worked so hard to make the Storytelling Project so special. It is a privilege to be able to share this wonderful experience with others.

1. First Steps is a language program from Australia. It provides developmental continuums, assessments, and ideas in the areas of oracy, writing, reading and spelling. At this stage we focused on the oral language component and the use of narrative.

REFERENCES

Booth, D., & Barton, B. (2000). *Story works: How teachers can use shared stories in the new curriculum*. Markham, ON: Pembrooke Publishers.

Brussat, F., & Brussat, M.A. (1996). *Spiritual literacy: Reading the sacred in everyday life*. New York: Scribner.

Lord Dufferin P. S. (1999). *Family stories from Lord Dufferin P.S.* Toronto, ON: Toronto District School Board.

Miller, J. P. (2000). *Education and the soul*. Albany: State University of New York Press.

Sanders, B. (1994). *A is for ox*. New York: Pantheon Books.

The storytelling project: Our community speaks. [video] (2002). Toronto, ON: Toronto District School Board. For information, contact Helen Bryce, Principal, Earl Grey Public School, Toronto, ON. E-mail: helen.bryce@tdsb.on.ca. Phone: 416-393-9545. E-mail: marnibinder@utoronto.ca.

Swartz, L. (1999). The best response to a story is another story. *ORBIT: Story Matters: The Role of Story in School, 30*(3), 14–17.

Zola, M. (1999). To story is to create space. *ORBIT: Story Matters: The Role of Story in School, 30*(3), 4–7.

CHAPTER 13

Journal Writing in Mathematics Education

Communicating the Affective Dimensions of Mathematics Learning

RINA COHEN

Journal writing has recently become an important tool in mathematics class-rooms, particularly in elementary schools and in preservice teacher education. This versatile tool helps broaden the scope of math education to include not only the cognitive dimensions of math learning but also the affective compo-nents. This helps make math learning more meaningful for the learners and gets them more personally involved with math. Learners are often encouraged to include not only text but also pictures and diagrams in their journals (Stix, 1994), which appeals particularly to younger students and visual learners. Jour-nal writing in math class is also one of the components of curriculum integration (Bean, 1995), where math is integrated with language arts, including various oral and written communication activities as well as the reading of math story-books (Elliot & Kenney, 1996).

Journal entries can deal with math content or process, as well as with stu-dents' ideas, experiences, attitudes, and feelings in relation to math. Each type of journal entry has potential benefits associated with it. For instance, asking stu-dents to write learning logs describing their ideas about or experiences with math concepts, procedures, or activities helps them clarify new material and deepens their understanding of math. As well, getting learners to reflect on and evaluate their own problem-solving processes helps improve their problem-solv-ing skills. In addition, math journals provide important diagnostic information for the teachers which allows them to adjust their programs accordingly, as well as respond to individual student needs (Burns, 1995; Cohen, 2000; Countryman, 1992; Edwards, 1999; Elliot & Kenney, 1996).

145

Journal writing in math can also be used as a personal reflection tool for gaining new insights and for therapeutic benefits (Tobias, 1993). Within a supportive learning environment and with a caring teacher, learners feel free to express their attitudes toward and feelings about math, both positive and negative. This often allows them to develop new perspectives on math and improve their attitudes. This chapter is concerned with the latter use of math journals as tools for personal reflection and for the expression and sharing of emotions, attitudes, beliefs, and experiences in relation to math learning.

The chapter, which is based on my 1999 presentation at the Holistic Learning Conference, will describe two different applications of journal writing in math education. Use of journal writing as a personal reflection tool for adult math learners will first be illustrated by describing a combined activity of guided visualization and journal writing that I conducted in the first part of the conference workshop. Similar activities are sometimes used in preservice and in-service teacher training. The second part will deal with an application of journal writing in a Grade 7 classroom. Implementation of journal writing in a unit on fractions will be described, including the teacher's journal prompts before, during, and after the unit and the students' responses, focusing mainly on their expression of feelings, beliefs, and attitudes in relation to their learning.

THE PERSONAL MATH AUTOBIOGRAPHY ACTIVITY

The conference presentation started with a guided visualization dealing with participants' mathematical history, immediately followed by meditative journal writing. Prior to the visualization, participants prepared their own notebooks or sheets of paper I distributed along with pen or pencil on the desk in front of them.

The guided visualization, done with very soft (new age) music in the background and with dim lights, started by guiding participants to sit comfortably, close their eyes, focus on breathing, and relax physically, mentally, and emotionally. After several minutes of that, participants were guided to go back in time to their earliest years in school, to recall their school, their teachers, peers, and so on and finally get in touch with their earliest memories in relation to math. How did they feel about math at that time? And how did they do in math? How did the teacher teach math? Did the teacher seem to enjoy teaching it? And how did the teacher treat them?

Participants were then guided to gradually go up in grade levels, from primary school, to junior level, then intermediate, then high school and college or university if applicable. For each level they were instructed to recall with as much detail as possible: the teachers who taught them math, the classroom environment, their peers, and any math-related memories they might have, and they were guided through a series of questions similar to those above.

As soon as they reached the end of their math schooling experiences, participants were asked to start writing in their notebooks while keeping their eyes still half closed and staying in a meditative state. They were encouraged to write very informally, as if they were talking to someone sharing their experience. The soft music was still playing in the background and the lights were dim.

When participants appeared to have finished their writing, I quietly suggested to them to continue to meditate if they chose to, or to slowly come back to the room and stay quiet in their seats. Once all participants were done, the music was discontinued, full lights were turned on, and we engaged in a lively discussion. The participants shared their experiences and their math autobiographies and reflected on how their early math experiences affected their later school years, their attitudes toward math, and possibly also career choices they had made.

It is important to point out that shedding new light on such early experiences and how they affected math learning and attitudes later in life can be highly beneficial for people with negative math attitudes or low math self-concept. It opens the door for change to happen. This will become clearer when we see some examples of the kinds of things people write about in this activity. Since I did not ask the workshop participants to provide me with copies of their journal entries, I am unable at this time to describe what was shared during that conference presentation. However, to illustrate the types of experiences that often surface during this math autobiography activity, I will draw here on another time I used this activity. The following example, based on the math autobiography of a new elementary teacher, was drawn from a recent workshop series I conducted with a group of elementary school teachers who were highly anxious about their math teaching.

Mary is a young elementary teacher, currently in her first year of teaching. Here she talks about her attitude toward math:

> All the way through public school I remember I hated it. And I recall doing mental math in Grade 4; I always hated that. And when teachers go around, and they ask you, you do it in order. . . . And I would sit going, "Oh, please, what question?" and I would sit there and count backwards to see which one I was going to get. And I remember I finally got one right one day, and my teacher went, "Look everybody, Mary *finally* got one right!" And it was that comment that threw me off for the rest of my life. I hated it since then. I remember just being horrified. And I don't know if she thought she was trying to be supportive, but it was the worst thing she could have said to me.

At least now, being herself a teacher, Mary realizes that this teacher might have meant well after all, in spite of all the suffering she had caused her. She continues to describe her Grade 4 challenges:

I remember math being very mechanical. It was just, this is how you do it, accept that's how you do it, and just move on. . . . There wasn't a lot of explanation as to why you do it, and I was always one of those kids who wanted to know why, and there wasn't that kind of thing. Just memorize this rule, use it, do it, and understand it. And I couldn't remember all those rules. And I didn't understand all of that.

And I remember math being a very competitive thing. . . . I was never one of those kids who got picked last for a team on soccer or whatever it was in phys ed, but when we had to do those mental math things we'd have teams. No one ever wanted me on the team. My best friends didn't want me on the team, because I couldn't do it; they knew they would lose because I would get every question wrong. So, it was very stressful. I hated it. It was awful!

Mary then goes on to her next significant math memory which was of a much more positive nature:

I did not like public school math at all, until Grade 8 when I had a really good math teacher. . . . She was very supportive, and I felt comfortable with her. It was difficult, but I didn't feel scared to ask questions. She was different in handling the way that I would ask a question. If I asked a question it wasn't, "Oh, that's so easy, that's how you do it." It was, "Oh, OK, let's look at this. You know how to do this part; what about this?" She guided you through it, it wasn't a competitive atmosphere. But I don't know if I necessarily gained a lot more skills. I was comfortable, but it all went away in Grade 9.

Unfortunately, the above experience with a helpful and accessible grade 8 teacher was an isolated one for Mary, who continued to have problems with math throughout her high school years.

Interestingly, in this math autobiography activity it is much more common for participants to come up with unhappy memories from math class than with happy ones. The next example is a Grade 8 memory of another young teacher, Karen:

I just remember very distinctly one teacher in Grade 8 and I remember he ordered the rows—I think it was from the windows to the doors on the basis of marks. So the students at the door in the rows were the smartest and they went from the smartest at the top of the row to the back of the row, and it went across the room to the windows. I was in the middle row. And I remember struggling with some math questions—I can't remember what they were—and my friend, my best friend Sherri, was in the first row, and I remember thinking, "I really can't figure out this question." So I asked people in my row and we were all at about the same level and couldn't figure it out either, and I remember I walked over to my friend in the first row and I asked her for help, and she started to help me. And the teacher got quite angry with me and said, "What are you doing? You're out of your seat." I said, "I'm trying to get some help," and he said, "You're supposed to ask people in your own row." And I said, "Well, we're all at the same point, or level, and we all don't know the answers, so I have to go to someone who has a better grasp of this." And he said, "Go back to your seat," and that was that.

Karen then goes on to share her recollections of how she felt toward her senior high school teachers:

I tended to be a little bit nervous about teachers, approaching teachers anyway, I guess maybe not wanting to admit perhaps that I didn't understand it. I can't really recall how open I was to going to teachers. I remember though distinctly in high school, one teacher, I think it was in Grade 12. She was considered to be an excellent math teacher. And I recall how she placed so much emphasis on teaching those students who did well in math, excelled in math. And some of us who were having difficulties—I remember her not giving much time to students who had problems or struggles. And when you approached her, I don't remember getting a lot of help.

The above excerpts from teachers' math autobiographies are quite typical. It seems that most of us have had some negative math experiences as children which may continue to impact us throughout our life.

The math autobiography activity, which involved recalling and visualizing childhood math experiences, then reflecting on them in writing and sharing with the group, often resulted in important insights for the participants. Such reflection, done from an adult perspective, can lead to reframing these experiences, which can help participants accept what happened during their school years and realize that at least some of those teachers who were unhelpful to them and caused them to lose their confidence may have actually tried their best based on their own understanding. Such acceptance of their childhood math experiences and of their teachers may lead to letting go of old resentments, and also to some new openness toward math and improvements in math-related attitudes.

The second part of my conference presentation was devoted to discussing journal writing in the elementary classroom with its various roles and associated benefits, and providing examples of various applications and student entries. The following is an example of one classroom implementation of journal writing as part of a unit on fractions.

JOURNAL WRITING IN A GRADE 7 CLASSROOM

Diane, a Grade 7 teacher, had a few years' teaching experience when she conducted the action research project described below. She integrated journal writing activities throughout her newly designed review unit on fractions. A few months prior to teaching fractions, she had a class discussion about fractions and then asked her students to write a journal entry answering the question, What are your thoughts about working with fractions? Typical responses included: "I can't remember the formulas, I always get the numbers mixed up"; "There are too many steps and I always get them wrong"; "I don't think I have been taught factions very well yet"; "I don't really mind working with fractions but I don't always understand them"; "Sometimes they are easy and sometimes they are difficult, I would like to understand fractions better"; "My thoughts on fractions are no good, I do not, I repeat, I do not like fractions. Why? Because they are hard. I don't understand plussing, subtracting or timesing." Out of the 25 students who wrote these journal entries, only 3 stated that they liked fractions and had little difficulty with them.

The teacher then went on to devise a fraction unit to help alleviate the frustration experienced by her students. The teaching of fractions would be accomplished via hands-on activities with concrete materials such as fraction strips, as well as with everyday experiences. She would not introduce formulas in group lessons, but rather individually when she thought the child was ready. Throughout the unit she would provide open-ended problems so that students could use their creativity, and develop different strategies on their own to solve the problems.

Math journal entries were also used for gaining feedback from students during the unit, and for assessing students' knowledge. As part of his answer to the teacher's journal prompt, "Have your thoughts on working with fractions changed from the beginning of this unit? Why or why not?", one student wrote, "No and yes. You see working with friendly fractions and plussing with the same denominator are easy, but making improper and whole fractions is a bit difficult, but I'm getting the hang of them very slowly."

In response to the teacher's journal prompt, "What do you like about the way we do math in our class (especially fractions)? What do you dislike about it? What would you like me to do to improve it?", one student wrote that "fraction strips are a real good idea because they help you see what fraction is bigger." He then went on to comment on the benefits of mental math: "I like mental math fractions. It helps you to see how much you know and how much you do not know." But then he also added:

> I dislike fractions a bit because they are too difficult. Some questions are so hard that you just give up. . . . When the teachers are not around almost every fraction question is hard to do. Some fraction periods are

so so boring. I guess I'm not the type to like fractions, right, Miss Jones. Sometimes they are so hard you wish that you could do something else beside fractions.

In response to the teacher's journal prompt, "What is the best way to do math?" this same boy provides his classmates with some very important advice:

> The very important thing is being calm, relax, try to not get mad because if you get mad you will get frustrated and you will have a hard time to do math. Keep saying to yourself, "I can do it," because if you say it's hard you will also have a bad time, but if you say it is easy every question will come like a cinch. So those are some ways to do your math. Just remember to keep calm.

The above entry is somewhat unusual for a Grade 7 student and makes one wonder whether this boy came up with it by himself, or whether this useful advice for students had originated from the teacher, or from some other significant adults in the boy's life.

The last example is a student's feedback about the fraction unit following completion of the unit.

> What I like about learning fractions is, now that someone actually decided to help me through the problems I had about understanding fractions, it is easier than I thought it would be. When I worked with fractions last year I was totally lost, and whenever I asked for help, I ended up more confused. Not understanding fractions made me feel really stupid. I feel better now that I know more about fractions. What I don't like about learning fractions is, for some reason, I feel slower than everyone else. However, when we mark our work I feel really good. Even though I get a few wrong, I get a lot of them right. Fractions are starting to come easier for me now.

CONCLUSION

The last journal entry above reminds us of some of the experiences shared by participants in the math autobiography activity described in the first part of this chapter. A learner's realization that some of her past teachers were unable to help her and even made her feel stupid, along with appreciation of a good teacher who finally came along, were common threads. But unlike the students in this Grade 7 class, the adult learners who participated in the math autobiography activity were also able to realize that some of their own teachers, even if they had been unhelpful to them and caused them to feel stupid, might have actually meant well and just didn't know any better.

School children, like adults, can greatly benefit from being able to reflect on their past experiences with math, and their thoughts and feelings about them. In the implementation of the fractions unit discussed above, analysis of the students' journal entries prior to, during, and following the unit indicated that the children's attitudes toward fractions have significantly improved. Clearly the innovative approach to the teaching of fractions, which included not only the integrated journal writing but also the use of specific teaching methods, has caused this change in attitudes. Yet further analysis of the journal entries made it clear that the journal writing activities had a strong impact on the students and were a major contributor to this remarkable improvement in the students' attitudes.

Hopefully the above examples helped illustrate some of the many ways in which journal writing in general, and specifically journal entries which enable the learner to deal with the affective dimensions of math learning, can be integrated with mathematics teacher development, and with school math. We have illustrated through these examples not only some actual journal writing techniques and approaches used in math learning, but also some of the important benefits associated with their use.

REFERENCES

Bean, J. A. (1995, April). Curriculum integration and the disciplines of knowledge. *Phi Delta Kappan*, 616–622.

Burns, M. (1995, April). Writing in math class? Absolutely! *Instructor*, 40–47.

Cohen, R. (2000). Journal writing in mathematics: Examples from elementary classrooms. *Orbit*, *31*(3), 45–47.

Countryman, J. (1992). *Writing to learn mathematics: Strategies that work, K–12.* Portsmouth, NH: Heineman Educational Books.

Edwards, M. E. (1999). Journal writing in an elementary math classroom and its effect on students' understanding of decimals. M.A. thesis, OISE/UT.

Elliott, P. C. & Kenney, M. J., (Eds.). (1996). *Communication in mathematics, K–12 and beyond.* Reston, VA: National Council of Teachers of Mathematics.

Stix, A. (1994, Jan.) Pic-jour math: Pictorial journal writing in mathematics: *Arithmetic Teacher*, 246–249.

Tobias, S. (1993). *Overcoming math anxiety.* New York: W. W. Norton.

CHAPTER 14

In Da Zone

Meditation, Masculinity, and a Meaningful Life

DAVID FORBES

At the bell twelve beefy, boisterous, high school male athletes burst into the classroom, joking, laughing, punching, and roughhousing each other. These varsity football team members from Brooklyn seem to be a rampant force of nature all their own. Yet soon each young man is seated in a circle, eyes closed, body upright yet relaxed, perfectly still. Except for a soothing voice emanating from a tape recorder and the slow, deep breathing of the students, the room is dead silent.

Welcome to "Da Zone."

Each week for an hour after school I have been meeting with these young men. Most of them are African Americans, along with Latinos, Arab Americans, and Italian Americans. They average around 16 years of age. I am a middle-aged, white, male college professor and mental health professional. Together we practice meditation and also discuss topics and readings that range from last week's football game to fathers, frustrations, and fears.

Why are they here? How is it possible to get them into a classroom on their own, let alone sit motionless and concentrate for any amount of time?

The young men are committed to coming because they want to enhance their ability to play sports in the zone (see Cooper, 1998; Murphy and White, 1995). What athletes call "the zone," or what Csikszentmihalyi (1990) and other researchers refer to as "flow," is the pleasurable experience of sustained, deep concentration, staying focused on the changing demands of an activity at each moment without falling prey to internal or external distractions. The flow response is incompatible with choking, the tendency during an athletic event or performance to think so much that one fails to do what one knows how to do. Meditation increases the chances that an athlete can find the zone during a game or performance. Phil Jackson, coach of the NBA champion Chicago Bulls and Los Angeles Lakers basketball teams and a practicing Zen Buddhist, has employed meditation with his players (Jackson & Delehanty, 1995). Many high school athletes are savvy about the zone and are highly motivated to find ways to improve their playing.

My primary goal was to work with male high school youth and figure out ways to help them move to higher levels of ego, moral, and gender identity development—to become more evolved. As part of their growth I hoped they would reflect on and challenge the problematic aspects of masculinity still common to many males: stoical inexpressiveness, toughness, the avoidance of qualities considered to be feminine, competitiveness, aggressiveness, and homophobia. Mental health professionals recently have characterized these tendencies as part of the Culture of Cruelty (Kindlon & Thompson, 2000), the Boy Code (Pollack, 1999), and performance-based esteem (Real, 1997). In each case a male often feels he never can let up the stressful need to prove his masculinity to himself and others.

I suspected that meditation, along with other psychological and educational approaches, could be a useful way to enhance young males' development. James Garbarino (1999), who has worked with troubled young males, showed how meditation helps teens find an alternative to either repressing unwanted thoughts or acting them out. By creating a space around a thought or self-concept, young people can more freely sit with their own experiences and become less attached to rigid, stereotypical notions of what one is supposed to think or who one is supposed to be. From readings as well as my own experience I know that as a meditator learns to compassionately witness thoughts and feelings and let them go, the individual may evolve from assuming a self-centered or conventional viewpoint to a more interconnected and spiritual one. Over time a person is then more open to seeing what is happening in the moment and more able to consider alternatives to do what is best. Evidence suggests that meditation is beneficial to health, reduces stress, and helps one deal with pain (Murphy, Donovan, & Taylor, 1997). I wanted to employ meditation as a developmental tool that could promote higher levels of self-awareness and identity specifically for young males.

At the outset I wondered how I could gain access to high school males and find a motivating factor that would pique their interest. Brooklyn College had developed an after-school program in a needy high school that seemed like a promising place to start. As Larson (2000) argues, in a voluntary structured activity such as an after-school program, unlike in most classrooms or even peer activities, students are both self-motivated and challenged to concentrate. At the school I considered recruiting for a discussion and support group for male students after class, but after running the idea past the school peer mediation club and their faculty sponsor, I decided that would be a tough sell. During a brainstorming session a colleague hit on the idea of recruiting members of one of the school athletic teams. The meditation to improve their game performance, a legitimate goal in its own right, would be the hook to get them interested in the rest of the program. I wanted them to play sports in the zone, but I also wanted them to consider playing life in the zone, and to come to see the two as inseparable. That is the more challenging part and is an ongoing process. As I go along, I myself am learning how to expand the lessons of playing sports in the zone to other aspects of everyday student life and development.

It is a challenge of course to start a new program in a public school, especially one of this kind. I approached the principal and assistant principal, who were supportive of the idea but were not happy about a draft of a recruitment flier I had submitted. Ironically, the objection seemed to be not over any reference to meditation and spiritual matters but to the invitation to speak confidentially—with the usual professional exceptions—about personal matters that might include sex and drugs. After the principal approved a revised flier he then summoned his coaches to a meeting where I explained what I wanted to do. The football coach was interested and cooperative but was properly cautious and protective of his own relationship and time with his players, and at first found it difficult to secure a weekly time to free them up. After a few meetings we worked out an arrangement and he invited me to address his players at a meeting after school. I gave a brief talk about the zone, said that parent consent forms were required, and handed out the fliers. Armed with a small pilot project grant, I told the team players I would provide snacks and handouts and show an occasional video. As an incentive I also promised I would do my best to invite a couple of New York Giant football players who I learned were interested in the meditative aspects of yoga (Williams, 2001). A number of the students already knew about the zone and expressed an interest in getting there. To my relief they also were open to coming to a group where they could talk about stress, anger, and other topics if they so chose. Some were even interested in finding a spiritual space and some peace of mind.

At the first session I administered pretest questionnaires. The promise of pizza when they completed the forms kept them in their seats but it wasn't easy. They complained that the questions took too long to do. I apologized, empathized with them, and kept encouraging them to finish, which not all of them did. I then set up the session as a group, putting everyone in a circle and establishing ground rules that would facilitate a climate of trust, confidentiality, and respect. I started out with a format for each session: snacks, discussion, and meditation. I later switched the meditation with the discussion and have found that to be more productive.

During the first few weeks there was some "dissing" and teasing, some of which was normal teen-male-jock-buddy interaction and some of which seemed hurtful. I did not hesitate to remind them of the ground rules to which they had agreed and intervened if things got out of hand. My aim, however, was not to repress their behaviors and criticize their values but to get them to notice and be aware of problems within the context of their own lives. I would use these disruptions and whatever occurred at the moment to get them to consider what was going on with them there and then: Is there a line that you cross from friendly teasing to hurtful comments? Some of the members did indeed admit that some dissing went too far and they were hurt by it. A few weeks after the World Trade Center attack, one young man, an Arab American, courageously confronted his teammates about their calling him and his family members "terrorists," and said it had crossed the line. I supported him and asked the group, "Can you be mindful of where that line is and when you cross it? Can you be open to listening to and understanding another's point of view?" I pointed out that being mindful in the group is like being aware of one's own mind during meditation and, by way of extension, on the football field. Some of the overt acting out lessened over time and the members began to take the group more seriously.

I had collected and distributed some articles on men and stress, meditation and sports, and relationships and encouraged them to read and talk about them. We discussed issues such as the relevance of fathers, the place of African American males in professional sports, and of course young women and how to treat them. We also discussed concerns the young men brought up themselves, such as a deep fear that they would fail as adults, a topic that resonated with a number of them. We would discuss a game, how they felt after a win or loss, and how they could employ a meditative approach to playing—not too nervous or slack, alert but relaxed at the same time. On occasion some of the young men initiated a discussion on the readings. Often, however, they were not interested in reading, and I have considered experimenting with a structured reading time and instituting some incentives to read as a way to integrate the program with their schooling and study skills. The principal was weighing offering one general credit for successful participation in the program, which could aid in this effort.

In any program that involves counseling and education it is crucial to establish a positive relationship with the students. I spent some time with team members in the weight room, in the hallways between periods, and outside after school, just hanging out. I also attended a number of their games on Saturday mornings and cheered them on. In the classroom both before and during the session I have tried to create a comfortable holding place that is neither academic nor anarchic but instead nonjudgmental and meditative in that it puts some space around our interactions. Some days, though, are better than others. Teens are known for their mood swings and uneven development. I am helping them (and myself) learn to take a mindful approach to changing feelings, concepts, and bodily sensations.

Many of the young males stated that they had a lot of stress in their lives, which was also reflected in their responses on a masculinity gender role stress questionnaire (Eisler & Skidmore, 1987). Meditation does help one relax and experience things in a calmer manner. However, besides learning to relax I also wanted the young men to be able to sit with and face some of the difficult feelings they admitted they had.

In the beginning I asked the students to write down the most important reason they wanted to meditate. They responded that they wanted to relax, release stress, and concentrate for a game. Meditation for them was another technique or skill they could employ to get what they wanted. I challenged this narrow view. Should, say, a drug dealer just use meditation to relax and focus on the job in order to pull off a better drug deal? Is meditation good in order to hurt your opponent or to win a game at any cost? They began to consider the holistic nature of meditation, an invitation to be fully aware in the moment and to strive to live a right-minded, enlightened life. I also encouraged them to learn to master an activity without needing to see it as an extension of their competitive ego or as an expression of power over others. That is a value that many of us adults find hard to grasp. For these reasons we do Vipassana, or insight, meditation, rather than practices that primarily emphasize relaxation through mantras or chanting. We used a tape by Jack Kornfield (1996), a teacher of insight meditation.

I also supported them to be mindful of certain patterns of thinking, for example to notice just when and how much they invested their identity in conventional notions of masculinity, such as having to act tough, deny feelings, and display verbal or physical aggression, and trace where those thoughts came from. We also have talked about the rough-and-tumble pecking order of a football team and how they could take a more responsible leadership position with the junior varsity players, whom some admitted to teasing in hurtful ways. On a postseason questionnaire one student wrote, "I've learned how to put myself in [junior varsity players"] shoes and think of their feelings." I also introduced the idea of their becoming role models and leaders within the entire school. As part of the program I hope later to involve them in some service learning, possibly mentoring or working with younger male children. At that stage I would introduce some metta (compassion) meditation that would also require more intensive attention to moral reasoning skills and development.

As some meditation teachers such as Jack Kornfield have pointed out, meditation needs to be supplemented with psychological and educational practices (Schwartz, 1996). Young people especially need supportive counseling, truthful and relevant information, and proper limit setting from caring adults. Schools themselves can benefit from mindful, contemplative, and holistic practices.

Some of the young men found that the meditation helped their playing. One reported back, "Meditation worked. I was able to concentrate on catching the ball, and not letting my mind get ahead of myself like I used to." Some said they could concentrate better on the football field by refocusing away from self-doubts, worries about the future, crowd noises, and trash-talking opponents. A number of students reported they had gained more awareness and control of thoughts and feelings since meditating. One student wrote, "During a game a kid kept cheap shooting me but I stayed under control." Others said it helped them relax and stay centered during a game. One student admitted he found it difficult to learn a new skill and perform it during practice. As a result we began to do more specific visualization meditations that related to performing during game time.

I also plan to help the students consider the problem of feeling pressured to play with pain. When professional football players are in pain from injuries most take painkillers to which some become addicted (Freeman, 2002). They do so because they want to play at all costs due to pressures from the team organization or teammates, or that they impose on themselves. The high school students first need to be aware of the feelings of pressure in their own lives and to develop a critical analysis of their sources. For example, some have spoken about wanting to please parents in the crowd or worrying about whether the coach will take them out if they mess up. Beginning in high school, athletes know that if they do well there are potential careers and big money at stake. With African American males there are still few channels other than sports to succeed in society. There is also the macho pressure to prove one's toughness to oneself and others. An athlete needs to consider how he will relate to these feelings of pressure. What values are most important to him? What are his options? Second, even if a young male does decide to play with pain because he feels pressured, he also needs to notice the pain and its degree of severity, given that many males are not in touch with bodily feelings or try to deny them (Levant, 1995). Pain is a signal from the body for the need to stop. When athletes keep playing in pain they are in danger of losing a sense of where that line is. If a player consistently ignores pain he can further damage his body. When pain is present, meditation also can help by breathing into the injured part of the body and attending to the more neutral sensations that comprise the experience. Instead of denying the pain, one can learn to disidentify the pain from a sense of self.

Some young men began to find meditation helpful in everyday situations like concentrating in school and noticing how they related to young women. One of the students admitted to struggling with his weight and asked if meditation could help him. I explained that if you feel anxious or upset you may reach for food, or even a drug, to medicate those feelings. Meditation can help train the mind to notice when those feelings arise, focus on breathing, and then, instead of mindlessly overeating, decide how to better deal with what is going on. In terms of group snacks, I learned I had to assume control over distributing the food, as leaving it up to them to share brought out some aggressive and competitive behavior. I used this as another opportunity for them to resolve this as a group issue as well as for each one of them to be more aware of how he behaved and what food and sharing brought up for him. I introduced a meditation on eating mindfully. Apart from all that, I needed to remind myself that adolescent males eat like there is no tomorrow. That of course is not what is meant by "Being in the moment"!

As a work in progress the project has reaped some benefits. During a stressful moment one of the students began to lose his temper. A number of his teammates told him, "Breathe!" and he was able to calm down. Today these young men—indeed, all young people—need to develop their full capacities to live a whole, meaningful life. Counseling students along with meditation as a means to promote higher development may be a way to help bring this about.

REFERENCES

Cooper, A (1998). *Playing in the zone: Exploring the spiritual dimensions of sports.* Boston: Shambhala.

Csikszentmihalyi, M. (1990). *Flow: The psychology of optimal experience.* New York: Harper & Row.

Eisler, R. M., & Skidmore, J. R. (1987). Masculine gender role stress: Scale development and component factors in the appraisal of stressful situations. *Behavior Modification, 11*(2), 123–136.

Freeman, M. (2002, Jan. 31). Painkillers a quiet fact of life in the N.F.L. *New York Times,* D1, D3.

Garbarino, J. (1999). *Lost boys: Why our sons turn violent and how we can save them.* New York: Free Press.

Jackson, P., & Delehanty, H. (1995). *Sacred hoops: Spiritual lessons of a hardwood warrior.* New York: Hyperion.

Kindlon, M., & Thompson, M. (2000). *Raising Cain: Protecting the emotional life of boys.* New York: Ballantine.

Kornfeld, J. (1996). *Meditation for beginners* (Tape No. A395). Boulder: Sounds True.

Larson, R. W. (2000). Toward a psychology of positive youth development. *American Psychologist, 55,* 170–183.

Levant, R. F. (1995). Toward the reconstruction of masculinity. In R. F. Levant & W. S. Pollack (Eds.), *A new psychology of man* (229–251). New York: Basic Books.

Murphy, M., Donavan, S., & Taylor, E. (1997). *The physical and psychological effects of meditation: A review of contemporary research with a comprehensive bibliography, 1931–1996.* Sausalito CA: Institute of Noetic Sciences.

Murphy, M., & White, R. A. (1995). *In the zone: Transcendent experience in sports.* New York: Penguin.

Pollack, W. (1999). *Real boys: Rescuing our sons from the myths of boyhood.* New York: Henry Holt.

Real, T. (1997). *I don't want to talk about it: Overcoming the secret legacy of male depression.* New York: Fireside.

Schwartz, T. (1996). *What really matters: Searching for wisdom in America.* New York: Bantam.

Williams, L. (2001, June 3). Taking a deep breath, N.F.L. tackles yoga. *New York Times,* sp9.

CHAPTER 15

Contemplating Great Things
in Soul and Place

SUSAN A. SCHILLER

INTRODUCTION

The holistic activity described in this chapter integrates mind, body, and soul in a process of harmonious interconnections among images, words, silence, and creativity. Images, words, and silence are used repeatedly to initiate a movement from outer to inner and back again. This "is a basic human rhythm" (Neville, as cited in Kessler, 2000, p. 56) that I also consider as a practical gateway leading to creativity and transformation.

Participants are asked to express the inner by creating their own poem about the greatness they have been able to see anew. Kessler (2000) informs us that, "When creativity breaks through . . . [m]ind, body, heart and spirit come together to spark the passion that fuels the motivation to learn to contribute and to savor our infinite capacity for growth" (p. 114). When participants share their creations at the end of the process, the capacity for growth is proclaimed and witnessed within the community. This validates their soul. In this context, "soul" refers to the inner depths from which feeling, knowledge, and change originate.

This process further creates the potential for participants to understand that greatness is accessible to us at any time if we allow the soul to transform our vision and to see that great things help our soul to emerge. While the outer shell of the process is linear, activities within each step are not; they awaken the participants to infinite opportunities for seeing greatness in soul and place. The relationship between linear and nonlinear ways of learning is created and

161

allowed to flow. Ultimately participants learn that greatness is everywhere if we just let our soul feel and see it, and that the soul itself is a transformative power we can access in order to resee the world.

Balance, inclusion, and connection, so vital to holistic learning (Miller, 1996, p. 3), are maintained as they lead us to see that the transformative power of the soul can be studied as a phenomenon. As a phenomenon, this power can be sought; it does not need to remain a mystery. Our soul, then, becomes a paramount and practical place of growth and infinite learning.

THE ACTIVITY

Step 1:   2–5 minutes of contemplating place as depicted in photos of Austria, the Czech Republic, and Hungary (poetic image)

Step 2:   5–10-minute silent meditation (reverie and imagination)

Step 3:   5–10-minute journal write on the greatness within these images of place (Linguistic experience: connecting soul to place; combining mind and soul)

Step 4:   5-minute scrutiny of potential greatness in the place where the workshop is held (poetic image)

Step 5:   5–10-minute silent meditation (reverie and imagination)

Step 6:   5–10-minute journal write on the greatness in the workshop place (linguistic experience: combining mind and soul)

Step 7:   Time for writing a poem about place and self (creative, imaginative, imagistic, and linguistic experience)

Step 8:   Discussion and evaluation (linguistic connections to community: Great things within and without)

In *step one*, photographs of indoor and outdoor European scenes offer a poetic image as a starting point for imagination. Although I find these foreign shots to be effective, primarily because they are unfamiliar and uncommon, any photograph of beauty or the unfamiliar would work as well. These photos become the "poetic image" as Bachelard (1969) describes it, and they function as an externally located "great thing" that initiates the subsequent process. I ask students to contemplate the image and to imagine where the greatness exists in such a place.

The subsequent process combines imagination, the poetic image as great thing, and reverie about the great thing. Participants are led to transforming the way they view place and self and then ultimately to seeing the transforming power of soul. They are transformed when they see that the transforming power of soul is primarily an internal event of viewpoint but is also a phenomenon within themselves that they can call forth at will. This means that when the poetic image and imagination are blended in reverie, the soul has the power to lead people to transformative viewpoints. Moreover, people learn that they can call on this power whenever they need it or want it.

Silent meditation is a natural choice to enhance or deepen the quality of reverie. In the silent space of meditation soul and mind can mingle; imagination can freely move in a state of reverie and without the restraints of order or structure. The reverie which *step two* permits is natural and inevitable because, according to Bachelard (1969) we cannot respond to the poetic image without a certain amount of reverie. For some people, particularly those who do not practice meditation, this activity can seem unfamiliar; five minutes of silent meditation feels extensive. Yet for those who do practice meditation five minutes may feel insufficient. Regardless of previous experience, however, each participant is likely to experience "a rest for the nervous system, a respite from the demands of others, and a chance to visit one's own inner life" (Kessler, 2000, p. 38).

The journal write in *step three* returns the participants to prose, a linguistic activity that is familiar and offers a time for personal yet private expression. It brings participants back to the outer, and as such it offers a bit of pseudoclosure that is calming. It also extends the intellectual reflection on place and self. The calming effect of this familiar linguistic activity helps to ready participants for the next step, which can be quite disarming for a number of reasons depending on the immediate environment.

In *step four* participants are asked to look for the greatness in the room they are in. As many of us know, classroom space can lack beauty. I generally find myself teaching in rooms made of painted beige cinderblock. Usually there is little daylight; shades are drawn and florescent lighting bears down unmercifully. Conference rooms are not much better either: chairs, tables, and perhaps audio-visual equipment are standard décor.

Creative tension arises when they are asked to do something that at first seems illogical or impossible. Palmer (1998) writes, "Awareness is always heightened when we are caught in a creative tension" (p. 74). At first participants react with surprise, thinking there is nothing great to be found in such a space, but then their perception takes a noticeable shift. As a facilitator for the process, I have been able to observe the way people suddenly acquire new vision when looking about the room. Some of them walk about to discover different vantage points for vision. I have seen people touch and even smell wallpaper or painted walls. The more inquisitive might even crawl under a table and take a look from that point or sit on the floor instead of in a chair. This kind of exploration is encouraged by me. I often suggest using movement at this step in the activity as a means for seeing differently and for knowing through the body. This step moves the participant into a deeper imaginative event that extends and further develops the potential for transformation.

Step five calls for additional reverie. It allows space for the imagination to again move toward transformation. The reverie in this step may actually be deeper because it may not feel as unfamiliar as it did earlier. The participant should be more relaxed at this stage. This is important, because "when a relaxed spirit meditates and dreams, immensity seems to expect images of immensity. The mind sees and continues to see objects, while the spirit finds the nest of immensity in an object" (Bachelard, 1969, p. 190). As one might assume, it is especially helpful at this point to extend the time for silent meditation. Even with people new to meditation or silence, I try to allow the full ten minutes. With more experienced participants, fifteen minutes is even more desirable. With this extended time, people are more likely to see the poetic image within the space around them and also see that the soul shapes what we see. Bachelard (1969) writes that "we are obliged to acknowledge that poetry is a commitment of the soul. A consciousness of the soul is more relaxed, less intentionalized than a consciousness associated with the phenomena of the mind" (p. xvii). In a meditative silent state, participants, when engaged with a poetic image, begin from a relaxed position and the mind is less restricted. The soul can rise up and emerge. Then its ability to shape the way we view our world can be recognized. At this point, participants should "realize within [themselves] the pure being of pure imagination" (Bachelard, 1969, p. 184). They might also reach a more holistic view, seeing that "the gifts of silence are intertwined; they cannot really be separated into cognitive, psychological, physiological, or spiritual" (Kessler, 2000, p. 43).

After the silent meditative reverie, participants are again asked to return to journal writing in *step six*. While it returns them to a familiar feeling and condition, it is also a prewriting activity for step seven. It is a stress-free way of releasing insights and realizations experienced during step five. I don't allow very much time for this journal writing—ten minutes at the most. Sometimes, though, people want more time for this. They seem to be overflowing with ideas and language and they want to let them out. I take this as evidence of what Palmer (1998) calls "the power of the living subject" (p. 103). He writes that "when we make the subject the center of our attention, we give it the respect and authority that we normally give only to human beings. We give it ontological significance" (p. 103). Furthermore, Bachelard (1969) writes, "The communicability of an unusual image is a fact of great ontological significance" (p. xiii). This ontological energy further primes participants for creative expression in step seven because its dynamism can take shape in the poetic image. In this way, participants are dealing with the nature of being, reality, and ultimate substance.

Step seven asks that participants write a poem about the greatness in place and self. By writing a poem, participants are taking space, their position in and view of it, and using it as an act of expansion. Bachelard (1969) states that "whatever affectivity that colors a given space, whether sad or ponderous, once it is poetically expressed, the sadness is diminished, the ponderousness lightened. Poetic space, because it is expressed, assumes values of expansion" (p. 201). Through creativity and expansion, participants will experience a new awareness and open themselves to the transforming power of soul.

They learn, as Parker Palmer (1998) tells us, that great things "are the irreducible elements of life itself" (p. 109). They also learn that to see great things we must turn inward to the soul and let it guide our vision.

It is essential to allow sharing time to close the activity in *step eight*. Facilitators can invite participants to read their poetry, share their emotions experienced throughout, ask questions, and give feedback or suggestions for changes in the process. The invitation must be sincere. Some people may not want to read their poem if it is too personal or if they just want to keep it private. Those who do want to share openly with the group do so with joy and excitement about the process. Their proclamations often encourage others to also share. More often than not, we have needed more time than I had scheduled for this part of the process. Yet, with just a little sharing, participants themselves validate creativity as a mode of knowing, and the phenomenon of transformation is manifested for everyone to see. It is demystified and appears as a normal and accessible function of soul.

To encourage nonjudgmental communication at this point, I sit quietly and let participants guide the conversation along lines they choose. I withhold opinions, but will answer questions whenever asked. Most of the time, people are eager to read their poems, have interesting comments about their experience throughout the whole process, and offer useful feedback about ways to alter the process. I can count on people to always share insight and growth, because they have reached a new awareness of their abilities to shape the world and understand the transformative power of soul in new ways.

VARIATIONS ON A THEME

Variations in this process are interesting to experiment with and have convinced me that the activity is extremely versatile without losing its transformative potential. For instance, weather permitting, the activity is especially potent for connecting to our Earth if participants can be taken out of doors and directed through the steps while sitting on the ground. Most recently, I inserted a step between six and seven when I asked students to pair off, hold both hands while gazing into each other's eyes, and simply look for the greatness in the other person. This variation elicited a stronger awareness of community and self. I have also asked participants to write letters (to their mother, friend, husband, significant other, or whomever they select) instead of a journal write or a poem. Rather than creating a poem, participants are sometimes directed to draw a picture or write a song. Currently, I prefer to end with a creative act because I believe creativity increases with practice and is directly connected to imagination. The imagination can lead us to break barriers, develop new consciousness, and experience the highest intuitive knowing. In this state, we can then experience the unity of inner and outer, seeing that all is interconnected.

CONCLUSION

This activity strengthens our relationships with soul, community, and place. At its core we find the soul; we find transformation as an ontological phenomenon of infinite capacity. This phenomenon can open us to the power we hold within to shape and live our lives. We learn to see that the inner and outer rhythms that shape life can be used for our benefit and growth. More importantly, we also learn that once demystified, the transformative power of soul can be accessible to us whenever we need it. We can understand and teach the transformative power of soul as a skill to use when we shape relationships with one another and with our world.

REFERENCES

Bachelard, G. (1969). *The poetics of space*. Boston: Beacon Press.

Kessler, R. (2000). *The soul of education*. Alexandria, VA: Association for Supervision and Curriculum Development.

Miller, J. P. (1996). *The holistic curriculum*. Toronto: OISE Press.

Palmer, P. J. (1998). *The courage to teach: Exploring the inner landscape of a teacher's life*. San Francisco: Jossey-Bass.

CHAPTER 16

Listening to Ancient Voices

Reaching Hearts and Souls through Benchmarks and
Rites of Passage Experiences in Schools

LESLIE OWEN WILSON

We must all search for alterable variables and processes which can make
a difference in the learning of children.
—B. Bloom, *All Our Children Learning*

Often variables and processes that are meaningful and relevant to students go
far beyond standards and tougher academic expectations, into exploring
the simple emotional aspects and connections to their hearts and souls. This
chapter is about making the processes of schooling more personal and meaningful to today's youth by redefining, redesigning, recapturing, or reinstituting rites
of passage and benchmarks as ways to help build confidence and community.

LOOKING FOR ALTERNATIVES: WHAT ARE RITES OF PASSAGE?

From a traditional sociological perspective rites of passage mark liminality
(threshold experiences) from one stage of life into another, or in the case of
death rites signify the threshold to another dimension or form, or into the
unknown. Rites of passage are both universal and yet highly diverse in their
designs, meanings, and forms of completion. But rites are always meant to signify
and mark profound changes in the reality or status of the participant. The traditional stages in rites are:

167

1. *Separation:* The individual is isolated.
2. *Margin:* a period of threshold or liminality as the isolate makes the transition from not knowing to one who has acquired skills, knowledge, maturation, or perspective.
3. *Aggregation:* acceptance and assimilation back into the main body or community in a new role. The individual is now initiated into the processes, skills, or knowledge shared by the larger body. The larger body or community acknowledges the passage.

Commonly shared rites of passage throughout the world include birth, ceremonies marking the transition from puberty into adulthood, marriage, and death. Add to this list modern rites of passage, or important benchmarks, have become such things as completion of schooling or training, or going on to more advanced forms of training; vocational promotions; landmark anniversaries or birthdays; retirement; completion of self-selected physical or personal challenges; surviving grave illness; divorce; and baptism, confirmation, and ordination.

All of these events indicate passages from one horizon to another and herald opportunities for personal growth or acknowledge changed perspectives or lifestyles.

PROBLEM: DISJUNCTURES AND TRANSITIONS

As I deliberate the importance of reinstituting rites of passage for today's youths there are several background points that are pertinent to my discussions. These points are about the importance of and the need for defining differently the educational passages of youths in transition.

The societal milieu that surrounds the concept of conventional family is in a state of chaos and flux in many parts of the world. This is especially true in the West. Here the traditional historic conceptualization of the nuclear family is disintegrating and being replaced with something more mutable, more mobile, smaller, and more diverse in its configurations. Extended family structures that once helped support the development of potential in individuals are changing dramatically too. In the past there was a sense of balance achieved as children explored their individualism while being supported and guided by families who provided them with some sense of belonging to a larger community, a larger whole. This change or absence of traditional supportive family structures, especially for youth in transition, is one of the elements that has caused a lack of balance, a sense of turmoil in our technosocial culture. It is one of the fine lines in life that has been fractured, and its fragmentation has decided repercussions for education.

Connecting this condition to the diminished stability of the family, many children no longer have or experience opportunities that clearly mark their passages from childhood into adulthood in positive ways. In today's rushed world personal progress on the path to adulthood frequently goes unnoticed; thus important benchmarks, milestones, and rites of celebration and passage often are missing or are ill defined in the lives of many children. As a result, personal, family, community, even spiritual identities are weakly formed, may never be formed, or are never reinforced in this current atmosphere of discontinuity. It is this absence of positive transitions into the world of adulthood that is causing concern over the fate of today's youth.

Since human beings tend to seek and create order in the world in which they live, often life becomes a balancing act, a series of journeys along separate fine lines in a precarious attempt to create or simply walk a straight, continuous path. In this time, many of us are seeking desperately to sort out certain aspects of our lives. We are trying to find balance, to find paths where we can walk with grace and dignity, and many of us are trying to find our spiritual centers as well. These adventures—trying to make order out of chaos, trying to connect with higher elements, trying to define inner space in positive ways—are not confined to any specific age group and may affect both young and old alike.

But something is very out of sorts with today's youth. Here the fine lines have become jagged and broken. While it is not unusual for successive generations to be at odds with one another, there appears here a huge generational split between members of newer generations and those of older generations. Part of the sense of nonfit may have to do with generations that are split apart by what Longstreet and Shane (1993) term "intergenerational disjunctures." This condition occurs when people of different generations fail to communicate at effective or common levels.

As a result of this disjuncture, members of different generations no longer share ideas and ideals through meaningful interactions, dialogues, or experiences. In this new century these types of schisms appear to be becoming more commonplace and more accelerated. Unfortunately, for many of today's youth the world is moving at such a fast pace that shared experiences that once united generations in some expectation of commonality and continuum simply no longer exist.

A KEY PARADOX

In times like these it is common for people to look to institutions to solve big problems. In the case of radical riffs with today's youth, parents, grandparents, and other adults are looking to schools to offer solutions—after all schools are one of the few remaining outlets that have direct access to today's youth. But schools are not meeting these expectations for action, partly because we live in a paradoxical world and the prevailing paradigm of schools is not the design needed to solve the problem.

Often we of the West pay lip service to valuing individualism. Much of our popular mythology romanticizes and idolizes characters with moxie, intestinal fortitude, and inner strength to challenge or stand up to the corrupt or the powerful. Characters that epitomize rugged individualism are common in our literature, entertainment, and music. Especially in times of chaos, uncertainty and social upheaval, we praise, recognize, and embrace the importance of having leaders with like qualities, ones who can make tough, insightful, and sometimes unpopular decisions—people who often openly celebrate their special form of individualism.

Here lies the heart of the paradox, because through the common practices of schooling we promote methods and principles that support conformity, blind obedience, and the importance of sameness and compliance. As stated earlier, for many of today's youth there are few experiences, beyond those aligned with either the performance arts or sports, where students can actively explore and nurture their intrapersonal intelligences, explore the multiple sides of their own uniqueness, or celebrate personal gifts—gifts of self.

While schools could help address both the problem of disjunctures between generations and the paradox between a culture that celebrates individualism and schools that perpetuate conformity, to date many Western educators appear more preoccupied with the maintenance of the status quo. Also, they appear unduly committed to the common, archaic, factory model of schooling. It is through being blindly tied to designs of the past that many people fail to perceive how larger, much broader forms of societal turbulence and cultural tension are impacting children. In education, one might say that many of the participants empowered to make changes are too busy being reactive to become proactive. This is especially true in regard to creating new educational designs that anticipate students' current and future needs.

Perhaps Chance (1994) makes the plea clear when he writes, "A new paradigm is needed to support a holist view of education from birth to death as a means of providing a basis for economic and social stability for our communities, states, nation and the world" (p. 70).

FRIGHTENING ALTERNATIVES

Within my exploration of alternative designs perhaps it is worthwhile to note that sometimes common popular culture gives us hints about society's evolutionary and developmental progression. Often members of a society actively, at times even desperately, search for and embrace what has gone missing, looking for replacements for what is meager or null. Currently humans seem to be looking for harmony, peace, tranquility, broadened definitions of love and family, and wellness at multiple levels—things which feed our minds, bodies, and spirits combined. On the other hand, youths are craving power and voice. We all appear to be searching for some sense of universal understanding, and perhaps more important, a sense of belonging—to something. This seems true for both adults and young people alike.

As stated before, in the recent past issues of exploring and developing self-concept and selfhood were tied to and supported by family units. For many children the resulting void has become corrupted by such negative forces as escalating gang membership. We are in a period of history where the proliferation of gangs and increasing teen violence have taken even the most astute sociologists by surprise.

What specifically is missing from home, community, and schools that gang membership offers today's youths? Gangs offer real or imagined stability or continuity of relationships; a sense of belonging or community; an immediate extended family; a rigid hierarchical structure; strong, personal role models; power and a power base; and clearly defined benchmarks, milestones, or rights of passage.

EXPLORING NEW DESIGNS: GUIDING QUESTIONS AND PROTOTYPES

Richard Weissbourd (1996) notes that:

> Over the past twenty years, various educators have begun independently to engineer new types of schools, taking into account the many dimensions and tangled nature of school problems. Although they have different visions, these reformers nevertheless share an assumption; the problems in schools cannot be fixed by reforming just one piece of a school. Responding to struggling children is not simply a matter of acquiring better teachers, better teaching methods, or more culturally relevant curricula. It is a matter of markedly changing the fundamental structure—and at times the function of schools. (p. 172)

I believe that there are methods available, and that many of these methods can aid youth in their maturation as both individuals and as members of larger communities. These goals are not mutually exclusive. Indeed, many of the answers to redesigning meaningful curricula lie in the examination and adaptation of ancient family structures and societal and cultural celebrations. Correspondingly, part of the primary and overt mission of modern educators must be to reconcile intergenerational disjunctures while they help redefine the institutional role in children's processes of maturation. Any meaningful educational reform must go beyond thinking about simply preparing students for graduation tests to creating curricula relevant to students' futures and preparing them for the arena of life.

Wood (1991), using a quote from George Wolfe, exposes the crux of the matter and the directive that challenges schools: "In a time of corruption, to nurture is a revolutionary act" (p. 3). This is what must happen in schools at accelerated levels—meaningful nurturing in order to provide students with positive alternatives to negative forces like gang membership. Schools need to pick up the responsibilities of giving today's youths some sense of belonging to larger communities while students are still allowed to explore their potential as individuals. Making schools more like families with clearly defined, incremental designations of maturation as students progress toward adulthood can help put some balance into a world gone astray and help mitigate the youthful need for darker, alternative rites of passage.

Changing the fundamental structure of schooling is not easy but there are prototypes that can certainly help, since rites have been part of the human condition for eons and are basic to understanding, exploring, and answering fundamental questions about one's humanity. A simple accommodation may be to consider the questions that are core to passage experiences. For example:

- Who am I?
- What is it that defines my humanity?
- Why am I here?
- Where am I going?
- Am I ready for the encounter offered?
- How am I to respond to the challenge?
- What is there to learn from the challenge? Or what has been learned for this encounter or transformative experience?

By adopting these same, or similar, questions it would be easy to incorporate types of reflective thought as a conceptual basis for subject-related problems. This accommodation would allow students to actively explore issues of both identity and community while learning new skills, content, and processes.

In addition to integrating meaningful questions into problem-based programs, there are also elements from preexisting programs that can be used as prototypes, foundations, or components for redesigned programs. Two excellent examples of preexisting programs are the Afrocentric Rites of Passage Program developed by Paul Hill, and a magnet high school program, Walden III in Racine, Wisconsin.

NGUSZO SABA: THE KWANZA MESSAGE

Hill (1992) has investigated reinstituting rites of passage as a way to help Black American youth. His solution revolves around returning to ancient African methods of education. Hill's ideas are based on the use of Afrocentric rites of passage and pivot around the seven moral principles of the Nguszo Saba, which is also the foundation for the Kwanza holiday.

These principles involve the following general areas: unity, self-determination, collective work and responsibility, cooperative economics, purpose, creativity, and faith. Using these seven principles, Hill offers the following suggestions to be incorporated into rites of passage used with youth:

> Rituals through ceremony are important to internal experiences. To become a rite or ritual, an activity need only be serious, established or prescribed by a legitimate authority, and formally performed at a designated time with appropriate symbolism. It is a ceremony and often a celebration of some kind. The following points are essential in implementing a ritualizing process:

> - Give definite initial directions.
> - Allow emotional expression and promote satisfaction at each step.
> - Allow for consideration of other family members.
> - Keep permanent records—snapshots, logs, etc.
> - Recognize an historic or ethnic connection from the past.
> - Establish future behavior expectations.
> - Makes appropriate and accurate custom references through research.
> - Provide appropriate recognition for initiating or culminating age period, year or skill levels. (p. 66)

Reflecting the focus of Hill's work with Ohio's Black youth, his original suggestions were specifically Afrocentric. Hill's work also includes an examination of basic, African education and social principles that are worthy of sharing. According to Hill (1991, p. 66), these principles reflect the following concepts:

1. Separating a child from the community and routines of daily life
2. Observing nature
3. A social process based on age
4. Reflection of childhood
5. Listening to elders
6. Purification rites
7. Tests of character
8. Use of special language
9. Use of a special name
10. Symbolic resurrection

THE WALDEN III PROGRAM

There is another nationally recognized program in Racine, Wisconsin, that offers a promising prototype. The program is called R.O.P.E. (Rite of Passage

Education) and is part of Walden III, an alternative magnet high school. As Feeney (1984) explains, in this program rites of passage have been conceptualized as events that evaluate students' readiness to graduate from high school as well as their readiness to enter the arena of adult life. The program targets 16 areas of human knowledge and skills. These are reading, English, self-expression, multicultural, personal growth, ethics, fine arts, mass media, human relations, science, U.S. history, mathematics, government, world, geography, physical challenge, and proficiency areas.

Within the listed categories, Walden students must demonstrate mastery before a committee in three ways: through portfolios, written projects, and oral demonstrations. This unusual program also stresses self-assessment, self-determination, and the building of self-confidence. Part of these exercises revolve around answering questions similar to the ones posed earlier: Who am I? What is it to be human? Where am I going? Am I ready?

Rites of passage at Walden III are demonstrated through authentic mastery and self-assessment. Reflective of true rites of passage, the threshold experience is reflected in the requirement for students to go through a series of probing exercises in intense self-examination. This magnet school's curriculum departs from traditional high schools in that there is strong emphasis on life skills. The school has a curriculum that is carefully balanced between the arts and academics, thus creating a more holistic view of high school and emphasizing schooling as a larger part of preparation of life.

From the vantage point of Walden III's example, rites of passage are redesigned and introduced as a time period in which students have opportunities to offer authentic proof that they are ready to leave the arena of schooling and face the challenges of real life. It is through their varied presentations that youths gain a sense of culminating excellence as their achievements become part of their ritualized passage into the world of adulthood. There is an important public element to this program in that Walden's students must make presentations before a committee of peers, faculty, and community members. Also, the program includes a series of self-defining questions. Walden III's efforts can be duplicated or adapted to many different types of programs.

SAMPLE SUGGESTIONS FOR ALTERING EXISTING CURRICULA

In addition to both Hill's program and Walden III's example, here are some of suggestions for incorporating rites of passage and celebration into existing curricula.

- Change the focus of projects or tasks, making them more introspective, reflective, and/or personalized. Deemphasize skill acquisition and highlight students' personal development or reflective growth, or focus on the exploration of connections beyond the classroom.

- Define the lesson or project focus as having emotional, physical, or cognitive growth potential, and encourage students to be reflective throughout the process through journaling, discussing, and making applications or connections to the community and the larger world.
- Keep permanent records (snapshots, logs, video, artifacts, and so on) as projects progress. Use these to encourage review, reflection, and interactive sharing. This is easy to do with today's technology. Digital cameras allow ways for teachers to document students' progress. With anonymous shots or with shots of students having parental permissions, digital pictures can also be posted on a webpage designed to give parents and community a glimpse of students' progression through the project.
- Emphasize connections to larger cycles and patterns—the universe, the earth, self-development, the past, and other peoples.
- Use the stages of traditional rites of passage to create challenging experiences:
  Separation: the individual is isolated by the challenge of solving a problem.
  Margin: a period of threshold or liminality as the isolate makes the transition from not knowing to one who has acquired skills, knowledge, or perspective.
  Aggregation: acceptance and assimilation back into the main body or learning community in a new role. The individual is now initiated into the processes, skills, or knowledge shared by the larger body.
- Celebrate the completion of tasks and create opportunities for students to share their journeys and processes, lessons learned, struggles overcome, and personal revelations.

MORE SUGGESTIONS: SIX STEPS IN MODERN RITES OF PASSAGE

Wilson (1996) lists the steps in rites of passage as follows:

1. Acknowledge the end of the old way and identify icons, symbols, and possessions that symbolize the past—the parts of the old self, or the old way to be left behind.
2. Cast off the old by engaging in a ceremony that actually destroys physical symbols or possessions that represent the old way. The destruction can be completed by burning, submergence in water, breaking or scattering, or burying symbols in the earth. Also, possessions can be given away to others in a ceremonial way.

3. Enter the void. The period of transformation is an authentic confrontation with the unknown. The participant attempts to see into the "beyond," to form new visions of perception and reality. This stage usually involves a task, or a period of isolation or introspection, or both.

4. Acknowledge the transformation. The teacher and a supportive group acknowledge the transition with gifts given to the participant. This may be done by giving the participant new material gifts, symbolic representations of new life roles and responsibilities, or symbols of changed perceptions of challenges or tasks completed.

5. Create celebrations that commemorate the transitions and allow for rejoicing in the newfound awareness and new roles and responsibilities.

6. Give thanks. Create a period of thanksgiving where the participant shows gratitude to those who have helped with life passages, and transitions.

The suggestions above can be incorporated into most classes or content with a little imagination. They create ceremony, meaning, and closure for tasks and events.

ENDINGS

Much of life's struggles have to do with power: who has it, who wants it, who gains it, who deserves it, who retains it. In modern societies we have created an artificially long period where children between ages eight to eighteen have little or no recognized power—political, financial, or personal. They are lost, and searching for their places in the continuum. Adults need to honor youthful journeys and give students and children some encouragement and serious markers of achievement along the way. Perhaps Hill (1991) says it best:

> Adults are not born but made. A tree without roots cannot survive! The development of centered and whole men and women will require a rediscovery and reactivation of some of the customs, traditions, rituals, and ceremonies we have lost. Customs, traditions, rituals and ceremonies are as veins and arteries to the body. Without connectors, there will be a breakdown in continuity. A shortage will occur somewhere in the system. Many of us have neglected, even shunned these processes at our peril. The benefits of custom, ceremonies, faith, and ritual acculturation have been discarded. . . .
> We have been educated away from ourselves. (p. 68)

Benchmarks and rites of passage are part of our human history, and part of our ancient cellular memories. Rites are beacons that help us traverse life's fine lines. They are like the tracks that served as markers for the childhood classic *The Little Engine That Could*. Thus rites and benchmarks are the incentives that help us say the Little Engine mantra, "I think I can, I think I can, I think I can" as we traverse our individual lines of life. Children deserve our support on their special life journeys. They deserve to know where they are going, and how far they have come. This is why it is important to consider rites as very real parts of their schooling experiences.

REFERENCES

Chance, L. (1994, Spring). Enabling, enhancing, empowering teachers through the supervision of pre-service teachers in the professional development schools. In R. J. Krajewski, (Ed.), *New roles for all: Fast forward 2* (70–74). Madison, WI: Wisconsin Association of Supervision and Curriculum Development.

Feeney, T. M. (1984). *R.O.P.E.: Rite of passage handbook.* Racine, WI: Walden III Alternative High School.

Hill, P., Jr. (1992). *Coming of age: African American male rites-of-passage.* Chicago: African American Images.

Longstreet, W. S., & Shane, H. G. (1993). *Curriculum for a new millennium.* Boston: Allyn & Bacon.

Van Gennep, A. (1960). *The rites of passage.* (M. B. Vizedom & G. L. Caffee, Trams.). London: Routledge & Kegan Paul.

Weissbourd, R. (1996). *The vulnerable child: What really hurts America's children and what we can do about it.* Reading, MA: Addison Wesley.

Wilson, L. O. (1996). *Making connections: Inside out, outside in.* Unpublished manuscript.

Wilson, L. O. (1998). Milestones: Integrating the celebratory elements of individual achievement and family tradition into the curriculum. In G. Benson, R. Glasberg, & B. Griffith (Eds.), *Perspectives on unity and integration of knowledge.* New York: Peter Lang.

Wood, C. (1991, Summer). Maternal teaching: Revolution of kindness. *Holistic Education Review,* 3–10.

PART 3

Inspiring Wholeness

The Poetics of Holistic Education

CHAPTER 17

In the Flame of the Heart

Toward a Pedagogy of Compassion

DIANA DENTON

I have presented three workshops at the Holistic Learning Conference: Breaking New Ground since its inception in 1997. Developing applications of my theoretical work on the phenomenology of the heart (Denton, 1998), each of these presentations offered opportunities for a reflexive exploration of the experience of the heart, both conceptual and somatic, through contemplative and imaginative practice. Each workshop addressed the primal question of my original research: How can I create the conditions for continually eliciting the kinds of ways of being in the world that I identify and describe in my study? Together with my workshop participants, I explored ways to integrate heart knowledge and experience with educational practice. In this chapter, I investigate how awakening the heart can be encouraged and guided through avenues of personal experience, imagery, and the evocation and exchange of learner responses. Engaging the heart as both inner method and attainment, as both practice and realization, I ask of myself and others how our sense of the awakened heart is embodied. How might perspectives and practices of the heart inform and expand our pedagogical praxis?

As educators we know that institutional environments, dominated by compartmental structure and bureaucratic procedure, can sometimes deaden our capacity for care and compassion. Yet a need for personal immediacy and presence, which underlies all effective intervention and support in learning environments, requires us to be fully ourselves, integrated, enlivened, and aware. Exploring elements of meditation, poetic symbolism, imaging, and metaphor can help return us to a deeper awareness and knowledge of ourselves, which can also open us to a richer knowledge and understanding of others. Such affective approaches often dismissed in the past as impractical and merely personal are now increasingly recognized as central to the generation of humane and compassionate teaching. A shared vision of the heart and of our interior geography of feeling may help to soften disciplinary and institutional boundaries and allow educators and students alike to reintegrate in a more vital and sustaining community. Ron Miller (2001) characterizes his vision of holism as "a vision of healing. It is a vision of atonement between humanity and nature. It is a vision of peace. And it is a vision of love" (p. xv). Miller's vision is consonant with my vision of the heart, and it is to this vision that I wish to speak. Our need to discover ways of being and of teaching grounded in compassionate self-awareness and empathy has never been more pressing than at present.

I begin each conference session with a period of guided meditation, inviting participants to "breathe into the heart center" and notice any textures, sensations, or feelings as they emerge. Common kinesthetic images reported include a sense of hardness or tightening, and alternately, feelings of warmth or comfort. I trace these surface signs toward a deeper understanding of our experience of the heart, and I wonder how the heart is embodied in our knowledge and experience by our perceptions and attitudes and how we might reshape and enhance these, both individually and culturally, through a possible shift in controlling images and metaphors.

Throughout time and across cultures the heart has been a symbol of compassion, eros, ecstasy, and spirit. It is the heart that soars and the heart that breaks. It is to the heart that we listen in times of solitude and in moments of intimacy. It is the heart that is stirred by the poet's lyric, the artist's eye. The heart is sacred, suffering, or triumphant. This concept of the heart has been linked to notions of the soul, a sacred inner center. Thomas Moore (1996) writes:

> Those who have written about the soul, both in the distant past and in the present, give the impression that the soul is something intimate, known to us more directly than anything else, and yet at the same time elusive, indescribably profound, not entirely knowable, not within our control, and not completely our personal possession. (p. 14)

Ancient Yogic writings refer to the heart chakra as the seat of the soul, as an embodied awareness of the infinite, a site of compassion, the very core of being (Ramana Maharshi, 1972/2001, p. 80). This heart or hrdaya is described as our innermost self, both known and unknowable, like Moore's soul. In many spiritual traditions the heart is often conceptualized as the site of liberation or enlightenment. Enlightenment is described as a perceptual shift—a process of recognition, an awakening to the immanent presence of the infinite (Singh, 1990). The enlightening self is literally illuminated: brightened, lightened, revealed. In the process of enlightenment, whether through a gradual awakening or a startling shift, we are thrown into a new epistemic domain (Nelson, in Hart, Nelson & Puhakka, 2000), but this new domain is not a region of disembodied knowledge possessed by the rational mind; it is rather a full realization of the infinite as intimate—an embodied knowing. Liberation has also been described as to "become something that moves in the heart"(Muller-Ortega, 1989, p. 2). In this formulation, it is no longer vision, the commanding bodily or intellectual eye, that orders experience, but instead, a sensation of movement, a tactile knowledge, which shifts perception by changing the avenue of perception. In seeking ways to facilitate such epistemic shifts, it is somatically mediated images of the heart derived from sensation that inform my perspectives and practice.

Recent theorists across various academic disciplines have pointed to the necessity of easing the gap between the researcher and the researched. In his exploration of the heart, Paul Muller-Ortega (1989) has recognized the limits of scholarly methods that objectify the phenomenon of study, and Paul Stoller (1997) has rightly called for a "sensuous scholarship" that involves a "mixing of head and heart—an opening of one's being to the world" (p. xiii). Entering the inner territory of the heart, I probe the self's own attempts to free consciousness through an examination of the tacit knowledge of poetics and the body. In my workshops, I offer a starting point for language and experience, helping participants embrace and experience their affective side. Muller-Ortega (1989) notes that a spiritual vision is not "something intellectual, emotional or imagined, but rather it is a pulsating powerful experience that completely transforms our ordinary and routinized perceptions of reality" (p. 3). To understand such a vision we must plunge directly into its depths. Phenomenological inquiry lends insight here. John Welwood (2000) writes that "phenomenological reflection is the putting aside of habitual conceptual assumptions in order to explore experience in a fresher, looser way" (p. 94). Understanding grows out of what is directly felt and perceived, narrowing the gap between observer and observed. Beyond phenomenological reflection, Welwood suggests a further mode of reflection that is transreflective—disclosing a way of being that lies beyond divided consciousness. We "become at-one with our experiencing—through overcoming all struggle with it, through discovering and abiding in the deep, silent source from which all experience arises" (pp. 95–96). In workshop environments access to this experience is mediated through language traces and the images constituted by affective and poetic speech, but the source and origin of these communicable forms is sought in a recovery of prelinguistic sensation and response, the rhythms of blood, breath, and heart.

THROUGH THE PERSONAL

As I turn toward the heart, I seek the sources of my own experience, which constitute and inform my vision. As a child, I frequently experienced an awareness of a compassionate presence within me. These flashes of insight would instantly, but only momentarily, collapse the distance between myself and the perceived world. I felt intimately connected with all that surrounded me. Peter Nelson (2000) discusses this transitory experience: "Although human experiential reality tends toward the everyday stratum, it is most often induced into the transition by aesthetic and religious experience. Leaping to new provinces of meaning is a metaphor for entering the sacred domain" (p. 69). I later referred to these instances of at-oneness, of a leap into meaning, as moments of presence—a nondual awareness. This could be described as the insight of inspiration. Tobin Hart (2000) refers to inspiration as a specific epistemic event, an activity of nonrational knowing. In inspirational knowing, the subject-object dichotomy is replaced with the "intimacy of contact" (p. 34), a condition of knowing removed from our normal waking state. Hart (2000) elaborates:

> It has a distinct difference from the kind of knowing characteristic of the typical normal waking state, in which a constant internal dialogue dominates. In the normal waking state awareness is subservient to analysis, the possibility of full participation in the event is often thwarted by the expectation of evaluation of it, and deep contact is prohibited by chronic categorizing of the other. This style of knowing is skewed by the acceptance of subject-object dichotomies and the objectivism that rationalizes this into place. (p. 31)

Nelson (2000) describes the different types of knowing as "epistemic frames that tend to highlight different aspects or perspectives of reality. The mystical epistemic frame carries with it an inclusiveness regarding the self-other dichotomy whereas our ordinary frame gives rise to a knowing in which self and other are exclusive" (p. 70). As a child, I developed a fierce longing for this inclusive presence—an intimacy of contact—and suffered from its frequent absence. Divisions of body, mind, heart and spirit haunted me. My later poetry (1977) gave voice to this dilemma:

> when I came
> with offerings
> of water
> wanting you thirsty
> your throat
> arched inward
> awkward & dry

I was confronted by the difficulties of the crossing, the uncertainty and impermanence of vision.

Drawn to meditation in my early teens, I began studying with a swami from India in 1974. Insights from Yogic traditions inspired my early inner journeying. In 1981 I began facilitating meditation retreats, workshops, and seminars. In my meditation work and in my daily life, I was often disturbed by a tension experienced between my embodied emotional self and my notions of an inner spiritual life. Contemporary and traditional literature pointed to a Higher Self, a Transcendent Awareness. In meditation there were glimpses of what this might be: an enveloping presence of peace and compassion, inner visions of light, and surges of subtle energy. Yet in my day-to-day existence these glimpses were fleeting and insubstantial, as I struggled to balance the demands of marriage, motherhood, and career. I began to take refuge in meditation as a retreat, resisting what I referred to as my "worldly" life. Meditation became an "ontological anchor" (Nelson, 2000, p. 80) that secured my place in the midst of nondual reality—within the precincts of an extra-ordinary consciousness. Increasingly I resisted the transition into my ordinary waking awareness, preferring to linger in meditative states for longer and longer periods. I refer to this now as a "flight into spirit." I was troubled by the divisiveness of this act, the splitting of self into a pure form of significance and a lower condition of essentially meaningless existence.

Strangely, it was this flight that finally returned me to embodied existence. During a meditation in 1986, I encountered a source of inspiration. As I sat in meditation, I became aware of a voice resonating inwardly, saying, "I have been with you but you have not seen—in the experience." Filled with a deep sense of compassion, I intuitively trusted this voice. It permeated my moment-to-moment consciousness for months to come with the words, "In this too I am present," sparking a subtle transformation in my relationship with the phenomenal world—a new, embodied, feelinged existence. What I had sought to distance in my flights of meditation became the nesting ground of spirit. It was in my all-too-human self that I was encountering this subtle compassionate presence. As I embraced the erotic quality of experience, tensions of subject/object dualism eased and I experienced an increasing intimacy with self. Drawn into the arms of experience—the mundane joys and the sorrows of mere existence— I awakened to feeling. The radical dichotomy between a higher spiritual self and the emptiness of daily life was annulled in a unified awareness of an essential, mutually sustaining interrelationship.

With this awakening of feeling, I was often shaken by an intensity of emotion. I likened this to a hand numbed by cold. Returning to warmth, there is initially severe pain. During these times I drew comfort from this inner presence. As I moved between epistemic frames my passage was mediated by this inner voice. At times the intensity was so great that I felt my heart to be breaking as if the shell of the heart were shattering. Jean Houston (1987) writes of this form of experience,

> Wounding involves a painful excursion into pathos, wherein the anguish is enormous and the suffering cracks the boundaries of what you thought you could bear. . . . Wounding involves the breaking or

penetration or opening into the human flesh or soul by a force or power or energy coming from beyond our ordinary recognized boundaries. (p. 105)

Yet this wounded, opening heart was a heart that was moved. As inner defenses dissolved, a tenderness arose. Nelson (2000) suggests, in his discussion of mystical experience, that whether or not this is an encounter with an actual existent ontological otherness is less important than the "sense of ontic shift" that arose as a result of the intensity of feeling engendered as I leapt "across an epistemic boundary" (p. 79). That this voice offered a comfort, a level of safety that facilitated this ontic shift, is undeniable. With this piercing of the heart my consciousness settled in the heart center, the heart chakra. And with this settling, the voice dissolved in silence. Nelson (2000) suggests that we must "understand mystical encounters as the remaking of one's epistemic frame of reference" (p. 64), which eventuates in a new style of knowing. I think of this experienced voice as the hand of a friend helping me traverse dangerous territory—the tangled waste of embedded restrictive inner patterns—without the terrors of isolation.

As I relaxed into the heart, I was aware that I had crossed a new threshold of consciousness. Perceptions of self were altering. I was aware of an immanent presence in the core of my own being. Fictions of some transcendent being that I aspired to become dissolved in this immediate presence of awareness. I was flooded with a deepening compassion for self. I felt softer, freer, and more grounded inside—rooted in the heart. With this came the understanding that the heart that moved moved "with a graceful stillness: firm, steady, even, beyond perturbations" (Levin, 1988, p. 239).

Emerging from the depths of this experience, I began to develop a phenomenology of the heart that provided new insights into both my personal and professional practices. The sharp dichotomy of a personal and professional life is precisely the commonly accepted and reinforced disjunction that my experience had removed. Assembling understandings, I sought a language and practice that could evoke and deepen this realization of the heart for myself and others. I wondered what practices were most useful for awakening the heart, what special conditions might be necessary to nurture and sustain a presence of the heart. It was in my workshops "In the Flame of the Heart" and my book "In the Tenderness of Stone" (Denton, 1998) that a discourse and practice evolved.

TOWARD A PRACTICE

Images of the heart volunteered by my workshop participants in discussions following meditation have been decisive in furthering and refining my understanding and methods. In returning to the core images of my own and others' experience, I repeatedly encountered the heart represented metaphorically as stone, ice, wood, or flame. Stone, ice, and wood pointed to the consciousness— the feelinged heart body—that in the midst of experience collects and retains impressions. As impressions are imbedded, conformations, deformations, and defenses arise. Consciousness hardens and contracts. As the movement of the heart diminishes, "the more does the subjectivity fall until it becomes inert like a stone" (Abhinavagupta, 1989, p. 209). The recurring image of flame seemed to reflect the vitality of feeling—the blazing fire that melts the hard core of the heart, the gentle warmth of the flame that warms and offers comfort, and the taper flame by which we see in the dark. These were vital and compelling visions that opened, released, and revitalized an awareness of the heart, of consciousness as a somatic experience made communicable in images. By "vision," I mean here the total experience of synaesthesia—"the concerted activity of all the body's senses as they function and flourish together"(Abram, 1996, p. 59). As attention moved to the heart center in meditation, I encouraged the engagement of sensational awareness. For some this was difficult. Abram notes that we "lose this awareness because we become estranged from our direct experience"(p. 62). He writes that restoring the intimate connection with experience calls for a recuperation of the senses. Sometimes a hand placed on the heart center was helpful. This making of contact often moved attention to an embodied consciousness. Always, the approach encouraged was one of gentleness and compassion.

I was aware that there had been two critical elements in my own experience that had allowed for the heart's awakening. First, the comfort of a compassionate presence gave me the courage to plunge into the depths of the heart, to engage experience not authorized and delimited as rational. And second, in this submersion I awakened the wounded experiencer. The embedded pains and patterns of a lifetime surfaced. It was the wound that stirred, moved, and melted the heart. As I reflected on my experience of the heart these two elements seemed especially significant. I wondered how my experience might be translated into a pedagogy, a teaching of the heart in the heart.

METHODS OF THE HEART

A search for method and means of teaching which could bring the heart into the shared experience of teacher and learner uncovered three related approaches. The first I identify as unintentional practice: those *woundings of the heart* that erupt in our human experience—moments of loss, rejection, trauma, and emotional pain. These have a profound effect on our consciousness, shifting our psychological boundaries. James Hillman (1989) refers to the deep hurts of experience as "salt mines from which we gain a precious essence. . . . The fact that we return to these deep hurts, in remorse and regret, in repentance and revenge, indicates a psychic need. . . . [T]he soul has a drive to remember"

(p. 125). The wound awakens us to experience. Flames of feeling melt and open the constricted places of the heart. Images of fire restore the heart's vitality, melt its frozen divides. In a meditation practice that makes contact with the wound, I invite others to return to a memory of wounding. Noticing where this is felt in the body and the emotions surrounding the wound often stirs the feeling of the heart. In the midst of wounding I ask, "What would bring you comfort in this experience?" Staying with the wound we invite in a source of comfort. In this practice we learn the difficult art of staying with the wound, releasing ourselves to suffering. (Jardine, 2001).

Pondering the intensity of my own experience, I wondered if the heart must necessarily be penetrated or wounded to be awakened. From what can come the comforting feeling, the warm hearth flame that soothes and heals? As I considered this, two further methods emerged. These are intentional practices. The first of these I refer to as a practice of *relaxing into the heart*, which cultivates a willingness to stay with experience, to recognize and listen attentively to feeling, similar to Welwood's (2000) notion of "unconditional presence" (p. 100). A key metaphor of the heart that surfaced in my early research (Denton, 1998) was described by a woman as she emerged from meditation. She reported that she felt as if her heart was a large stone, as if a hard boulder was suspended in her chest. Over a period of weeks, as she relaxed into the stone, she sensed it softening until it gradually dissolved. This was accompanied by a sensation of lightening, as if a burden had been lifted. Nelson (2000) describes an experience of recurring images in which he makes a similar discovery: "[T]he more I suspended the judgement process and became an impartial observer, the more I could see and accept them with the subsequent diminishment of their power to offend" (p. 59). It is the tendency to judge an experience that contracts and tightens the heart, that closes her doors. Welwood (2000) notes that "when we no longer maintain distance from a feeling it cannot preserve its apparent solidity" (p. 102). The emergence of durable images in meditation often attests to sensations that are imperfectly experienced, postponed, or excluded, the somatic form of a wounding. By sustaining attention on the image, by experiencing it fully, in its immediacy over time, the image is often transformed: dissolved, attenuated, or reformed. Feeling and seeing are unified in the suspended judgement of immediate, embodied perception, and the solidity of emergent visual and linguistic metaphors becomes a prelude to redistributed awareness, an opening and centering of the heart.

In these practices of relaxing into the heart, images of tightening and contraction recurred. One woman felt as if her heart was grasped by a clenched fist. Puhakka (2000) notes that

> there is a kind of "solidity" that mental images and thoughts possess
> that is similar to the solidity of physical objects. Like physical objects,

mental images are in varying degrees permeable. When they are solid, they tend to clash with other images and thoughts, and deflect attempts to make contact. (p. 17)

I would dramatize this process with an image of my own, one which I have used in the form of a concrete object in workshops: a large black pillow. The pillow is representative of the soft, malleable stuff of consciousness—a consciousness that hardens, is compressed, in the midst of experience, as impressions are embedded and reactive defences formed. This hardening of the pillow is akin to the tightening of the ego—the crust or shell that hardens around the self—constricting the heart.

Tracing my own steps, I am aware that it was my love for a sense of inner presence that allowed me to draw close to my innermost feelings. My trans-reflective awareness of compassion, which had aided an increased intimacy with self and experience, was essential to achieving an inner crossing from moments of illumination to a steady sensation of presence in various aspects of my daily life. As a possible approach to this experience, I invite workshop participants to think of something that frightens or repels them. I ask them to close their eyes and imagine their discomforting situations or objects and to move toward them, noticing as they do so accompanying feelings or images. Typical responses include tightening, tension, and resistance to touching or seeing the offending object. When I ask these same participants to visualize a loved object, they report that their sense of connection is immediate. I point out the parallel in our relationship with self. When we are disapproving of self and our experience we stand at a distance. Having compassion for what arises allows us to move inwardly. With compassion we begin to relax into experience, into feeling. Welwood (2000) notes that "here there is no effort to transmute the emotions; rather, transmutation happens spontaneously through opening fully to them" (p. 99).

The second of the intentional methods involves conscious practice of *filling the heart*—learning to nourish the self in thought, feeling, and action. I often tell a story drawn from my own parenting experience. As a child, my son, along with a neighborhood friend, decided to bake chocolate chip cookies. Their cookies were yellow and shockingly bitter. "What did you add?" I asked, simulating casualness. "Tumeric" came the reply. "That's like cinnamon, right Mom?" In the bittering of these cookies I see a metaphor for our bittering of consciousness. What we offer to the self bears fruit. Our thoughts, feelings, and actions resonate inwardly. I frequently ask participants to contemplate, *What am I offering myself in experience?* The ingredients of our consciousness form and direct our experience, or taste of self.

As we acknowledge our conscious participation in the patterns that surround and fill us, we awaken new possibilities in experience. We discover that these hardened patterns, the stones of our heart and life, have a malleable quality. They are not as fixed as we had thought. In my workshops I work with the physically malleable medium of clay to explore this possible shifting. I invite participants to think of a feeling that would nourish them. Feelings that arise include peace, gentleness, spontaneity, vitality, and fulfillment. Through memory, we invite these qualities into the body. As the memory dissolves we stay with the feeling, breathing it into and throughout the body. At the close of meditation, I invite participants to imagine the feeling moving through their arms and into their hands. Letting the feeling move through their fingers they offer this quality to the clay itself. The molding skin is wet and gentle. We notice how easily the clay receives this quality. Years later these pieces of hardened clay may still resonate with the same feelings that were part of their formation. In another contemplative exercise I invite participants to reflect on a moment of fulfillment and to allow these feelings to flood the body and consciousness. The inner shift is often immediate.

These three methods: *the evocation of the wound, relaxing into the heart* and *filling the heart* represent the core of my heart practice. I've developed numerous exercises within each of these practices to facilitate awakening the heart. Beyond these of my invention, I often encourage others to find practices, actions, and images that stir, fill, and move their own hearts. Here one's unique experience becomes the mantra of choice.

The ancient and persistent somatic and poetic identification of the heart as a center of being, as the place of the soul, provides the orienting metaphors of my approach to a compassionate pedagogy. In accordance with Nelson's view of the phenomenological integrity of mystical experience, my exploration of emergent heart images does not demand any peremptory decision concerning the objective causation of experiences which elicit them, neither in myself nor in my students and colleagues. It is enough that a working level of intersubjectivity involving these images is culturally available and evident in the responses of participants. The traditional concept of the heart provides a point of entry to a thinking with and through the body, seeking to free new energies of feeling and imagination through the generation and exploration of images and sensations awakened in meditation. Methods for facilitating this exploration involve freeing experiences and images of pain and loss, accepting and attending to these images, and opening the self to regeneration and transformation through guided imagery exercises and shared reflection. My approach resists genetic or causal explanation of experience and examines instead the somatic and conceptual texture of experience in its immediacy, as it unfolds in the language and images of the reflective subject. The heart as a center of physical and psychic being becomes the ground of a shared experience of images and their affective significance: the stone, ice, and flame. An openness to poetic reflection, a relaxation into the experienced, a freeing of associative and affective imagination, all these contribute to exchanges and interrelationships of meaning which can nourish community and regenerated vision. Instructional pedagogies based on mechanistic cognitive models and increasingly directed by quantifiable measures must be balanced by an awareness of the heart.

REFERENCES

Abram, D. (1996). *The spell of the sensuous: Language in a more-than-human world.* New York: Vintage Books.

Denton, D. (1977). Tasting: Hunger & thirst. *West Coast Review, 11*(3): 41–42.

Denton, D. (1998). *In the tenderness of stone: Liberating consciousness through the awakening of the heart.* Pittsburgh: Sterling House.

Hart, T., Nelson, P., & Puhakka, K. (Eds.). (2000). *Transpersonal knowing: Exploring the horizon of consciousness.* Albany: State University of New York Press.

Hillman, J. (1981). *Blue fire.* New York: Harper SanFrancisco.

Hocking, B., Haskell, J., & Linds, W. (Eds.). (2001). *Unfolding bodymind: Exploring possibility through education.* Brandon, VT: Foundation for Educational Renewal.

Houston, J. (1987). *The search for the beloved: journeys in mythology and sacred psychology.* Los Angeles: Jeremy P. Tarcher.

Jardine, D. W. (2001). Unable to return to the gods that made them. In B. Hocking, J. Haskell, & W. Linds, (Eds.), *Unfolding bodymind: Exploring possibility through education* (269–281). Brandon, VT: Foundation for Educational Renewal.

Levin, D. M. (1988). *The opening of vision: Nihilism and the postmodern situation.* New York: Routledge, Chapman & Hall.

Maharshi, R. (1972) *The spiritual teachings of Ramana Maharshi.* Boston: Shambhala.

Maharshi, R. (2001). The heart is the self: From the spiritual teachings of Ramana Maharshi. *Parabola, 26*(4): 80–82.

Moore, T. (Ed.). (1996). *The education of the heart.* New York: HarperPerennial.

Muller-Ortega, P. (1989). *The triadic heart of siva: Kaula tantricism of Abhinavagupta in the non-dual shaivism of kashmir.* Albany: State University of New York Press.

Nelson, P. (2000). Mystical experience and radical deconstruction: through ontological looking glass. In Hart, T., Nelson, P., & Puhaka, K. *Transpersonal knowing: Exploring the horizon of consciousness.* Albany: State University of New York Press.

Singh, J. (Trans.). (1990). *The doctrine of recognition: A translation of Pratyabhij-nahrdayam*. Albany: State University of New York Press.
Stoller, P. (1997). *Sensuous scholarship*. Philadelphia: University of Pennsylvania Press.

CHAPTER 18

The Creative Journey

Personal Creativity as Soul Work

ISABELLA COLALILLO KATES

As I open, you open, we open.
—Emerson, *source unknown*

CREATIVITY AS A SPIRITUAL PATH: HOLISTIC PREMISES

Imagine a world made up of creative individuals doing their own thing! Choosing to use personal creativity in an ever more complex, consumerist, and flat-liner world is a decision to live soulfully. Creative work nurtures the sacralizing power that connects the head and heart and taps into spiritual sources of wisdom. William Blake considered personal creativity a gift of the spirit. " I will not Reason & Compare," he wrote, "My business is to Create" (Euland, 1938/1987, p. 158). Creativity is an inner fire that stokes the passion of self-growth and offers us a shared and shareable language. It fosters holistic modes of learning that develop multidimensional intelligences, from intellectual to spiritual intelligence (Gallegos Nava, 2000). Through our creative voice we claim a personal space within the public space and thereby enrich our character and the evolving character of our social milieu. Creativity is the soul's gift to the self in time and needs our time and intent to grow and flourish.

In my workshops and classes with aspiring creators, who come from all age groups and walks of life, we explore personal creativity from the perspective of a spiritual activity. It is a spiritual choice to nurture our creative powers by reconnecting to the creative source. Although writing is the chief expressive mode in my classes, the passion to do, to create, and to express our knowing aesthetically, is what we are after. Two questions invite participants to ponder the nature of creativity and its relationship to life and work: *What are the ways in which I am creative? Am I willing to use my souljuice to expand the purpose of my life?* These questions open up discussion on the importance of choosing or ignoring our innate, creative talent and how either choice affects our life and health and delineates the quality of our relationship to the larger community.

Taking time and responsibility for our creative powers nurtures our innate talent and satisfies our need for personal growth. *How is creativity connected to my aspiration to be more authentic, empathetic, and compassionate?* asks students and workshop participants to reflect on opening locked creative doors by nurturing their synaesthetic sensoria. They perceive the creative journey as part of a larger healing journey toward wholeness and wholeheartedness. Creativity is as much about nurturing the self as it is about producing works of art. Rhudyhar (1977) perceives personal creativity as a personal need that responds to the larger need of a cultural transformation:

> The essential value of the creative process, as I see it, is the answer it gives to the collective need of a culture and a society. . . . To create is to transform; but the basic issue is what is being transformed. It may be raw materials (clay, wood, words, pigments or the patterns of social behaviour) to which a more integrative and meaning-realising form is given; but it also could be the consciousness of human beings and their capacity to respond effectively to the challenge of a greater life. (p. 176)

As a poet, writer, holistic educator, and psychotherapist, I am interested in how personal creativity, qualified as holistic sensing, contributes to the integration of consciousness and well-being. I have presented my work with creativity, developed through writing classes and workshops, at four holistic world conferences. Each workshop highlighted aspects of the creative journey and its relationship to holistic practice, personal integration, and soul work. Experiential exercises framing the theoretical tenets of the creative process allow participants to gauge their creative process and explore the larger principles that guide the creative odyssey. In this chapter, I discuss three main premises of personal creativity as soulwork: the creative process as a spiritual path; the recovery of creative voice as healing act; and the social importance of activating personal creativity in an age characterized by obsessive consumerism and violence.

THE CREATIVE JOURNEY: THE CREATIVE SELF

In my classes and workshops we use insightful tools such as creative visualization, focusing activities, and spontaneous art to access inner flow. Inner explorations encourage aspiring creators to recover the sound and quality of their authentic imagery and to use their voice to express their experiential "I." Stories, poetry, and other forms of writing restore their faith in their inner world and innate talent. The spiritual context considers how the creative journey consoles and heals the wounded, fragmented self by engaging a shift in consciousness that awakens the heart, empowers the creative voice and tames the critical self. The creative experience unfolds from a deeply felt sense, until it bursts free in a moment of inspiration. This is the moment when the tendril of creative aspiration propels us to search for our authentic voice. Crafting a poem or prose piece requires opening and attuning to the inner and outer sensoria while plucking at the rhythms and cadences of emerging imagery and its expressive language (Rico, 1983). This process takes time, patience, and sometimes great courage. As a guide, I am deeply moved by the varied experiences of students and workshop participants. In many ways, their journey toward awakening the power and purpose of their creative energy reflects my own. Over time, I have come to understand how my own creative work serves to nourish my spiritual senses. Personal creativity links me with my soul's vision of myself in time. A paper (2000) given as a lecture and poetry reading expresses the fullness of these ideas:

> Creativity is a large gift, at once shamanic and phenomenological. I never know where my creative spirit will lead me though I know that its source is deep within my pre-verbal self rooted in the sacred core of being. Creative journeys into the timeless self are not unlike the shaman's journeys into other realms. For me writing is a kind of time travel that uses the fuel of creativity to sojourn into and beyond time and place using the mnemonic maps of the creative spirit. Creativity, like grace, privileges and guides me to new depths of consciousness; it functions like spiritual myelin, like a magical/mantic elixir that allows consciousness to unknot and flow into multidimensional journeys of discovery. My writing is a discovery of the bridges linking the ordinary and the sacred spaces of my life, lending me courage to live through phases of darkness and confusion. Writing is a sacred act of survival that allows the self in time to prevail and flourish. (p. 1)

CREATIVITY AS *THERAPEA*: WHOLING THE SELF

As products of modern education, which still favors logic and analysis over affect and creative exploration, my students have learned to subdue their feelings—the door to the creative imagination. After the age of eight or nine, most people are urged to develop the logical, classifying mind, associated with the left-brain mode. This mode makes use of the technical aspects of the imagination while ignoring its more whimsical, analogical ones. Imaginal tools such as creative visualization reopen our creative channels by exercising the right-brain mode. This analogical feeling mind draws on our playful, preverbal knowing and provides us with holistic resources for reacquainting ourselves with the power of imaginal play. When we are creatively engaged we broadcast our aliveness, wonder, and curiousity.

Engagement and intentionality are two main tenets of my work with creativity. I remind students that the creative path begins with choosing to make time to create and learning to prevail over the nagging critical voices that tell us to give up; that make us consumers rather than creators. Robert Bly (1988), the poet and social activist, warns that when people don't use their creative juices, the powers-that-be pounce on their unused creativity and use its power to wage war and grow in political dominance. As this shocking idea sinks in, my students begin to understand the importance of taking responsibility for their creative talents. Uncovering the layers of resistance that keep us from consciously using our latent creativity involves commitment and risk. The odyssey of recovering our creative voice brings us face to face with the conflict between our Innate Creator and the Inner Critic. Affirming the presence of the Creator is the only way to the dim the power of the Critic. As each of us matures creatively and spiritually, we create new behavioral and perceptual structures for expanding the self and establish our creative visions for personal and social change (Eisler, 1987).

A fundamental role of art and aesthetic reflection is to decode the quality and baggage of our encoded imagery and to provide us with the opportunity to explore its meaning. Creative energy has the capacity to shift our ego-based perspectives and propel us into increased states of awareness and integrity (Ferrucci, 1982/1989; Goldberg, 1986, 1990). In my educative work, I propose that as we reacquire the dynamic capacity to reactivate our spiritual senses, we take small, sure steps in helping to reduce violent, addictive, self-destructive behaviors that characterize life in modern societies. I remind aspiring creators that making time to reflect in solitude is an essential prerequisite for creative activity (Storr, 1988). Creative reflection can take many forms: creative visualization, daydreaming, or walking in a quiet place in solitary contemplation are some activities that inspire the imagination, unlimber intuition, and provide a framework for engaging the creative senses and cultivating insight.

WRITING AS A SPIRITUAL PATH: THE INNATE CREATOR

In each class or workshop, creative reflection guides participants to discover their own imagery. I remind people to feel rather than analyze their imaginal experiences. Creativity activates latent emotional intelligence; feelings open us to intuition and insight and inspire creative expression (Rico, 1983). Intuition has been described as the imagination of the soul (Bailey, 1974). I remind participants that creative intelligence, centered in the heart, is a resonant aspect of our holistic and spiritual intelligence. The epistemological thread highlighting the natural relationship between creativity and spirituality first emerged in one of my writing classes. After reading her written piece on the nature of her creative process, a student remarked that for her, creativity and spirituality were part of the same continuum of consciousness. This insight lent a new resonance to my work as a writer and teacher of creative process. At the end of the class where we discussed this important connection, I recorded the following observation:

> R said the class was *amazing*. Yes is a "maze" to the Self, I said laugh-ing. . . . Tonight, D finally stopped feeling fearful. . . . His eyes were softer, more receptive. . . . At the end of the class he trusted me enough to hand me a short one-page piece. . . . He was smiling with his eyes. . . . I think that by opening up the discussion at that point we were able to put our feelings of diminishment, shame, self-doubt out on the floor. (Creativity and Writing Journal, 1998)

Rooted in the wonder and curiosity of childhood, creative energy nurtures our memory of spirit (Keen, 1969; Steiner, 1924/1974; Rico, 1983). It prevails even when dimmed by the slaying power of carping, critical voices. In the cre-ative journey, we reanimate the wonder and curiousity of our early years as we engage the experiences of the ordinary life and relate them to our inner life. From this perspective, creativity is soul work and creates a sacred bridge between the inner and outer realities of self. We track the soul's circuitous movements toward degrees of wholeness as we experience and express insights through cre-ative work that promotes wholeness and transformation. We move from thresh-old to threshold both vertically and horizontally—or as Salinger (1963) put it: "All we do our whole lives is go from one little piece of Holy Ground to the next" (p. 213).

The human being is made up of the triangle of mind, soul and spirit. The soul, at the center of this relationship, expresses the creative fluidity of the self in time. Mind (*manas* in Sanskrit) is the incarnating principle between soul and spirit, with soul as the creative principle (Bailey, 1974). Our word *human*, derived from *manas*, reflects the incarnated, localized aspect of spirit working through the agency of soul—the generative principle behind material reality. We use the noetic and poetic modes of mind to experience reality and in cre-ative acts we learn to build a relational bridge between the linear rational mind (noetic) and the nonlinear imaginal (poetic) mind. Creativity is the "magic syn-thesis," says Arieti (1976) and Czikzentmihaly (1996) calls it "flow."

We embark on the creative journey by making meaningful connections with the creative source, which I have named the Innate Creator—the source of our wonder, exploration, and discovery. As children, we played, imagined, and expressed our wonder until we entered into the rational world of measurements and logical consequences. This shift dimmed the power and influence of the cre-ative imagination. Our *poesis* (from the Greek, *poein*, "to do," "to create") gave way to *noesis* (from the Greek for "to think"). The voice of our Innate Creator belongs to the realm of *poesis*, which represents the active, creative power of the human spirit. Experiencing the mythic language of the imaginal mind expresses our intuitive sources of knowing. Visualization journeys and other imaginal technologies reveal rich archetypal imagery reflecting the source of the vision or idea ready to be expressed in a work of art. Through creative activities we become pilgrims into the sacred sites of the psyche. Creative writing is an aesthetic activity that decompresses stored emotional experiences in order to make sense of them in new ways. Writing and creating from the source of *poesis* may come through moments of great pain or sudden inspiration.

Visualization exercises bypass the critical gates of the Inner Critic by tapping into the playful visions of the Innate Creator, whose voice encourages us to create with pleasure and nourish ourselves through our creative contributions. The Innate Creator belongs to the life of the soul and embodies its qualities— beauty, harmony, rhythm, discernment, joy, love, and truth. We express our soul's knowing through aesthetic processes: writing, painting, music, dance, and other expressive arts. As the soul's advocate, the Innate Creator encourages us to take risks and expand the perceptual, intuitive, and affective parameters of self. Its main role is to midwife expressive freedom and nurture the affective domains.

RE-CONNECTING TO THE CREATIVE SOURCE:
IMAGINATION AND VISUALIZATION

Aesthetic forms communicate what we know and understand about an experience—a work of art invokes new, subjective understandings that invite others to commune with our own understanding. A creative activity, like other spiritual practices, awakens and sharpens our spiritual senses. Using the healing power of the imagination, creative acts teach us the secret of self-re-creation so that each time we fall, or like Humpty Dumpty are pushed off the wall, we can reconstruct the shape of our reality. Imaginal technologies offer direct access to the pathways of the creative self as we feel and sense images. "Images," writes Hillman (1999), "come to us from the world's imagination with which ours corresponds" (p. 183). Images are a kind of aesthetic DNA projecting the perceived value of experience through the imagination: "More than a faculty," adds Hillman, "the imagination is one of the great archetypal principles, like love, order, beauty" (p. 183). "Imagination," proclaimed William Blake, "is the divine body in everyman" (as cited in Euland, 1938/1987, p. 10). The imagination is the soul's window on time and experience and uses the grammar of images to organize our understanding and elaborates the soulful dimensions of self through aesthetic expression.

Creative works embody the magnitude of the soul's inspirational dimensions. Within the word *aesthetic* is the "aha" moment of inspired seeing when we become aware of what we need to express (Rico, 1983). The Greek word *aisthou*, meaning "gasp," is a sudden intake of breath (Hillman, 1999). Aesthetic activity emerges from moments of deep illumination—a moment of surprise catches the breath, yielding images, metaphors, and expressive direction toward a work of art. We write a poem, dialogue or short story without knowing beforehand what genre it needs to embody its message. The vision shapes its own literary form.

Visualization journeys evoke inspiration by pulling at the sinewy threads of emotional memory where the experience is stored. The right brain mode, associated with the sensing aspect of unbounded exploration, is also the seat of the emotions (Rico, 1983; Murdock, 1987). Brain-mind research posits that the brain encodes experiences in images stored in the cell body of its dendritic web. Emotional bias shapes the memory's encoding process: the more we feel an experience, the more myelin (brain glue) is produced in the creation of the brain cell storing the memory (Sperry, 1973). Images are preverbal perceptual patterns, recursive and whole, stored in the affective domain of the mind. In visualisation there is an inherent relationship between the right mode, which engages and discerns images, and the left mode, which expresses their meaning through rhythm and structure. Creating and writing from the source of images takes us inside the feeling tone of the experience and gives our communication its vivid aesthetic significance (Rico, 1983).

As we awaken the imaginal mind, we octavize our nested creative potential. The word *octavize* is a musical term that comes from Gurdjieff's philosophy concerned with bringing into rhythmic correspondence the misaligned parts of the self (Ouspensky, 1949). Octavization, in this sense, signifies an integration of two loci of consciousness. In the journey toward wholeness, we bring the fragmented personality self (the timebound social ego) under the guidance of the timeless spiritual self influenced by the soul. William Blake understood that our creative power represents life itself, that it is spirit (Euland, 1938/1987). In creative moments of illumination we feel a sense of unity and oneness, a deep sense of beauty and harmony.

The soul, our locus of spiralling creative power anchored in the heart, mediates the concerns of the material self focused in timebound noetic thinking. During aesthetic exploration, the higher spiritual self—the bridge to the soul—engages the nondual rhythms of the imagination and senses larger reality clusters, both visible and invisible. This perceptual shift from linear time to cyclical time produces "a very liberating effect on the heart" (Y. Toufexis, personal communication, 2002). Creating works of art articulates our deepest yearnings and serves to mend the heart while nurturing mind and spirit. This is the essential healing value of artistic expression. Unexamined experiences, like thorns or slivers, irritate our hearts, disturb the psyche and bring disquiet to the spirit.

AWAKENING CREATIVITY: USING IMAGINAL PRACTICES

Exploration through imagery is an ongoing activity in my classes. A multidimensional exercise called "The Tree" imaginally explores the hidden qualities of the creative self and anchors trust in our personal imagery. A short visualization invites participants to imagine they are walking in a forest. They observe a special tree and using their synaesthetic senses discern its spiritual and physical qualities. Eyes open, students spontaneously choose two colors and draw two images of the tree, one with the dominant hand and the other with the nondominant hand, while staying close to the feeling quality of the experience. After completing their drawings, participants revisit the imaginal tree and perceive its essential qualities (friendly, open, caring, gentle, wise, centered, and so on) as well as its functional qualities (tall, strong, beautiful, green, old, bent, and so forth). Focusing on the drawings and qualities, they quickly write words or phrases associated with each tree in and around the drawings with the dominant and nondominant hand. The dual power of image and words ferrets out raw patterns of buried emotional states. Taking a final overview they ask, Do the words fit? What is the feeling tone for each tree? Do I want to add or change anything?

A clustering exercise prepares students to write. Clustering is the creation of word maps from a single word to draw out associations, connectivity and resonance from the psyche to locate the abstract message encoded in the drawings (Rico, 1983). Students choose a quality word (from each of the drawings) and as new words resonate with the key word they create a word web. The emerging word map charts emotional strings of memory until a moment of "aha" offers a story thread, engaging the final act of writing. After taking a final overview of the cluster, students write a short paragraph for each tree using the pronoun *I*. Taking an overview before writing refocuses attention and shifts the imaginal, explorative mode towards the logical, generative mode of consciousness. After clustering, students write quickly and effortlessly without censoring or editing their flow of ideas.

The experiential journey into the imagination (*poesis*) followed by the expressive, thoughtful (*noesis*) writing stage provides personal meaning for the writer. The power of the Tree exercise evokes deep levels of insight and inspires powerful, dramatic texts. Trusting the authenticity of their inner imagery helps writers to appreciate the unique quality and depth of their creative process. Interpreting their own imagery is an important step to reclaiming authentic voice. In the sharing circle, participants are free to share their writing and aspects of their process or simply to listen without making any interpretive comment on another's work.

"The Tree" exercise reawakens childlike wonder. Students experience deep feelings of joy and discovery reminding them of their young years, before the fear of doing things wrong or in a particular way dimmed their imaginal spontaneity.

They experience an embodied flow of feeling, thinking, and sensing. "This is fun! This is freeing! I haven't done this for years! Wow!"(CW Journal, 1998). They also discover the ease of expression of the dominant hand (symbolic of the outer, constructed self) and the shy clumsiness of the nondominant hand (the inner, more silent self). Symbolically, the drawings represent affective snapshots suggesting perceptual aspects of inner and outer tensions between overt and hidden talents represented by the qualities of self characterized by each hand. "The drawings are live transmissions from your inner self," I say, and suggest that hanging them up where they may see them may inspire new insight and produce more writing.

CREATIVITY AS SOUL WORK: PRINCIPLES AND PRACTICE

The soul speaks to us through intuition and inspiration. When we experience great beauty or great sadness we are connecting to the realm of soul. "The Ladder" exemplifies a guided imagery exercise that helps participants to perceive the nature of their commitment to the creative journey. The exercise shifts everyday perception into an expanded state of consciousness. The imagery reflects the self's engagement with the creative energies of the soul. Symbols of resistance, as we climb the ladder, signal the personality's tentative relationship with personal creativity.

The exercise begins with participants imagining themselves on a star. They are invited to climb a ladder leading from the star into space. The top of the ladder dissolves into brilliant white light. Can they reach the top and merge with the light? At the end of the exercise, I invite them to make a drawing of their imagery and write from the experience. Reflection through art and writing engages the creative antennae in decoding the deeper archetypal message of the imaginal language. Symbolically, the Ladder exercise offers participants a glimpse into the nature and depth of their choice to be creative. It is important to remind people to suspend all judgement about their place on the ladder and to merely reflect on the experience and its meaning *for them*.

In each class or workshop, I ask people to consider the question, What are the ways in which you express and nourish your creativity? Participants share their answers in the circle so everyone can hear the many ways we nourish creativity. As we discuss the holistic, integrative potential of personal creativity, we uncover some principles that characterize the creative process and its rela-tionship to our life and work: (a) Engaging the creative sensoria develops keener powers of observation, through which we gain insight into life's problems. (b) We are all creators and we each have something important to say; we have a sacred responsibility to communicate our understanding in ways that nourish our spirit and console our woundings. (c) Personal creativity nurtures our need for beauty and wholeness and is the expression of our soul's light. (d) The expressive arts reconnect us to our inner life and nurture our evolving consciousness, contributing to the evolution of the world soul—the *anima mundi*. (e) Using personal creativity fosters personal growth and self-transformation so we become more courageous, authentic, and self-directed. (f) Personal creativity as soul work enhances our character and restores degrees of self-trust and self-love so we may embody our inner vision and identify our personal purpose for creating.

RECOVERING OUR SUBLIME NATURE: POSITIVE SELF-TALK

We tend to suppress our sublime nature out of habit and discouragement: "I'm not sure I can write or draw well, I don't want to try." We ignore the creative call out of neglect or habitual laziness: " I have no time to be creative," or out of fear and shame: "People will laugh at my work." In these and other ways, people manage to silence their Innate Creator and leave the management of their creative house to the Inner Critic. We are all subject to the internalized tyranny of critical voices (Elbow, 1994). The Inner Critic, the composite voice of the many external critics that try to govern our life, wants us to obey its overbearing, commanding voice. The more we do so, the more victimizsed and uncreative we feel. Our resident Critic uses our creative energy to machinate against the will of the Innate Creator. Associated with the ego, which seeks permanence, the Critic resists flow and transformation (Goldberg, 1990). Its main role is to protect us from taking risks, from overreaching our dreams. In its attempts to spare us from failure, usually through shame and fear, the Critic cuts us off from the explorative energy of the Creator. When we give the critic this parenting responsibility, we shift our locus of willpower and derive our self-image from the opinion of others. We draw energy from external power sources and learn to speak with false, socially constructed voices in order to fit in. In time we become ventriloquized and forget the sound of our original voice.

Negative self-talk damages our self-esteem and weakens our trust in our inner sources of power (Fiore, 1989). Our discernment becomes negative judgment and turns our hearts away from pursuing our dreams. Negative self-talk is a subconscious mental activity that creates a state of creative numbness. Many students complain that they don't have the discipline to engage in or complete creative work, a symptom pointing to an absence of passion. The Latin root of *discipline* means "to learn," to dedicate oneself completely to an area of study. To have discipline suggests having passion for something. When we are cut off from the energy of creative passion of the Innate Creator, we become distracted by the protective voice of the Critic, which says, "If you don't try, you can't fail." The quantity and quality of our negative self-talk literally separates us from the heart, the center of passion and exploration.

It is useful to examine how redirecting self-talk can change the trajectory of the subvocal mental scripts that determine the nature of our emotional responses and inhibit our will to choose. An exercise I have named "Positive Talk: Turning the Critic into an Ally" calls upon our skillful will to rebalance and redirect negative self-talk. It begins with a focusing exercise (Gendlin, 1992) in which participants observe, without judgement, the many self-negating messages of the Inner Critic: "I *need* to finish this work"; "I *must* begin this project", "I *have* to be perfect." Noticing how oppressive modals—*should, need to, have to, must*—engage murky feelings of shame, participants learn to feel the embodied quality of negative admonitions (feeling cold, hot, nausea, tight muscles). After writing down some negative messages, they search for verb forms that suggest more encouraging choices: "I can be human" rather than "I must be perfect"; "I choose to complete this work" rather than "I don't have time." Rebalancing the warnings of the Critic turns it into an ally. Each negative message represents a potential opportunity for doing creative work without fear and affirms our creative intentions. Positive self-talk is self-care. The creative shift from fear to intent reminds us of the original relationship between discipline and passion.

SOULFULNESS AND CHARACTER: ENGAGING THE CREATIVE SPIRAL

Creative activities are integral acts of "therapea," of making whole what has been fragmented (Houston, 1982). The creative journey begins with making time to explore the imagination through wonder and inspired moments, allowing aesthetic expression to transform desire into action. Blake wrote that creativity is the journey of the self reconnecting with the soul's vibration (Euland, 1938/1987). It is a spiraling musical journey. The philosopher Plotinus wrote that the circling soul reaches for all things in living its life (Hillman, 1999, p. 128). Creative activity attunes us to the soul's rhythms and its creative purpose for our life, allowing us to move toward wholeness with more courage, grace, value, power, and wisdom. William Blake's dictum, "He whose face gives no light shall never become a star," reminds us of the essential need to create. Euland (1938/1987) writes, "Gradually by writing you will find more and more of your true self . . . to be free to say what you think. . . . [O]nly by writing and by long and patient true work you will find your true self" (p. 111).

Creative power neither comes from nor feeds ambition. Blake burned many of his manuscripts to avoid the trap of self-importance that injures the creative spirit and its will to create: "People confuse the human and the divine ego" he proclaimed (as cited in Euland, p. 82). We create first and foremost for ourselves, for our own spiritual nourishment. A creative life is richer, more meaningful, and insightful and guides us to become more self-aware, sovereign cartographers of our own life, work, desires, and destiny.

REFERENCES

Arieti, S. (1976). *Creativity: The magic synthesis*. New York: Basic Books.

Bailey, A. A. (1974). *The soul: The quality of life*. New York: Lucis.

Bly, R. (1988). *The little book on the human shadow*. San Francisco: Harper & Row.

Colalillo Kates, I. (1990–1999). Unpublished Creativity and Writing research journals.

Colalillo Kates, I. (2000). *Identity and Gender: Self creating the self*. Paper for Iacobucci Centre Conference, University of Toronto.

Colalillo Kates, I. (2002). Awakening creativity and spiritual intelligence: The soul work of holistic educators. Unpublished dissertation, Ontario Institute for Studies in Education at the University of Toronto.

Czikszentmihalyi, M. (1996). *Creativity*. New York: Harper Collins.

Eisler, R. (1987). *The chalice and the blade. Our history, our future*. New York: Harper SanFrancisco.

Elbow, P. (1994). *Writing without teachers*. London: Oxford University Press.

Euland, B. (1987). *If you want to write*. St. Paul, MN: Greywolf Press. (Original work published 1938.)

Ferrucci, P. (1989). *What we may be: The visions and techniques of Psychosynthesis*. Los Angeles: Jeremy P. Tarcher.

Fiore, N. (1989). *The now habit*. Los Angeles: Jeremy P. Tarcher.

Gallegos Nava, R. (2000) A multidimensional, multilevel perspective of holistic education: An integrated model. A paper presented at the 8th Holistic Education Conference, Guadalajara, Mexico. Retrieved from www.neat.tas/edu.au/HENT/world.rgm/integration.htm

Gendlin, E. T. (1978/1982). *Focusing*. Toronto: Bantam Books.

Ghiselin, B. (Ed.). (1952). *The creative process*. Los Angeles: University of California Press.

Goldberg, N. (1986). *Writing down the bones*. Boston and London: Shambhala.

Goldberg, N. (1990). *Wild mind: Living the writer's life*. New York: Bantam Books.

Hillman, James. (1999). *The force of character and the lasting life*. New York: Ballantine Books.

Houston, J. (1982). *The possible human*. Los Angeles: Jeremy Tarcher/Perigee.

Keen, S. (1969). *Apology for wonder*. New York: Harper & Row.

Murdock, M. (1987). *Spinning inward*. Boston & London: Shambhala.

Ouspensky, P. D. (1949). *In search of the miraculous*. New York: Harcourt, Brace & World.

Rico Lusser, G. (1983). *Writing the natural way*. Los Angeles: J. P. Tarcher.

Rudhyar, D. (1977). *Culture, crisis and creativity*. Wheaton, IL: QuestBooks.

Salinger, J. D. (1963). *Raise high the roofbeam, Carpenters, and Seymour: An introduction*. Boston: Little Brown.

Sperry, R. (1973). Lateral specialization of cerebral function in surgically separated hemispheres. In F. J. Mc Guigan & R. A. Schoonover (Eds.), *The psychobiology of thinking* (pp. 209–229). New York: Academic Press.

Steiner, R. (1924/1974). *The kingdom of childhood*. London: Rudolf Steiner Centre.

Storr, A. (1988). *Solitude. A return to self*. New York: Macmillan.

CHAPTER 19

A Gathering of Orphans

Struggling for Liberation and Awakening within the Goal

F. CHRISTOPHER REYNOLDS

As we work as teachers working in an emancipator (Henderson, 1995), prophetic (Slattery, 1995), or initiatiory (Moore, 1997; Reynolds, 2001; Fideler, 1993) style, to comfort the afflicted and afflict the comfortable, we soon encounter the image of the orphan. In fact, there seems to be no working in those styles without having suffered our own versions and visions of orphanhood. While the orphan is a guiding image of movements of change, we can stumble upon the very source of our wisdom if we are unable to separate from the archetypal energy of the One Who Belongs Nowhere and take on a more human attitude and workload.

The orphan path carries with it the challenge of belonging nowhere. If acted out too unconsciously, that path can take us from city to city, from institution to institution, driven on at times by an inner necessity, at others, by outer crises. However, having nowhere to lay one's head, if taken up consciously, can also represent the stance of teachers working in relation with their deepest power. The difference between getting burned on the job and bringing a truly transformative fire into the world seems to be related to getting to know the archetype that has called us.

We gain consciousness of the archetypal by psychologizing or seeing through (Hillman, 1975). That work requires many orphan images. The alchemists would say that we need to dissolve the matter in its own water. We will consider the orphan as biology, symptoms, and secrets; as history, culture, and cosmology; as iconoclast and chosen one; as trickster, as elder; and lastly as a bearer of planetary consciousness.

ORPHAN AS BIOLOGY, SYMPTOMS, AND SECRETS

Here, the image is of the abandoned one who is literally not good enough to keep. Suffering from a broken home because of divorce, sickness, death come too soon, or because of some crime or shameful secret, deeply felt worthlessness seems to be the start of orphan life (Piirto, 1998). For me, the reaction was to hate my parents and most things that they found valuable. With that hatred came blame for what felt like a life damaged from the start. I suffered from the symptom of chewing on my own hands, detesting my father's drunkenness, my mother's control.

The orphan life can be lived out at this level of hating your source and compulsively feeding on yourself. A life caught in this image though is a kind of hell that seems to lead to greater hates and more ravenous self-eating until breakdown, the image is broken through, or death brings relief. In the song, "My War" (2001), I wrote:

This is my war
I have fought from every side
I have conquered and I have died
This is my war
I am the blood on the steel
I am the chariot and the wheel

ORPHAN AS HISTORY, CULTURE, AND COSMOLOGY

Seeing through the personal wounding and neglect can be done by learning the history of the family and the culture. I eased up on my parents when I realized how wounded they were. I also saw the genealogy of the wounds they suffered. The energy that orphans us has a family history that has the reach of centuries.

Understanding the family wound as a seeing through of history opens to how the family wound is suffered by Western culture at large. Malidoma Some (1999) makes us aware of this wound with his description of the village life of the Dagara tribe of West Central Africa. In premodern cultures like the Dagara, the grandparents play a role in finding out an individual child's true name, in the sense of that child's reason for being born. In our culture, where that is not done, we suffer neglect in the form of ignorance of our life's purpose and a general dis-empowering of the grandparents. Further, without meaningful rites of passage at puberty, another opportunity for the individual to take possession of the deepest meaning of life is missed. These are two very powerful orphan wounds.

Ultimately, the cultural wound rests upon cosmology. By cosmology, I mean the story we tell of how and why our universe got here, its nature, source, and destiny, and how culture, family, and individual fit into it. Reading of the care of soul done by Egyptian culture (Lamy, 1981), it soon becomes evident how the age of individual soul and the age of the physical cosmos were always kept in harmony. The age was not only a scientific fact, but also a psychological one that could be known through initiatory experience. We currently suffer a tremendous wound, knowing consciously that our universe is billions of years old, but having no sense or experience of soul that is in pace with that. Our planetary sense itself is orphaned and not at home in its own cosmos.

Life can also be lived at this level of orphanhood. It is another form of hell, a prison of materialism. For me the symptom was a hatred of all things Western, all things "White." In extremis, there was a virulent seeking of the revolution to overthrow that system with the belief that non-Western cultures were unconditionally better. In dreams, I experienced a doubling of myself, the theme of the evil guy who looked like me, who always seemed to get me in trouble. To be honest, within all the suffering, I also held a constant secret superiority, looking down on even my own friends who I felt had bought into the system.

It is possible to stay at this level, but it requires alcohol, medication, or manic energy as the hatred grows and the doubling becomes more pronounced. It's a dangerous place because of the potential for violence.

Seeing through this image of the orphan requires what Jung (1959) called work on the "Shadow," what Campbell (1968) called, "entering the forest where it is darkest." It is a movement out of a wasteland in search of what has been lost, a felt connection to the Source. Of this I wrote in the song, "Into the Dark" (1991):

The lady lays in waiting
The king is sealed in his tomb
Held bound in silence by forgotten wounds . . .
The way to all, the casting off
The final lot
The way to all, into the dark

ORPHAN AS THE ICONOCLAST, THE CHOSEN ONE

At this level, the solo flight to the Source is a direct dealing with the image of God. Meister Eckart called this "taking leave of God in search of God." I call it "god smashing," because that's what it was like for me. It has tones of patricide. After the smashing of the image of God given by the traditional faith, there is an initial high of freedom from bondage that can last years. The down side is the spiritual ordeal that comes one day after the old image of God is gone. Loss of the central image sets forth a rush of raw spirit. This is not unlike the twister that comes and tears the home from its foundations in the Wizard of Oz. A good understanding of the psychospiritual terrain is in Stan and Christina Grof's (1989) *Spiritual Emergency: When Personal Transformation Becomes a Crisis.*

Spiritual transformation and mental illness often have the same appearance. This is important to know going in. It also bears upon how we get through. The Grofs warn that we can be held in a perpetual state of in-between if the psychological community applies drugs to stop the transformation from completion. We can also become overly inflated and too good for the world, refusing to return from the place of visions. That means becoming Jesus, Mary, Mohammed, Crazy Horse, or some mythic figure on a permanent basis.

It is possible to live life in the in-between in a disembodied and detached state. However, this seems to court its end in physical self-sacrifice. As an image cage, it is another form of hell if we choose to stay there or are forced to stay there by a community that is unfamiliar with spiritual transformations.

The way through is by an experience of psychological death and rebirth, very much an initiation in the classic sense. My making it through was more a question of giving up self-will and commending my life into the hands of a loving deity. I think a successful death and rebirth are not possible without some leap of faith. A connection with a higher power seems to require letting go of personal power, when we learn from experience what the words "not my will, but thine be done" really mean.

I wrote of this passage in, "Marilyn of the Whirlwind" (2001):

> Maybe it was three days,
> Maybe it was forever
> On the morning of the golden dawn
> There was a new creation
> Now a vessel to the underground
> Now an anchor to the heavens
> Now a woman in the kitchen sings
> The bread is ready from the oven
> Come the rushing of the whirlwind
> Come the opening of the door
> Come the sounding of the hour
> No preparing for what's in store

ORPHAN AS TRICKSTER, AS ELDER

There is a robust sense of well-being and health that comes from a successful passage through the death and rebirth of a spiritual transformation. There is also a time of grieving for the person we were, the person who died. As teachers on the orphan path though, when we begin speaking in the light what we have seen in the dark, we experience with our students what Plato in the *Phaedrus* called "the horses of the student rushing toward the teacher." The temptation is strong to use for our own gain the very Grail we have recovered.

There are two orphan images which can ease the possessive and compulsive energy of the archetype. Together they can function to balance, to redeem, even to lovingly betray each other. The two are the Trickster and the Elder. Without the help of the Elder image, the Trickster can catch us when we overly personalize the results of our work. I am talking about an erotic inflation well described by the image of the trickster, Coyote: He Who Has Intercourse with Everything in the World. The overpersonalization can be as strong as being in love with several persons at once, but the love is in close proximity to very destructive forces. The love also has a recurring theme of "You are the only one who can save me," or "I'm the only person who can save ————." In a lesser form, the love dismembers our energy through good intentions. We are torn apart in the service of others. I wrote in the song, "One Good Thing Blues" (1999):

My woman needs a lot of love
That's why I'm always standing by
My woman needs a lot of love
That's why I'm always standing by
I keep trying to find the one good thing
to give her
to keep her
satisfied
Brothers listen to me
Cause I finally got the news
You never keep your woman satisfied
Once she gets them one good thing blues

The awakened orphan archetype sets up what is like a conduit to the divine. I mean here that we begin to receive healing information for other people. The more we share, the more we receive. You would think this would be a good thing, but it is exhausting if unbalanced. When I teach at a conference, I can tell how well I'm doing with the Trickster energy by a quick look at where all my things are. On a bad day, my guitar is in one room, three different people have three different books I loaned them, my suitcase is up in my room, my pullover is over in the theater, my shoes are missing, I can't find my car keys, and so on. At the end of a day like that, it can take me four hours to slowly gather all the things together into one place. Even then, I may forget my coat.

I think the Trickster's wildness is essential to the spontaneity of good work. I also think that the Trickster's challenge to become aware of our own contradictions is a required passage. Make no mistakes: the path can end there, end tragically. Hopefully, when wisdom prevails, the way through the Trickster opens to the Elder, who can finally ground us.

To be blunt, the Elder represents one who sees through the bullshit. That capacity seems linked to having made many mistakes. The Elder is a very deep stage of the parentless life—as far as I know, the deepest. From that stance, the parentless and homeless life can be seen in proper context. What supports the Elder is invisible. The chair over nowhere rests upon the unseen history, initiations, visions, ancestors, a special relationship with death, and the Source. Consider the orphan passage as a slow movement of the Elder outward through phases out of context.

For another portion of the invisible support I think we must turn to the soul of the teacher. It is due time for a Western conception of the Eastern concept of the Boddhisattva. It's time to say that there are some teaching souls that embody again and again, who choose to participate in the becoming of this cosmos, who work for the liberation of all. Jung (1959) seemed to hint at such an idea and more recently, Robert Sardello (2000), in a talk called The Heart of Archetypal Psychology, suggested the existence of such a concept running through the Christian Sophianic tradition of Jakob Boehme, among others. The Western version of the Boddhisattva is a democratization of what was formerly a form of soul monarchy. At this time, there appears to be many teaching souls, outside established tradition. They are orphan souls. They work in distant places, but they show up together at conferences like the Holistic Learning Conference.

Of the orphan soul, I wrote a song (2001), a small instruction guide for teaching souls when they meet:

> When you meet the Orphan Soul
> may you talk all night, because the time is full
> may you know the growing edge of you
> the secret questions, what your dreams told you.
> Where did you wake up in this world?
> These are the meanings, the signs I explored.
> Feel your words grow thick, the synchronistic clues
> feel the golden chills for the beautiful and true
> Minds from All Times
> visit our time
> Minds from all times
> are visiting Our Time
> When you meet the Orphan Soul
> talk of erotic love, the southern and the northern pole.
> As philosophers held out their mirror
> again you know yourself.
> Together the Mind is clearer.
> Once in painted caves, cathedral rooms
> in Alexandria, the temple and the sweatlodge too.
> Know each other by laughter and heart,
> by the passion for your work and your Art.

Minds from All Times
visit our time
Minds from all times
are visiting Our Time
When you meet the Orphan Soul
talk of your loved ones from the young
to the invisibles.
Share this ritual, bless the human kind
with an immortal Heart
that's in love with Time.
Minds from All Times
visit our time
Minds from all times
are visiting Our Time.

ORPHAN AS CARRIER OF PLANETARY CONSCIOUSNESS

The full embodiment of the educator's life called forth by the orphan archetype arrives at a nowhere that circulates or alternates among its many images. Surprisingly, the ever-wandering path has an unexpected gift. A small turn of the idea of belonging nowhere renders the idea not of homelessness but a home that is always in motion. The word *planet* means "wanderer." With that in mind, consider the orphan's home as a wandering home, a planet. *Planetary consciousness* is another name for the goal of the orphan's path. The orphan's voice leads us home to the wandering place. We return to earth and image of the earth marks the orphan's return.

So, I close with words from the song, "Is It Time?" (2001):

Through the violent heavens stars fly like sand
I know that I love you, I have a place to stand
I have a place to stand
Kai lai lai lai, is it time?

REFERENCES

Campbell, J. (1968). *The masks of god: Creative mythology*. New York: Penguin Books.

Fideler, D. (1995). Reviving the academies of the muses. In D. Fideler (Ed.), *Alexandria: The journal of western cosmological traditions*, (213–226). Grand Rapids, MI: Phanes.

Grof, S., & Grof, C. (Eds.). (1989). *Spiritual emergency: When personal transformation becomes a crisis*. Los Angeles: Tarcher.

Henderson, J. G., & Hawthorn, R. D. (1995). *Transformative curriculum leadership*. Columbus, OH: Merril.

Hillman, J. (1975). *Re-visioning psychology*. New York, NY: Harper and Row.

Jung, C. G. (1959). The archetypes and the collective unconscious (R. F. C. Hull, Trans.) In *Collected Works*, (Vol. 9, 1). Princeton, NJ: Princeton University Press.

Kaplan, A. (1978). *Meditation and the bible*. New York: Sam Weiser, Inc.

Lamy, L. (1981). *Egyptian mysteries*. Singapore: Thames & Hudson.

Moore, T. (1997). Ways of knowledge. In *The Salt Journal*, 1: 37–38.

Piirto, J. (1998). *Understanding those who create*. Dayton, OH: Gifted Psychology Press.

Reynolds, F. C. (1991). *A suburban nigredo* (cassette recording). Berea, OH: Shirtless Records.

Reynolds, F. C. (2001). *Creation: The pyramid and the suns* (CD). Berea, OH: Shirtless Records.

Sardello, R. (2000). *The heart of archetypal psychology* (sound recording). Dallas, TX.: Sounds True.

Slattery, P. (1995). *Curriculum development in the postmodern era*. New York: Garland Publishing.

Some, M. (1999). *The healing wisdom of Africa*. New York: Penguin Putnam.

CHAPTER 20

The Eros of Teaching

CELESTE SNOWBER

Arbutus Skin

Arbutus
burnt umber torso
you unwrap your skin
ever so lightly
slip off sienna
mint green beneath

You keep your skin
half on
I want to peel it off
like birch bark peeled
from trees of childhood
I want you
to keep it too
revealing both edges
multi-layered
Triple beauty

I've been told
my boundaries
are too big
Bounteous
walking around with no skin

My olive skin has layers
like summer arbutus

Some skins
are for shedding
Relinquish
sea of forgetfulness
Be in the skin of now

Other skins
for finding—
liver
heart
breast

Living into your own skin
protecting enough skin
to hold
shedding enough skin
to release.
Inhabiting epidermis
Flesh and skin
go on a singing adventure

I will never tire
sitting
in arbutus presence
Grace of standing tall
in seasons of skin

I don't rise with
such elegance
in my layered seasons.

Perhaps it is time
of the singing skin.

The act of teaching is an act of eros, an act of creation, an act of love. This act is embedded in the physicality of flesh—breath, tone, voice, and muscles are central to each breath we utter. Knowledge is released through every sinew and gesture, posture and glance, as we engage both heart and body. The nuances of smell, touch, sound, and sight shape and inform our lives; they are sensuous knowledge, not that different from the arbutus. Teaching is the art of word becoming flesh. This chapter focuses on eros being the enlivening force which is present in teaching, whether with children or adults, in or out of the classroom.

No matter what we are teaching, whether it is spirituality or science, meditation or methodology, what is often remembered is what is captured between the words—the echoes and whispers, the gestures and sighs, the quality of presence. I explore the geography of physicality as a place to live, be, and dwell; a place where both body and soul unite in the enlivening action of teaching.

Eros is the underlying thread through this chapter, yet I would like to consider eros in the broad sense, not only confined to the erotics of sexuality, but the element which infuses life into all our partnerships and interactions. Eros springs through the partnership between ourselves and colleagues, students, friends, children, partners, lovers, creation, and ultimately in relation to our selves. Eros is the life force that breathes through us and beckons us to the life that wants to be lived in us. It is the blood and passion running through our bodies, or as Gunilla Norris (1992) says so poignantly, "As we enter into exquisite awareness of the life that wants to live as us, we learn to love deeply. We claim our passion" (p. 8). This blood stirring the body and soul is what infuses love. Love infuses teaching. Love is transformed into knowledge in the act of relationship. And knowledge is transformed into love. If we are open to an embodied way of knowing, we become partners in this dance. A dance infused with sacred interaction. Student to teacher. Teacher to student. Love infuses the cells within the relationship of learning. So well said many centuries before by the poet Rumi (1995): Human beings are discourse. That flowing moves through you whether you say anything or not. Everything that happens is filled with pleasure and warmth because of the delight of the discourse that's always going on (p. 76).

It is in this live exchange, this fertile place, where words become flesh and dance amidst each other's body and soul. Whether one is teaching chemistry or spirituality, it is a ground for the relationship between knower and known. To know or to be known is an intimate act. It is the act which we desire for in relation to other. Other could be person, god or goddess, spirit, ourselves, or knowledge. In this rich exchange of word becoming flesh, the soil of ripe hearts sprouts into the newness and excitement of what it means to know. Knowing unfolds into being and being unfolds into knowing.

We can only know partially in the long run. Our longing and thirst to know has the capacity to animate the relationship between teacher and student. Yet we are all teachers and students at the same time, if we are open to all of life as teacher, to all the pedagogical pieces of our lives to touch our intellect, body, mind, and heart. The teacher changes. Sometimes teacher is in the form of a person, in fact it may be our elementary teacher, professor, mentor, or kayaking instructor, for that matter. The teacher may also take the shape of an elderly woman, an artwork, a budding child, a dance, or a crinkled leaf on the ground. We have the capacity to be taught by all if we continue to cultivate receptivity. The teacher changes form, but the teaching does not. It is an act of flesh, of our flesh being ripped open, sometimes subtlety and other times with a storm into the exquisite beauty of knowing.

In the end, our deepest engagement with knowledge may be mystery. We can plan the curriculum, study the course, pursue the best teacher or the most suitable college, but often our most profound engagement with knowledge is mystery. Mysterious as the pulse of life and the pulse of eros flowing through our veins. For in the long run it is about a relationality, oozing with a vitality so deep we are drawn into intimacy. Knowledge woos us. The creation bursts with this kind of knowledge, and it is not surprising that teachers come in many shapes, textures, and forms. Even as a child, I think I learned more from trees, waves, and sea glass than I did from the third grade. The teacher changes form. Sometimes it will be in the form of a classroom teacher, and hopefully this will be true. But perhaps many other times it may be friend, mother, neighbor, father, sister, or even stones, trees, water, and wood. Life is erupting with teachers encompassing us. The land, stars, air, and water all hold a holy place as teacher, if we can let ourselves be receptive to their invitation to the eros of the everyday.

I remember that as a child my biggest teacher was often the sea. The sea in all its moods, colors, and motion taught me more about seasons, flow, acceptance, expression, and surrender than all the Sunday school lessons I encountered. The sea became a place of solace; the deep beauty of New England salt and light caressed the flesh of my torso. I listened with my heart to the rhythm of waves. I released my body to the aftermath of a storm and gave my olive-skinned arms to ocean spray. The changing colors of lavender gray, blue, and sea green melted into my soul and I came to embrace the rhythms of my own internal life. The sea was my essay of knowledge. In its ebb and flow I became intimate with a beautiful teacher. I was schooled through beauty, the beauty of change. Change is a constant companion with me now. It continues to be my teacher.

This is not to underestimate the value of teachers as human beings in our lives. After all, this is a big part of my personal vocation, as I work in teacher education at a university, yet what continues to be crucial is the ability to foster an enlivened relationship between teacher and student where knowledge can be given wings. In this resounding relationship between knower and known, the teacher can be found in various forms: creation or friends, elementary school teacher or college professor, rabbi or priest, suffering or joy. What can be true for all of these is that the relationship between teacher and student can be a space where knowledge is ripened within the torso of our bodies.

I am speaking here of a kind of engagement which encompasses bodily, heart, and intellectual knowing. A kind of engagement where we become truly present. In this presence we become known as we know. I like to refer to this presence as "a physicality of presence." This expands on the notion of attentiveness of mind to include the full attentiveness of the body as well. Essentially it is a bodily mindfulness, a place where we are cracked open to both the interior and exterior realms of experience.

I wish to unsilence the body, bring it out of its boxes, to let it breathe, play, and have a voice, and to listen to its rhythms in the practice of life and work. To let it be a site for knowledge, a place for the deep wisdom available to us. So often in Western culture there is the understanding that we *have* bodies rather than that we *are* bodies. Yet whatever we do, we do through our bodies: eat, sleep, type, teach, drive, or love. We live, breathe, and dwell in and through our bodies, but more often than not they unfortunately have been relegated to the status of instrument or tool, rather than being a place of discovery. The questions I continue to dwell in and pose to student teachers are these: How do we foster a connection to our own knowing, our own eros, our own bodies, our own internal landscapes? How do we continue to honor the body in all its paradox and joy as a place for discovery and wonder, a place for living into our own knowing? As teachers, the most important thing we can do for ourselves in our practice of teaching is to stay keenly alive in the practice of living and being. So beautifully articulated by Parker Palmer (1998) in his important work, *The Courage to Teach:* "We teach who we are" (p. 2). Our invitation is to continue to notice and access the raw details of our souls and bodies that shape our own internal landscapes. To stay alive to the eros flowing through our own bodies, the pulse of creation in our inner geography. The body is a huge teacher in our lives if we listen and our bodies can be a sacred space for continual knowledge and wisdom. A physicality of presence can allow us to stay close to the pulse of our own hearts, to the raw details of our own lives where all of life can be a sacred space for embodied knowing. Textures, sounds, gestures, smells, and sights become an alphabet all to themselves, shaping the alphabet of life, giving voice to a way of being attentive, to learning in the margins.

I will never forget an experience where one of my twins was in the beginning stages of elementary school and was having trouble with counting his numbers. His teacher was very concerned that he was not getting his numbers in order, nor did he have any enthusiasm to repeat them or practice them. Ultimately, he was not conforming well. And we know it is often the children who conform who are the ones who succeed. "Con form"—with form, without passion. One needs both form and passion, a passionate form. Later in the same week when the teacher was concerned with my son's number progress, we were walking the dog in the woods near our house. Laced with green moss and cedar, the smells of the Pacific Northwest swept us up into a delightful rhythm. I saw my son drop into the dampened earth alongside an old tree stump and shout with exclamation, "Look, Mom, at the tree rings!" He proceeded to count them with an enthusiasm of his whole body, he exuberantly counted up to twenty two, each number a point of joy on the scale. I will never forget his passion for counting the rings on the tree, his knees nestled in the soft earth, his jeans full of wet mud. I leapt with gratitude for him so pragmatically demonstrating the relation-ship between eros and knowledge. His energetic body struggles with the confines of the normal pedagogic containers: desks, halls, vertical and horizontal spaces squeezing each limb. My three boys are often restless in school. I empathize for I am a dancer; a significant part of life is movement to me. I too conformed to the sedentary postures of my schooling in the 1960s, but I now wonder what the price was for that conformity. Did I minimize knowledge which my lived body spoke? The knowledge from outer sources always took precedent: math tables, spelling charts, maps of the world. The map of my body was relegated to the back door. The consistent message was to control the body with the mind; the body serves the mind.

My children continue to be my teachers as they skip with glee, run into my arms, or spontaneously fall to the earth and count tree rings. They do not fear trembling with agitation or joy, knowing that knowledge carries within it an ele-ment of eros. Children teach us to make friends with our bodies and give them back their voice. Of course this is in an invitation to navigate places of both joy and discomfort, for our bodies can be a huge place for paradox as well (Friedman & Moon, 1997). Yet it is these uncomfortable spaces which hold the fires of transformation. Eros slices through the polarities and shatters our categories. We are invited to release to the movements of our lives which compel, turn, and ultimately mutate our ways of being and seeing in the world. The eros of creation bursts through cedars and sky, salt and arbutus. It lives in my child's desiring to snuggle, counting in the mud, or to look at a bug, pulling me into his moment of possibility. In this place of waiting for something else to happen, an invitation to life emerges. I am caught and drawn into this present moment, one which dis-rupts and erupts. A rupture of time perhaps, but more an invitation into another kind of time, a timelessness within time. Not so much a pace that can be meas-ured, but an invitation to release measure and be enchanted by the adventure of life. The life force of eros infuses our lives as teachers, igniting the flame of pas-sion in all we do, think, say, and ultimately, love.

Earth Altar

Earth is my altar
where I can
  absorb her
    natural patterns
I am a spiral section
  splattered
across her
  Mystery.

She is where
I can trust
to let the Mystery BE
encase my heart.

Lifting the tyranny
of my own
frets, worries
pebbles of problems
wade to sea
against
her soft wind
changing color
of water sky.

Every weed
tree and rock
manifests
diversity of shape
tone

I too,
am in her tones
the sway of breeze
Baking my
weariness
against her breasts
of sun
I take in
whispers
of earth's altar.

REFERENCES

Friedman, L., & Moon, S. (Eds.). (1997). *Being bodies: Buddhist women on the paradox of embodiment*. Boston: Shambhala.

Norris, G. (1992). *Sharing silence: Meditation practice and mindful living*. New York: Bell Tower.

Palmer, P. (1998). *The courage to teach: Exploring the inner landscape of the teacher's life*. San Francisco: Jossey Bass.

Rumi. (1995). *The essential Rumi. (Trans. C. barks)*. San Francisco: Harper Collins.

CHAPTER 21

Flowing Together in the Rainbow

Experiences from Two Workshops on Art Making and Meditation

AYAKO NOZAWA

NIJI	RAINBOW
Nana iro no niji	*Rainbow in seven colors*
Nagareru youni	*As if it flew*
Arau youni	*As if it washed everything away*
Yuruyaka ni	*Gently*
Burashi no oto	*The sound of brush*
Mizu no oto	*The sound of water*
Tori no koe	*The sound of birds singing*
Issho ni nagare-yo	*Let's flow together*
Mina issho ni	*All together*
Tokeru yo-ni	*As if we all melt away*
Watashi mo	*Me, too*
Anata mo	*You, too*
Arigato	*Thank you*

—Ayako Nozawa, 2001. written after painting at the 3rd Holistic Learning Conference Workshop

(translated by myself)

INTRODUCTION

In this chapter, I will describe experiences of two workshops I facilitated at the second and third Holistic Learning Conferences in 1999 and 2001. In 1999, four doctoral students at the Ontario Institute for Studies in Education at the University of Toronto including myself cofacilitated the workshop "Contemplative Art as a Way to Know: Animating the Inner Landscape." In 2001, I facilitated the workshop "Sacred Space for Connecting with Our Soul within and with Others through Art."

In both workshops, it was considered that starting with ourselves is vital (Pinar, 1974; Hunt, 1987; Palmer, 1993; Miller, 1996; Moustakas, 1990). They focused on individuals connecting with their deeper selves, which is important for personal and professional lives and also supports the earth's community. These workshops were also ways to show that art is a way of knowing (Allen, 1995) and art making is a form of meditation. Art making as meditation was one of the techniques explored in these workshops to enhance our self-awareness and gain deeper understanding of ourselves. Such learning can be utilized in broader educational settings such as holistic education, teacher education, adult education, and health care education.

MEDITATION

Meditation is a way to keep in touch with our "inner lives" or "our essence" (Pinar, 1974, p. 5). It can take us beyond the boundary of self by focusing on the awareness of our physical, intellectual, and emotional states, bringing attention to and being in the moment (Aoki, 1983; Miller, 1996). This self, our ego which is the socialized sense of who we are, can be the source of our sense of separateness (Pinar, 1974; Miller, 1994). In meditation, we can let go of self-control, and dive into the free realm of interconnectedness. Merton (cited in Miller, 1994) describes it as "reconnecting with the fundamental unity of life, or Source" (p. 24). Dewey (1934/1979) describes it as the experience of "inner harmony" (p. 17); while Csikszentmihalyi (1996) refers to "flow experience," a natural, effortless unfolding of our life in a way that moves us toward wholeness and harmony (Belitz and Lundstrom, 1998).

Through meditation, we can bring more attention to the experience of our being interconnected with the whole. Based on this profound connectedness, we may experience humbleness, awe, appreciation, and indescribable connection with others. We can go beyond our ego's tendency to create negative reactions by practicing these techniques. Meditation is one way to create an inner harmony, which can be shared throughout educators' personal and professional lives (Mulvaney, 1994; Miller, 1996; Miller & Nozawa, 2002). Miller (1994, 1996,

2000) emphasizes the importance of meditation as connecting ourselves to Source, or Self, in the notion of holistic education.

Meditation in daily life is one way to develop alternative attitudes and values in our lifestyle. Many prominent scientists and educators in Western and Eastern societies share the view that nothing exists as a compartmentalized mechanism but instead as an interconnected whole at a deeper level. They express concern that we have been overemphasizing the compartmentalized and rational-industrial view.[1] Swimme (1992) and O'Sullivan (1999) describe that after a long prevailing compartmentalized, rational-industrial mode of living in Western society, it is time to evolve toward a new "ecozoic" era characterized by a holistic, planetary-aware, and interconnected mindset. Meditation could help us develop this mindset by connecting our souls within and with others.

The form of meditation can vary from person to person. In his *Contemplative Practitioner*, Miller (1994) described forms of meditation such as insight (being aware of what happens in each moment starting with the flow of the breath); mindfulness (bringing awareness to acts that we do each day); mantra (using a word or phrase as a vehicle to awakening); visualization (eliciting images that can foster positive growth and awareness); movement (bringing a heightened awareness to bodily movement such as yoga or walking); and loving kindness (sending thoughts of peace and wellness to self and others). With awareness, walking or washing dishes can be an act of meditation.

ART MAKING AS MEDITATION

In my workshops, painting, drawing, and clay sculpting were introduced as forms of meditation in addition to a means of expressing our inner selves. As one way to tune ourselves into the ego-free state, art is a powerful means.[2] By living the process in the here and now, creating art can be a way to take us to the deeper self, and to go beyond the ego boundary. In *Creative Healing*, Samuel and Lane (1998) explain:

> Transcendence has to do with going into the place in yourself where the spirit resides and then coming out with spirit in your life. . . . You go into the moment, within your body, and then go deeper. . . . the way to get into the experience of transcendence is to spiral deeper and deeper into the breath, the movement, the flow of creativity. (p. 270)

McNiff (1998b) states:

> Training in creativity requires the ability to relax in periods of uncertainty and to trust that the creative intelligence will find its way. The education of imagination involves giving up what I call "ego" control.

It requires an inclination to step into the unknown as well as the ability to persist when there is no end in sight. (p. 3)

This describes what meditation requires: a radical openness in which the individual does not try to control what is happening. Creating art can be used as a way of meditation with a heightened awareness of interconnectedness with a whole, the Source. Making art is a means to transform individuals and communities[3] as well as bringing them together.

WORKSHOP EXPERIENCES

Contemplative Art as a Way to Know: Animating the Inner Landscape

The desks in the center of the room were filled with art materials such as brushes, acrylic paints, water in containers, and paper. These desks were surrounded by other desks on which an inviting Indonesian wood sculpture, a straw decoration from a Japanese shrine, slightly scented candles, and sliced apples on Thai cloth were placed. Twelve educators from both Canada and overseas, with various professional backgrounds, chose to become part of this calm setting.

First, four of us, as cofacilitators, introduced ourselves and briefly explained our own group process and our philosophy. We emphasized the use of art for the process of exploring ourselves rather than emphasizing a product in this workshop. The first activity was designed to encourage the participants to engage in the process by allowing them to paint. Participants painted on eleven pieces of paper from thirty seconds to five minutes each. By limiting the time, we could eliminate the tendency to judge what we were painting and our desire to care about the results of painting. For the first four paintings, each participant chose three colors and spent thirty seconds for each painting. For the next four paintings, four colors were chosen by each participant and one minute was given for each painting. Participants could choose two colors from the first three colors they were using. After painting the second set of four paintings, participants were asked to choose one painting, which appealed to them the most. Then they used the chosen painting to get prepared for the last five minutes long painting experience. Without thinking about what to do next, participants became very engaged in painting and did not stop the process. The four facilitators were busy changing water, adding paints and preparing for the second clay activity while the participants painted. Finally, participants shared their experiences of the painting process in pairs. We specifically asked them not to make judgmental comments regarding their partner's painting. This included positive ones in order to stay away from judgmental thinking. Comments needed to be focused on facts such as "Red and yellow repeatedly appear in these paintings" and "There are more lines in this painting than the other ones" or simply open-ended questions. The discussion quickly became very active.

The next activity was to animate the inner landscape by using clay. Two questions were offered to participants to contemplate: Where are you in your inner space now? Where would you like to be in the near future? All participants quietly closed their eyes to ask the first question. They waited for what came to their mind after connecting with themselves within. Whenever they were ready, keeping their eyes closed, they slowly started to mold their clay. Some looked very confident and kept molding quickly. Others took their time as if they had searched for the form to come. Most of participants looked calm, radiant and even joyful as if they were back in their childhood. They opened their eyes and wrote down what came to their mind when they felt ready. In the same way, they started the second sculpture reflecting on the second question: Where would I like to be? Their hands led their movements in silence. I had a strong feeling that the room was filled with calm yet vibrating energy.

We shared our experiences in a group at the end of the art session. There were comments on the experiences as well as questions on how to apply this activity in educational practice.

One elementary school teacher asked how to apply this activity to lower grade classes as the students cannot understand abstract questions nor express what their process was like. In one of the past workshops for teacher and students, young participants were asked to create objects using natural materials such as leaves, branches, pebbles, and wools. In this case, students can create an art form they like and simply explain what it is in detail, as in "show and tell." Without using difficult vocabulary, children can explore and express themselves at their own level if proper questions are asked. This is also a great way to include environmental elements in education if gathering natural objects is used for discussing the natural environment in the area. For adults, questions similar to the ones asked at the conference workshop could be asked, as well as extended questions such as what the objects remind them of.

Some expressed frustration during the first painting activity as the time made them feel pressured. We explained that it was because participants were not given a chance to stop and think about the painting but were forced to just paint. This strategy was needed as people are accustomed to expect to create something "good" and constantly judge what we can be creating and adjust accordingly. Participants agreed with this argument. I added that it was beneficial to explore this feeling of frustration by asking questions: Where did you feel frustration in your body? When did you feel it? What did the frustrating feeling mean to you? How did the experience relate to your daily life? The negative emotions from the process can also help them in animating their inner landscape.

Participants shared that they could free themselves in these activities and realized how important it was to spend time for themselves in this way. Some agreed that they would like their students to explore themselves through art, and that they would create time for these activities in their classroom settings.

One person shared that she felt deep caring from facilitators during the workshop, reminding her of a warm blanket, and thanked us for creating such a warm and comfortable space. This comment warmed my heart. It made me realize that we did everything in such a flow that we did not have to speak to each other during the workshop. I assumed that this was because of the trust and comfort brought about through our own group artistic process that prevailed in this workshop. I was personally moved by the fact that participants could feel that.

Sacred Space for Connecting with Our Soul within and with Others through Art

In a spacious room in the center of the circle of chairs, my Japanese water color paintings were decorated between the drapes of a soft cloth printed with the brown and yellow plants. Around the central chairs, tables and chairs were set in a big half circle for painting and drawing activities and two tea candles were lit at each table. Dim light and quiet nature music ("Algonquin Suite" from Northern Ontario) welcomed six participants from Canada, the United States, Japan, and the United Kingdom.

The session started with our quiet moment together. Then we introduced ourselves and participants were asked to share what attracted them to come to the session. Their professional backgrounds included a psychologist, a psychotherapist, an artist, an elementary school teacher, and educators in higher education. One participant from higher education said that she was creating a curriculum which involved meditation and she wanted to learn ways to incorporate it. Another educator in higher education used body movements in her courses to enable students to connect with their body, mind, and soul and wanted to explore visual art. The artist said that she wanted to take advantage of all opportunities to try different approaches to enhance her skills in art. The psychotherapist expressed his interest in using his left hand to experience how free he could be from his judgmental position. The elementary school teacher said that she had never done this kind of activity before and it was her urge to get into painting freely that was leading her to the session. The psychologist never planned to attend this session but somehow she ended up coming to this experiential learning style workshop.

Then I introduced how I came to use painting and drawing as contemplative practice. I described how this contemplative space was influencing me and I showed some of my drawings and paintings. I was pregnant with my son then. One of the images, which emerged during my mediation, was my birth in a deep sea. In this image, the young dolphin received our newborn baby and two other old dolphins were surrounding us. I was floating in the water, and my husband was holding my back. Participants were looking at images while listening to my artful stories. Sometimes they were smiling and nodding.

After sharing my own process with art, I invited participants to use this space for quieting their mind and expressing what they experienced through art. They were asked to choose their seats in the activity area and their media for visual art, either watercolor or oil and soft pastels, or both. As soon as the participants came back to their tables, they went into their own space. I walked quietly to each table to light the tea candles. It was an initiation of the important ritual—to open the gate of the sacred space. We could only hear the music, the sound of brushes rubbing the paper, and the stirring of water. Participants all looked vibrant and freed themselves into this space. Sometimes they stopped, looking at the painting, and pondered. Other times, it seemed that they kept moving brushes and pastels diligently as if these materials were moving them. I did not want to walk around them to observe how they were doing as I felt it would be invading their space.

Their faces were filled with calm and a childlike quality. I became aware of a tingling sensation slowly emerging in me. "I want to paint!" I felt my heart beating faster with excitement and anticipation. I had never planned to participate in art making myself during the session. The thought that a facilitator should not be the participant came to my mind. I could no longer deny the tingling sensation. I was moving to the spot, which was vacant. I could hardly wait to start painting myself and sat on the chair impatiently. I lit the candle slowly to allow myself to enter my sacred space. I closed my eyes and took a long deep breath. Then slowly I opened my eyes and let my hands choose the mediums. It was watercolor. Next, my right hand grabbed purple. A purple line was making a big wave from the left center to the right center. Then red, then orange, then yellow, green. . . . My eyes found these colors together and the words "It is rainbow!" echoed in my mind. I felt calm and focused. After a while, I checked the time and also how the participants were progressing. When I finished the last stroke and felt done with this painting, I looked at my creation. Japanese words emerged and I wrote them down on the other piece of paper. I felt that not only participants and I but also all other beings were in this flow of rainbow. I felt a strong togetherness and an indescribable deep appreciation. When I put down the purple pastel I used for this poem, I was experiencing an overwhelming emotion in my whole body. The poem written at the beginning of this chapter was born in this way.

I stretched out the session time as long as possible for participants to enjoy what they were doing. I had to warn them several times to wrap it up. When I finally announced that the time was up, participants had a hard time leaving the table, as if they had been glued to it. They were invited to the circle to share any feeling, thought, or bodily experience during the session. All participants looked relaxed and happy.

We took turns sharing our experiences. Everybody was open enough to show their paintings or drawings. The images that they shared were full of colors and lines, shapes, and different brush tones. The varieties of images celebrated the diversity among us.

They spoke about their experiences when their turn came. One said that the image was emerging from the music and memories that she never imagined would come to her. One found that what she saw in the images was interesting and explained the meaning. One said using the left hand for right-handed people was freeing the judgmental element and made it possible to explore more. Some realized the connections between the images that they created to what they were experiencing in their daily life. Some said that this could be used in their own educational practices.

One said that her feelings of being rushed and guilt that she was going to be late totally vanished after the session. Her body felt free and light. As she spoke, I was thinking about these questions: How many negative feelings do we tend to carry in our body? With these in our body, how are we relating to others: to our coworkers, family, and friends, to anybody and any being around us? How different could it be to relate to people from this free and light state!

We shared every little discovery. Art making seemed to have evoked something in every participant. Our sharing filled with laughter and lightness was followed by a concluding quiet time. Warmth and strong connection existed in the room for a while after we opened our eyes. After the participants left, I felt that excitement remained in the air. To me, this feeling was what our profound connection with our souls within and with others had left behind.

CONCLUSION

On the basis of what I saw, I felt that participants could free themselves and that something shifted in the process. Many participants agreed that they were so engaged in art making that time passed very quickly and they enjoyed it as if they had been children. They were lost in time and space through art making. They were in the realm where we connect within ourselves and with others beyond the ego world. There is no boundary between myself and others there. This is where my poem "Rainbow" emerged. We are all flowing together in this realm. When we touch our soul in this profound connection and express what emerges, some shifts occur in our mind and body, as participants felt free and cheerful like children. It is an uplifting experience that we can feel in our body as one participant also shared. Fenner (1996) writes, "[T]he 'body shift' experienced by focusing is necessary for all real change (p. 30). This shift is a transformation.

The process of art making can lead to the experience of our interconnectedness with the whole. With our awareness, art making can become a way of meditation. Carrying the special space within us through meditation helps us connect deeply with others in our personal and professional lives. Even if we forget, I hope that our bodies remember the experience of meditation and help in bringing us back from time to time to this sacred space in our stressful life.

NOTES

1. See Capra, 1987; Berry, 1988; Pike & Selby, 1988; Swimme, 1992; Funai, 1994; Miller, 1996, 2000; O'Sullivan, 1999; Fox, 1999; Lerner, 2000.

2. See Jung, 1989; Cameron,1992; Hunt, 1997; McNiff, 1996, 1998a, 1998b; Samuel & Lane, 1998; Ganim, 1999.

3. Cane, 1983; Jung, 1989; McNiff, 1998a, 1998b; Allen, 1995; Csikszentmihalyi, 1996; Samuels & Lane, 1998.

REFERENCES

Allen, P. (1995). *Art is a way of knowing.* Boston & London: Shambhala.

Aoki, T. (1983). Towards a dialectic between the conceptual world and the lived world: Transcending instrumentalism in curriculum orientation. *Journal of Curriculum Theorizing,5*(4), 4–21.

Belitz, C., & Lundstrom, M. (1998). *The power of flow: Practical ways to transform your life with meaningful conincidence.* New York: Three Rivers Press.

Berry, T. (1988). *The dream of the earth.* San Francisco: Sierra Club Books.

Cameron, J. (1992). *The artist's way:A spiritual path to higher creativity.* New York: Tarcher/Putnum.

Cane, K. (1983). *The artist in each of us.* Craftsbury Common, VT: Art Therapy Publications.

Capra, F. (1982). *The turning point.* New York: Bantam.

Csikszentmihalyi, M. (1996). *Creativity.* New York: HarperCollins.

Dewey, J. (1979). *Art as experience.* New York: Paragon Books. (original work published 1934)

Fenner, P. (1996). Heuristic research study: Self-therapy using the brief image-making experience. *The Arts in Psychotherapy, 23*(1), 37–51.

Fox, M. (1999). *One river, Many wells.* NY: Penguin Putnam.

Funai, Y. (1994). *Mirai e no hinto* (Hints to the future). Tokyo: Sun-Mark Shya.

Ganim, B. (1999). *Art and healing: Using expressive art to heal your body, mind and spirit.* New York: Three Rivers Press.

Hunt, D. (1987). *Beginning with ourselves: In practice, theory and human affairs.* Toronto: OISE.

Jung, C. G. (1989). *Memories, dreams, reflections.* New York: Vintage Books.

Lerner, M. (2000). *Sprit matters.* New York: Hampton Roads.

McNiff, S. (1998a). *Art based research.* London: Jessica Kingsley.

McNiff, S. (1998b). *Trust the process.* Boston and London: Shambhala.

McNiff, S. (1996). Auras and their medicines. *The Arts in Psychotherapy, 22*(4), 297–305.

Miller, J. (1994). *The contemplative practitioner.* Toronto: OISE.

Miller, J. (1996). *The holistic curriculum.* Toronto: OISE Press.

Miller, J. (2000). *Education and the soul: Toward a spiritual curriculum.* Albany: State University of New York Press.

Miller, J., & Nozawa, A. (2002). Meditating educators: Qualitative research. *Journal of Inservice Education, 28*(1), 179–192.

Moustakas, C. (1990). *Heuristic research: Design, methodology and applications.* London: Sage.

Mulvaney, A.(1994). *Seeds from silence: The impact of meditation on the lives of five educators.* Doctoral Thesis. Toronto:OISE.

O'Sullivan, E. (1999). *Transformative learning: Educational vision for the 21st century.* Toronto: OISE.

Palmer, P. (1993). *To know as we are known: Education as a spiritual journey.* New York: HarperCollins.

Pike, G., & Selby, D. (1988). *Global teacher, global learner.* London: Hodder & Stoughton.

Pinar, F. W. (1974). *Heightened consciousness, cultural revolution, and curriculum theory.* Berkeley, CA: McCutchan.

Samuels, M., & Lane, M. R. (1998). *Creative healing: How to heal yourself by tapping into your inner creativity.* New York: Harper Collins.

Swimme, B. (1992). *The universe story from the primordial flaring forth to the ecozoic era: A celebration of the unfolding of the cosmos.* New York: Harper-Collins.

CHAPTER 22

Conclusion

Seeking Wholeness

JOHN P. MILLER

A lthough there are a wide variety of issues and approaches discussed in this book, I believe there are a few themes that run through all three parts. These include a critical perspective, spirituality, embodiment, and wholeness.

CRITICAL PERSPECTIVE

The first theme, a critical perspective, is perhaps the least evident of the four, yet it is important to the future of holistic education. Ron Miller (2000) and others have argued that holistic educators need to find common ground with feminists, antiracist educators, and critical theorists. Holistic education is connected, then, to what Deborah Orr calls "anti-oppressive pedagogies." Clearly Riane Eisler's call for partnership education is written within this perspective. In contrast, educational practices drawn from what Eisler calls the "dominator model" are oppressive pedagogies that perpetuate racism and sexism. Partnership education provides a perspective for teachers and students to remake the curriculum. Many recent political and social movements such as women's liberation, the civil rights movement, and environmental reform can be seen as efforts to build a society that is based in the partnership model. I believe that schools described by Gary Babiuk and Marni Binder in the second part of the book reflect efforts to build schools where partnership and mutuality are central.

Edmund O'Sullivan's chapter on emancipatory hope is also written from a critical perspective. O'Sullivan is critical of current economic and social structures that make the GNP and consumerism the main goals of the global economy. He calls for us to be aware of "strange attractors" that can provide the creative edge to personal and social transformation. The term *strange attractors* is drawn from physics and chaos theory and refers to individuals or small institutions that are providing alternative ways of living and being in today's world. Christopher Reynolds discusses the concept of "orphans," who can be viewed as the "strange attractors" that O'Sullivan writes about. For Reynolds these are people who can bring "a truly transformative fire into the world."

SPIRITUALITY

The second theme in this book is the importance of spirit. Sometimes spirit is referred to as "soul" (Moore, Sloan, Orr, Kessler, Schiller, and Colallilo Kates) while others prefer the term "heart" (Denton) or "heart-mind" (Park and Song). As I mentioned in the introduction, the acknowledgment of the spiritual dimension of existence is one of the critical elements of holistic learning. One of the persons who has been central to reclaiming a vision of soul has been Thomas Moore. Moore believes that "soul-centered education would emphasize the many dimensions of poetic existence." Such an education would also be comfortable with paradox.

Douglas Sloan, working from the Steiner/Waldorf tradition uses the term *soul/spirit*. Sloan does not separate soul and spirit but views soul within a more inclusive wholeness in relation to thinking, feeling, and the body. All the authors in this text, I believe, have tried to take this integrative approach to spirituality.

Deborah Orr has explored the concept of soul in relation to the work of Wittgenstein and the second-century Indian Buddhist philosopher Nagarjuna. She argues that they both see the "human soul as fluid, every changing being (empty) which exists in a complex web of relationship with other souls and the nonhuman world." Again this is a holistic view of soul as something not disembodied but intimately connected to all that surrounds it. In part 2 David Forbes picks up on the Buddhist theme in the work that he does with male athletes in high school. He introduced them to meditation and mindfulness practice. His chapter is a good example of the antioppressive pedagogies that Orr discusses in the first part of this book.

Rachael Kessler and Leslie Owen Wilson focus on soul in relation to adolescent development. Both argue that we can meet these spiritual needs in public school classrooms without threatening a person's religious beliefs.

The heart is also a symbol of spirit. Korean educators Young-Mann Park and Min-Young Song describe Won Hyo's central idea was One Heart-Mind (OHM). The ancients often referred to the "thinking heart" and Won Hyo is also describing that place where heart and mind are not separate but are deeply interconnected. One Heart-Mind can be facilitated through various contemplative disciplines such as meditation.

Diana Denton focuses on the heart in her work. She describes various exercises that she uses in her workshops to nourish the soul. She has found that various images of the heart can arise, including stone, ice, wood, or flame. Denton suggests that these images point to what she calls "the feelinged heart body." Again we have another image of spirit connected to the body.

EMBODIMENT

Embodiment is another major theme that runs throughout this book. I have already pointed out how authors such as Sloan, Orr, and Denton have linked spirit and body.

In part 2 Atsuhiko Yoshida describes how his experience of writing Japanese characters resonated in his body. For example, he wrote the character for "river" and felt that "it is something living in me."

Susan A. Schiller and Isabella Colallilo Kates use imagery as central tools in their teaching which focuses on creative writing. Citing Kessler, Schiller believes that the experiences that arise in her workshops are holistic and the learning "cannot really be separated into cognitive, psychological, physiological, or spiritual."

WHOLENESS

To link body, mind, and spirit is to seek the wholeness that is at the heart of holistic learning. To seek wholeness, however, it not striving for perfection. On the contrary, it is to recognize and accept the darkness as well.

Occasionally one comes across a book that touches a person below the surface. I have just finished reading such a book, *Learning to Fall: The Blessings of an Imperfect Life* by Phillip Simmons. Simmons wrote this book while he was suffering from Lou Gehrig's disease, or ALS. He writes:

> Think again of falling as figure of speech. We fall on our faces, we fall for a joke, we fall for someone, we fall in love. In each of these falls, what do we fall away from? We fall from ego, we fall from our carefully constructed identities, our reputations, our precious selves. We fall from ambition, we fall from grasping, we fall, at least temporarily, from reason. And what do we fall into? We fall into passion, into terror, into unreasoning joy. We fall into humility, into compassion, into emptiness, into oneness with forces larger than ourselves, into oneness with

others whom we realize are likewise falling. We fall, at last, into the presence of the sacred, into godliness, into mystery, into our better, diviner natures. (p. 11)

Holistic Education also involves falling. In falling we recognize our humanity and, as Simmons so wisely acknowledges, our divinity. This is not to celebrate falling. Falling can be painful. However, it does mean not shoving it aside or denying we are falling. By accepting and working with the falling we enter more deeply into the mystery of being and the cosmos. Clearly this entry is not just an intellectual journey, but one that engages our entire being. It is such engagement that is at the heart of holistic learning and the visions that underly much that is written in this book.

REFERENCES

Miller, R. (2000). *Caring for new life: Essays in holistic education.* Brandon, VT: Foundation for Educational Renewal.

Simmons, P. (2002). *Learning to fall: The blessings of an imperfect life.* New York: Bantam.

Contributors

Gary Babiuk is an assistant professor in the Department of Education at the University of Minnesota in Duluth, Minnesota. His current teaching area is social studies education with emphasis on social justice and diversity. His research interests also include such areas as team teaching, integrated curriculum, authentic student assessment, and community connections as they relate to the development of relationships in holistic and transformational schools. He is a runner and outdoor enthusiast. His e-mail and Web site are gbabiuk@d.umn.edu and www.d.umn.edu/~gbabiuk/.

Marni Binder, Ed.D, has taught in the inner city of Toronto for 23 years, with primary students, as a literacy coordinator, and librarian. She has worked extensively with teacher candidates in the Central Option Preservice Program at OISE/UT. Teaching through the arts is at the heart of her holistic philosophy of education. Her doctoral studies explored the phenomena of the visual arts and literacy for young children in the inner city. Marni is currently a Course Director for The Faculty of Education, York University. Marni can be reached at marni.binder@utoronto.ca.

Rina Cohen is a professor at OISE/UT, Department of Curriculum, Teaching and Learning, where she specializes in holistic education approaches in mathematics education. Recently, through teacher workshops and a new graduate course, she has been developing and researching a holistic approach to empowering math-anxious elementary school teachers in overcoming their anxieties.

Diana Denton integrates spirituality and the arts in her work as professor, poet and consultant. Her publications include her book *In the Tenderness of Stone: Liberating Consciousness Through Awakening the Heart* (Sterling House, 1998) and articles in various journals. A faculty member at the University of Waterloo, she teaches in the Department of Drama and Speech Communication.

Riane Eisler is best known for her bestsellers *The Chalice* and *The Blade* (Harper & Row, 1997), translated into 19 languages, and *The Power of Partnership* (New World Library, 2002), a guide to personal and cultural transformation. Her other books include *Tomorrow's Children* (Westview Press, 2000), applying her interdisciplinary research to education, *Sacred Pleasure* (Harper Collins, 1995), and *Women, Men, and the Global Quality of Life* (Center for Partnership Studies, 1995). She is President of the Center for Partnership Studies, PO Box 51936, Pacific Grove, CA 93950, www.partnershipway.org.

David Forbes teaches in the School Counseling program in the School of Education at Brooklyn College/CUNY. He worked in a school-based substance abuse prevention program and is the author of *False Fixes: The Cultural Politics of Drugs, Alcohol, and Addictive Relations* (State University of New York Press, 1994) and *Boys 2 Buddhas: Counseling Urban High School Male Athletes in the Zone* (Peter Lang, 2004).

Selia Karsten teaches full-time in The School of Marketing and eBusiness, Seneca College, and part-time at OISE/UT. Her area of expertise and research is web-based instructional design, curriculum development, mixed modes of course delivery and enhancing holistic learning with computer technology. Her recent awards, provincially and internationally, are for innovation and excellence in teaching and learning.

Isabella Colalillo Kates (pen name Isabella Colalillo Katz) is a poet/writer, holistic educator, and creativity consultant. She is the co-creator of the award winning children's audio tape *Crocket, Carob and Crystals: the C3 Trilogy* and the author of two books of poetry, *And Light Remain* (Guernica, in press) and *Tasting Fire* (Guernica, 1999).

Rachael Kessler is the author of *The Soul of Education: Helping Students Find Connection, Compassion and Character at School* (ASCD, 2000), and coauthor of *Promoting Social and Emotional Learning: Guidelines for Educators* (ASCD, 1997). She is the founder and director of The PassageWays Institute in Boulder, Colorado. She can be reached at passagewaysrk@aol.com. For more information, visit www.passageways.org.

Bok Young Kim is associate professor in the Department of Education at the University of Incheon in Korea. He received his doctorate from the University of

Connecticut-Storrs and has translated several books into Korean including *A Post-Modern Perspective on Curriculum* by William Dorr (1993), *Understanding Curriculum* by William Pinar (1995), and *The Holistic Curriculum* by John Miller (2001). He is also vice president of the Korean Association for Holistic Education.

Anna F. Lemkow, a Canadian of Russian birth, lives in New York City. From 1946 to 1975 she worked in the United Nations Secretariat as an economist. In 1981–82 she prepared and submitted papers on peace education curriculum to the UN-sponsored Univeristy for Peace in Costa Rica. She is author of *The Wholeness Principle* (Quest Books, 1995).

John (Jack) P. Miller has worked in the area of humanistic and holistic education for over 30 years. Currently he is professor in the Department of Curriculum, teaching, and Learning and head of the Centre for Teacher Development at the Ontario Institute for Studies in Education at the University of Toronto, where he teaches courses in holistic education and spirituality in education. He is the author of 13 books, including *The Contemplative Practitioner* (Bergin & Garvey, 1994), *Education and the Soul* (State University of New York Press, 2000), and *The Holistic Curriculum* University of Toronto Press, 2001). His writing has been translated into 7 languages, including Korean and Japanese, and for the past 10 years he has worked extensively with holistic educators in Asia.

Thomas Moore was a monk in a Catholic religious order for twelve years and has degrees in theology, musicology, and philosophy. A former professor of psychology, he is author of several books including *Care of the Soul* (Harper, 1993) and *Soul Mates* (Harper, 1994). He lives in New Hampshire with his wife and two children.

Ayako Nozawa is a holistic educator and researcher, and the mother of a three-year-old. She completed her Ed.D. dissertation on contemplative practices in educators' lives at OISE/UT. She is investigating the impact of contemplative practices on holistic community development, and developing and facilitating series of workshops in Canada and Japan.

Deborah Orr is a philosopher teaching in York University's interdisciplinary Division of Humanities. She has published in the areas of Wittgenstein scholarship, gender, ethics, informal logic, and mindful pedagogy. She is currently finishing revisions to a book on embodied spirituality, *The Art of Love: The Logic of a Feminist Spiritual Erotics*, and working on *Mindful Pedagogy*. She has practiced yoga and meditation for approximately 30 years and teaches both in Toronto.

Edmund O'Sullivan is coordinator of the Transformative Learning Centre at OISE/UT. From 1983 to 1992 he was professor of applied psychology at OISE. He is the author of numerous books, including *Critical Psychology and Pedagogy* (Bergin & Garvey, 1990) and *Transformative Learning: Educational Vision for the 21st Century* (University of Toronto Press, 1999).

Young-Mann Park is the president of Dr. Park's Spirituality Center, a vice president of the Korean Holistic Education Society, and a professor at the Clinical Pastoral Institute in Korea. He taught at Graduate Theological Union at Berkeley, and at Mercy College in New York. He studied both at Graduate Theological Union and at U. C. Berkeley, and graduated from GTU with a Ph.D. in spirituality and religious studies. He has written many books and articles in Korean and English, including *Dr. Park's Soul-Body Discipline*. E-mail: young-mann@lycos.co.kr.

F. Christopher Reynolds, M.Ed. Also known as Christopher, Chris Reynolds is a songwriter, artist, teacher, and founder of the Urrealist Art Movement. A recording artist with six CDs under his belt (www.urrealist.com), Christopher is also a high school French teacher in Berea City Schools in Ohio and an adjunct professor in creativity studies at Ashland University, Ashland, Ohio.

Susan A. Schiller is a professor of English and member of the Graduate Faculty at Central Michigan University. She teaches composition, American literature, film, and English education. Her research interests include spiritual approaches to writing and learning, holistic education, and imagery and affect in meaning making. She has published in *JAEPL, Innovative Higher Education*, and *Transformations*, and is coeditor of a collection of essays titled, *The Spiritual Side of Writing: Releasing the Learner's Whole Potential* (Heinemann, 1997).

Douglas Sloan is professor emeritus of history and education at Teachers College, Columbia University. He is currently editor of the *Research Bulletin* of the Research Institute for Waldorf Education in North America. Among his books are *Insight-Imagination: The Emancipation of Thought and the Modern World* (1983) and *Faith and Knowledge: Mainline Protestantism and American Higher Education* (1984).

Celeste Snowber, Ph.D., is a dancer, educator, writer, and assistant professor in the Faculty of Education at Simon Fraser University, British Columbia. She has authored several books, including *Embodied Prayer* (Northstone, 2004), and has published numerous essays and poetry in journals. She continues to create improvisational performances in various venues, and dances through motherhood with her three lively boys.

Min-Young Song is a research professor at Seoul National University, research and education director at National Yul-Gok Education Center in Korea, and vice president of the Korean Society for Holistic Education. She graduated from Tokyo Metropolitan University in Japan with a Ph.D. in education. She has written several books and many articles in Korean and Japanese, including *Holistic Science Curriculum: A Holistic Curriculum and Education for the Whole Person* (in collaboration with Young-Mann Park). E-mail: smy626@chollian.net.

Leslie Owen Wilson is a professor at the School of Education, University of Wisconsin–Stevens Point. Her graduate courses include curriculum, newer views of learning, creativity, models of teaching, brain-based education, and reflective educational practice, in addition to undergraduate courses in educational psychology. She has authored the book *Every Child, Whole Child* (Zephyr, 1994), and written and administrated several large grants related to reformed educational practice and to educational technology. She maintains a large, comprehensive Web site (http://www.uwsp.edu/education/lwilson) used by educators around the world.

Atsuhiko Yoshida is a professor at Osaka Women's University in Japan. He is the author and editor of several books, including *Holistic Education: Philosophy and Movement* (Nippon Hyoron-sha, 1999), *Waldorf-Inspired Education in Japan* (Seseragi Publishing, 2001), *Inquiries into the Psychology of Religion* (University of Tokyo Press, 2001), *Cosmology of the Child* (Jimbun shoin, 1996), and *Introduction to Holistic Education* (Hakuju-sha, 1995). He is the president of the Japanese Holistic Education Society.

Index

243

Made in the USA
San Bernardino, CA
17 February 2019